Verbatim Theatre Methodologies for Community-Engaged Practice

Verbatim Theatre Methodologies for Community-Engaged Practice offers a framework for developing original community-engaged productions using a range of verbatim theatre approaches.

This book's methodologies offer an approach to community-engaged productions that fosters collaborative artistry, ethically nuanced practice, and social intentionality. Through research-based discussion, case study analysis, and exercises, it provides a historical context for verbatim theatre; outlines the ethics and methods for community immersion that form the foundation of community-engaged best practice; explores the value of interviews and how to go about them; provides clear pathways for translating gathered data into an artistic product; and offers rehearsal room strategies for playwrights, producers, directors, and actors in managing the specific context of the verbatim theatre form.

Based on diverse, real-world practice that spans regional, metropolitan, large-scale, micro, independent, commercial, and curriculum-based work, this is a practical and accessible guide for undergraduates, artists, and researchers alike.

Sarah Peters is a playwright and senior lecturer in drama at Flinders University, Australia.

David Burton is a playwright and researcher in Queensland, Australia.

Verbatim Theatre Methodologies for Community-Engaged Practice

Perspectives from Australian Theatre

Sarah Peters and David Burton

LONDON AND NEW YORK

Designed cover image: © Photograph by Markus Ravik.

First published 2024
by Routledge
4 Park Square, Milton Park, Abingdon, Oxon OX14 4RN

and by Routledge
605 Third Avenue, New York, NY 10158

Routledge is an imprint of the Taylor & Francis Group, an informa business

© 2024 Sarah Peters and David Burton

The right of Sarah Peters and David Burton to be identified as authors of this work has been asserted in accordance with sections 77 and 78 of the Copyright, Designs and Patents Act 1988.

All rights reserved. No part of this book may be reprinted or reproduced or utilised in any form or by any electronic, mechanical, or other means, now known or hereafter invented, including photocopying and recording, or in any information storage or retrieval system, without permission in writing from the publishers.

Trademark notice: Product or corporate names may be trademarks or registered trademarks, and are used only for identification and explanation without intent to infringe.

British Library Cataloguing-in-Publication Data
A catalogue record for this book is available from the British Library

ISBN: 978-0-367-72640-9 (hbk)
ISBN: 978-0-367-72639-3 (pbk)
ISBN: 978-1-003-15570-6 (ebk)

DOI: 10.4324/9781003155706

Typeset in Times New Roman
by MPS Limited, Dehradun

Contents

	Introduction	1
1	Histories, Definitions, and Applications	13
2	Community Immersion	42
3	Interviewing and Listening for Aesthetics	65
4	Transcription, Exploration, and Community-Engaged Workshopping	87
5	Playwriting: Translating Stories into Performance	113
6	Verbatim and Community-Engaged Work in Rehearsal and Beyond	142
7	Ethical Practice: Private Lives, Public Stages, and Making Space for Stories	165
	Afterword	*194*
	Index	*196*

Introduction

This book is our love letter to storytelling; specifically to the process and practice of stories told by engaging with communities and using the methods of verbatim theatre. We love working with people to tell engaging and dynamic stories. We also love research and teaching, and through this book, our aim is to bring these three porous areas of our work together in a way that is useful for others. This is a book for artists, academics, teachers, students, community arts practitioners, emerging creatives, and seasoned professionals. In part, this is our way of thanking those communities we have worked with. Some parts of this book will resonate and click with you, and some parts won't – and that's ok! We encourage you to skip through to the bits that sound most useful or intriguing, hop from one chapter to another, put the book down and pick it up later and discover something else that hadn't seemed relevant before. Sections of the book are more conversational, some are incredibly practical, and some sections are more theorised. What we hope to emphasise throughout are examples and reflections from both our own projects and the work of other Australian artists, with plenty of suggestions and options for you to try in yours. Having more people engaging with communities, telling stories, and experimenting with their creative practice is surely a glorious thing.

We refer to each other as Sarah (who uses she/her pronouns) and David (who uses he/him pronouns) throughout the book, and use "we" when something is from both of us. We are both originally from Queensland, Australia. We acknowledge the Traditional Custodians of this country and their stewardship of the many lands across the continent on which this book was written. Sarah's ancestors are originally from England and Germany, and she was born on Mandandanji country (colonially known as Roma). David's ancestors are originally from England, and he was born on Jagara and Turrubul land (colonially known as Brisbane). We both studied on the traditional lands of the Giabal and Jarowair people at the University of Southern Queensland (Toowoomba). Sections of this book were written as part of Sarah and David's respective Doctor of Philosophies in Theatre, and sections of the book were written while Sarah was living on Kaurna land in South Australia, and David was living on Jagara and Turrubul land in Queensland. We pay our respects to

DOI: 10.4324/9781003155706-1

their Ancestors and descendants, who continue cultural and spiritual connections to the Country. We acknowledge that we are living and working on stolen lands; sovereignty was never ceded.

The words in our title are our best attempt to represent the work we share in this book: Verbatim Theatre Methodologies for Community-Engaged Practice. In Chapter 1, we will discuss each of these words and ideas in greater detail, looking at their history, the practice they refer to, and how we are using these terms in our work. Chapter 1 is our acknowledgement of the work that has come before us in this space, historically contextualising the development of Verbatim Theatre and modes of performance based on lived experiences, casting a wide net to explore the porous edges of verbatim theatre and how it connects to and overlaps in some ways with oral history, documentary, and political theatre forms (just to name a few!). We introduce the guiding framework for this book – Engaged Verbatim Theatre Praxis, and conclude with a series of activities designed to get you thinking about verbatim theatre methods, storytelling, and performance based on lived experiences.

Chapters 2–6 each focus on an aspect of creative practice. Community immersion means spending time in and with the community you are engaging with, and can also mean finding ways to support that community's goals. In Chapter 2 we describe the strategies we have employed in our community immersion across different projects and provide some prompting questions to get you thinking about how you might structure and implement your own practices of getting to know and support the communities you work with. Chapter 3 focuses on the interview - one of the central methods for many verbatim theatre artists - and explores this practice through the lens of research and preparation, creative practice, ethics, and how teachers and educators might negotiate interviews in a classroom environment. In Chapter 4 we look at what you might do next, after you've spent time with a community and conducted your interviews. Sometimes the next step is transcribing the interviews, sometimes it might be workshopping stories. Chapter 4 steps you through a variety of methods for exploring the stories, content, and dramatic meaning that will go into your creative outcome. In this chapter, we've also included a short section on devising, with a particular focus on a variety of projects we have facilitated with young people, as many of the same principles and values which underpin our approach to community-engaged verbatim practice are employed in this context as well.

Chapter 5 focuses on the practice of playwriting. We discuss a variety of conventions, dramatic languages, and structures used in the playwriting process, and give some examples from our own drafting processes where the story or character in a text has stayed the same, but through a shift in convention or structure, the story has shifted in rhythm and theatricality. Chapter 6 takes us into rehearsal, reflecting on how this process can be quite different when the acting company and the participating community are the same people, compared to when they are not. We reflect on some of our experiences as the playwright in a rehearsal process, and how taking a story into production means inviting new collaborators who are going to interpret and represent the text you have composed. We also talk briefly about the audience experience when watching a verbatim informed performance, and the impact it can have on a community when they see their stories reflected back to them through performance.

Finally, Chapter 7 is our deep dive into ethical practice, and what it means to work with real people, telling stories based on lived experiences, and sharing these stories in a creatively interpreted way. We have aimed to embed a consideration of ethics and a theory of ethical practice across the book as a whole, so Chapter 7 is an opportunity to pull each of these threads together and spend a little more time theorising and critically analysing our own theory of ethical practice. We name this Engaged Verbatim Theatre Praxis, and spend time discussing in Chapter 7 how this has been informed by critical theory, critical pedagogy, feminist theatre practice, and an ethics of care.

At the end of every chapter we have compiled a series of activities, frequently asked questions, and prompting questions for you to consider in your own practice. We hope that somewhere in this book you find an idea or a practice that excites, energises or challenges you. This is just one of a growing number of books dedicated to discussing, analysing, and sharing verbatim theatre and community-engaged practice. At the end of every chapter, you'll find our list of references, and we encourage you to read wildly and widely. As mentioned above, in this book we'll spend a good chunk of time talking about the language and terminology of verbatim theatre and community-engaged practice. Before we dive into that, we thought it would also be worthwhile to have a quick chat about the words we use to describe what we do.

1 The Words We Use to Describe What We Do

Playwright

Playwright is often a word we use to describe ourselves and our creative practice. When we are responsible for putting words on a page that are intended as a blueprint for performance, we are being playwrights. Some of that writing conjures setting and mood, and other words introduce us to characters and actions and objectives – but they all work together to create the world of a play and communicate dramatic meaning to an audience. This is the playwright's challenge – to tell a story through words that will evoke action, movement, breath, emotion, and dramatic meaning. Paul Castagno describes playwriting as being language based, "as such, language prevails as the dominant force in the shaping of characters, action, and theme. The playwright orchestrates the voices in the text" (Castagno 10). Orchestrating voices in text, writing a play, putting into words a story for performance – when we do these things we are playwriting and describe ourselves as the playwright (even when the voices haven't come from our imagination, but from another source, such as an interview). As Foxon and Turvey qualify, while playwriting is as diverse as "an individual scribbling away on a literary masterpiece, to a devising ensemble with one person nominated to turn collective ideas into a single text-based story, through to teams of writers coming together to edit verbatim material into a script", the word playwright comes from the words "play", meaning brisk movement, and "wright", meaning work, so a playwright is someone who "works to make movement happen" (xiv). We love this framing, as it broadens the understanding of what it is that a playwright does, making the word for our practice more inclusive – particularly for the telling of stories that might never be written down formally on the page. While sometimes this work to make movement happen through the telling of stories sits well under the title of playwright, sometimes we shift to use the word facilitator instead.

Facilitator

We might use the word "facilitator" when it's clear that our role is primarily to help a group of people work towards a mutual goal, and to do some of the thinking and organising that will help that process go as well as possible for the group. While being the facilitator we might also make creative contributions to the group's goal and take on a variety of other roles throughout the process. The facilitator is inside the project/process, while also keeping an eye *on* the project/process itself – looking at the process from the outside to identify opportunities, assist with challenges, and generally keep the work on track. This dual sense of being both within and without is one of the ways our approach to facilitation aligns in some ways with the role of the Joker in Boal's theatre of the oppressed (check out *A Boal Companion* edited by Jan Cohen-Cruz and Mady Schutzman for more on this), undoing hierarchies and "standing in-between, keeping things as fluid as possible, and inevitably serving as a translator, an interpreter" (Schutzman 144). Our facilitation is relational, and often involves navigating the ongoing dialectic within a group from action to reflection and back again (Mutnick 42), moving through processes of trialling ideas, figuring things out, experimenting, expanding, refining, and progressing towards an outcome.

Dramaturg

The dramaturgy of a play refers to its composition. It is the way that the play has been structured or composed to convey dramatic meaning through the rules and world of the play and how that meaning is communicated to audiences through theatrical languages. As a dramaturg, you might analyse a plays' dramaturgy (its composition, structure, meaning) and you can also be involved in helping craft and shape a play's dramaturgy. As Turner and Behrndt explain, dramaturgical work might include "an engagement with the actual practical process of structuring the work, combined with the reflective analysis that accompanies such a process" (3). In this way a dramaturg can be both "map maker and compass bearer" (176), looking at all the different parts of a play in relation to each other. In our work in community-engaged performance-making projects, we are often working as a dramaturg. Sometimes this might be during the interview in a verbatim process, when we consider how a story might be written into performance. Sometimes it might be when we're working collaboratively with an ensemble to tell a particular moment in the story through movement, sound, and mood. A dramaturg often works adjacent to a playwright or a director, and it's this sense of companionship that makes the role of dramaturg resonate with the work we do in many of our community-engaged projects. We are working alongside a community to tell a story, so sometimes the word "dramaturg" best describes the work we are doing, especially when that work is connected to the story of a performance and how that story is communicated to an audience.

Community-Engaged Theatre Artist

Like the term facilitator, "community-engaged theatre artist" is another broadly defined role and so we might use this to describe our work when we are doing many things in a project, or when we want to emphasise the community-engaged aspect of our practice. As we talk about further in chapter 1, community-engaged practice is fundamentally relational – it is about working with a community in an engaged way, meaning that you are considering the social, cultural, political, and economic context of the community you are working with, alongside your creative and artistic goals. Engaged practices "rely on dialogue and interaction among participating individuals ... emphasize the role of personal relationships and the need for teachers and practitioners to bring themselves fully to an engaged process" (Alrutz and Hoare 28). A community-engaged theatre artist is deeply connected to the people in a project: "the most important element of our work is to develop and nurture our relationships ... A relationship is the state of being connected. Without connection to the people we are working with, we're not able to design or create a truly community-engaged process or experience" (Lillie 159). In the field, or conversationally, "community-engaged" may become synonymous with "community-based" or simply "community artist". In a theoretical context, it is important to note that in recent years, the field has settled upon the notion of "engagement" as crucial to our definitions of these working artists. We discuss the historical roots of these titles in chapter 1.

2 Case Study Overview

We weave examples from our personal practice across this book, referencing particular projects and giving detailed insights into the processes and practices we have applied in our own community-engaged creative work. In this section, you'll find a short introduction to each of the main projects that we reference. Examination of these case studies reveals that even though the final products might seem worlds apart regarding style, conventions, and audience, similar methods and community engagement processes have been applied across their development.

In addition, we reference many other Australian playwrights throughout the book, which we highlight in sections titled "Principles in Practice".

April's Fool *(2010)*

Empire Theatre Projects commissioned *April's Fool* in Toowoomba, Queensland, Australia. The play focuses on the death of a teenager due to illicit drug use. The project was initiated when the family of the deceased connected with the Empire Theatre and the theatre then commissioned David Burton as a playwright to begin work on the piece. The initial brief was to create a piece of verbatim theatre suitable for secondary school audiences.

The deceased's father, David Terauds, had written a journal while his son was in a coma for seven days. This document provided a dramaturgical spine for the resulting script. The script also drew on over twenty-four hours of one-on-one interviews between the playwright and family, friends, hospital staff, and the deceased's drug dealer.

Interviews began just under six months from the actual events of the play. All interviews were recorded over audio and then transcribed and edited by the writer. The play toured Queensland in 2010, then Australia in 2012, and was published by Playlab Press (playlabtheatre.com.au). Sarah analyses some of the play's conventions in a 2018 article for *Drama Australia Journal*, titled "The Function of Verbatim Theatre Conventions in three Australian plays".

Queensland Music Festival Signature Community Works *(2013–2019)*

These unique productions are community-engaged projects on a massive scale. Occurring once every two years, the QMF Signature Community Works took a team of professional artists into regional and remote communities, where they built an original musical theatre production over eighteen months. The results were outdoor, free "spectaculars" with local cast numbers in the hundreds and audiences in the thousands. In addition, the shows featured not only local musical and dramatic talent but aimed to celebrate the region's specific culture (productions have included stunt motorcycles, tugboat "ballet", and live cattle and horses).

These productions began in 2001, but David has been the commissioned playwright since 2013s *Boomtown*. The professional artistic team engage with the community on multiple levels and David utilised verbatim theatre methodologies. This happened most explicitly in specific "verbatim theatre moments" of each production. David interviewed community members, recorded and edited that interview, and then gave the data back to the participant as a short monologue to be delivered on stage. The productions also utilised verbatim theatre methodologies in less explicit ways, frequently using the interview form as a way of gathering data that would then creatively inform how the artists engaged with the community. These works were the focus of David's published doctoral thesis, "Playwrighting methodologies in community-engaged theatre practice" (2021). The 2015 production *Under This Sky* was the focus of a feature-length documentary, *The Logan Project*, produced by SBS Australia and available through their streaming service, SBS On Demand. One community participant's journey of the 2017 production, *The Power Within*, was also the focus of a journal article co-written by David Burton and Janet McDonald, "Performance 'Training' in the Dirt: Facilitating Belonging in a Regional Community Musical Theatre Event" (2021). Excerpts of the 2019 production, *The Mount Isa Blast*, are available on the Queensland Music Festival YouTube channel (https://www.youtube.com/@qldmusicfest).

twelve2twentyfive *(2013)*

twelve2twentyfive is a verbatim performance piece by Sarah that gives a unique insight into the language and experience of youth mental health and wellbeing in regional areas. Developed in collaboration with mental health providers who interviewed young regional clients in Toowoomba and the Darling Downs (Queensland, Australia), *twelve2twentyfive* seeks to ignite conversation, stimulate thought, and push the boundaries of negative perceptions surrounding mental health. The stories are messy, touching, sometimes awkward, and often beautiful. Initially commissioned for performance at a medical conference (funded through support from the Queensland Regional Arts Development Fund and Medicare Local), *twelve2twentyfive* was subsequently workshopped and revised for a school's tour in 2015 with support from Toowoomba's Empire Theatre, Headspace, and First Coat Festival. *twelve2twentyfive* is published by Australian Plays Transform (apt.org.au).

bald heads & blue stars *(2014)*

bald heads & blue stars is an original verbatim play that explores the female experience of Alopecia, an autoimmune condition that results in varying degrees of hair loss. Sarah (who has had Alopecia since the age of three) spent three months interviewing 15 women from across Queensland to share stories about what it meant for them to experience this condition. These stories were then workshopped with acting students training at the University of Southern Queensland and written into performance. The play integrated direct excerpts from every interview, but also focussed on the journey of "Violet". Violet was a protagonist informed by many of the interviewee's stories. The audience sees Violet experience high school, try out wigs, survive embarrassing social situations, and "come out" as bald with a personified Alopecia by her side. David directed the first production of *bald heads & blue stars* and aspects of the rehearsal process and the project's impact on participants has been published in the following journal articles:

- The Impact of Participating in a Verbatim Theatre Process. *Social Alternatives*, 36(2), 2017, pp. 32–39

- Acting in Verbatim Theatre: An Australian Case Study. *Australasian Drama Studies.* La Trobe University, 2016

The production was supported financially by the Australian Alopecia Areata Foundation, the Queensland Regional Arts Development Fund and Artsworx USQ. It is published by Australian Plays Transform (apt.org.au).

St Mary's In Exile *(2016)*

David first pitched *St Mary's In Exile* to Queensland Theatre as an explicitly verbatim theatre production. The story focused on the events surrounding St Mary's South Brisbane Catholic Parish in 2009, where two progressive priests were effectively fired from their roles for breaking with Vatican doctrine. Burton gathered over thirty hours of interviews and began constructing a script. However, in drafting and working with Queensland Theatre, the work shifted from an explicitly verbatim theatre performance into a dramatic, fictionalised work based on actual events. The resulting production, which premiered in 2016, featured a combination of invented and verbatim dialogue. *St Mary's in Exile* is published by Playlab Press (playlabtheatre.com.au).

Eternity *(2017)*

Eternity is a contemporary exploration of identity, belonging, and family in a regional Australian community written for and with the 2017 first-year theatre students at the University of Southern Queensland. Two of the key strategies employed within the collaborative development of *Eternity* were workshops and letter writing. Three workshops were conducted across the semester, focussing on exploring rituals, traditions, and difficult conversations. A key "question" emerged from each workshop, and students were asked to write a letter in response to that question. Students used the letters as a vehicle to share individual perspectives and ideas that they felt may typically be marginalised in group settings, and these informed the playwriting process. The undergraduate cohort, directed by Lucas Stibbard, designed, rehearsed, and performed *Eternity* in 2017, and it is published by Australian Plays Transform (apt.org.au), with an excerpt of the play also published in a 2018 edition of *New Writing: The International Journal for the Practice and Theory of Creative Writing.*

Blister *(2019)*

Blister is a verbatim play that tells the story of Rosie, an Australian woman who is walking the Camino de Santiago. The Camino is an 800km pilgrimage across Northern Spain that begins in the French Pyrenees and traverses mountains, vineyard-covered hills, mesetas (plateaus), and urban centres before concluding at Santiago de Compostela. Pre-Covid, two hundred thousand people from across the world walked the Camino every year, often carrying their minimal belongings in a backpack, staying in dormitory-style accommodation with fellow pilgrims in local albergues, and walking between 20–35 kms most days. Sarah walked the Camino in 2016 (as well as a few extra hundred kilometres, walking from Santiago de Compostela to Finisterre and Muxia, and then also from Porto to Tui on the Portuguese Camino). She documented her travels and conversations through reflective journals and photographs. The production at Holden Street Theatres (Adelaide, South Australia) in 2019 was supported through funding by the College of Humanities, Arts and Social Sciences at Flinders University and in-kind support from the Australian Friends of the Camino. *Blister* is published via Australian Plays Transform, and an article outlining some of the writing process was published in a 2019 special issue (*Walking in/as Publics* edited by Stephanie Springgay and Sarah E. Truman) of the *Public Pedagogy Journal* titled "The pedagogy of pilgrimage on the Camino de Santiago written into performance".

LockDown *(2021)*

Sarah was the lead artist on the collaboratively created *LockDown* with Carclew's ExpressWay Arts. ExpressWay Arts is a joint initiative between Carclew and City of Onkaparinga to nurture young artistic leaders in the southern suburbs of Adelaide, employing experienced professional artists to work with the ensemble. *LockDown* was supported by the Australia Council, the federal government's arts funding and advisory body, the Department of Premier and Cabinet through Arts South Australia and Adelaide Fringe. Sarah worked with the ExpressWay ensemble once a week from October 2019 through to the sold-out season of performances at Adelaide Fringe in 2021. Through these weekly workshops the group collaboratively built the world of the play, created characters, explored themes and plot points through devising, improvisation, and writing tasks. In 2020, when the Covid-19 pandemic meant that workshops had to shift online, the ensemble began reworking the medium of the play, and subsequently recorded and produced a shorter radioplay version for the DreamBIG Children's Festival in Adelaide. Initially, the ensemble were exploring the themes (and their lived experiences) of violence in schools and communities (the title LockDown initially referred to how a school responds if there is a violent event on a school campus), however, in response to their experience of living through a pandemic, this came to inform their redirection of the final creative outcome which is set on the eve of lockdown. Access to the radio play, Educational resources relating to the production, and further information about ExpressWay Arts can be found online at carclew.com.au.

The Time is Now *(2021)*

David worked as a facilitator with two other lead artists, Ari Palani, and Aleea Monsour, to work with a group of ten young people and create original work. Working in part-time rehearsals over eight weeks, *The Time Is Now* premiered as part of La Boite Theatre Company's mainstage season in 2021. The lead artists were briefed to work with the young people on individual political speeches that would be used to provoke, challenge, and inspire the audience. The artists used the formation of the speeches to inform a list of themes that were then explored in a workshop setting. The final performance ended up being a collage of political monologue, physical theatre, and a wealth of scenes derived from verbatim sources, as discussions the participants had in workshops were then transcribed and edited for the stage. Themes covered included climate change, sexual harassment of young people, domestic violence, bullying, racism, and self-empowerment.

Stuck *(2022)*

Prospect Theatre for Young People (PTFYP) commissioned Sarah and two other writers (Carla Phillips and Jace Grummet) to each create fifteen-minute plays that would be performed as a triptych by PTFYP's senior ensemble at Adelaide Fringe in 2022. The writers worked with the ensemble to decide on a theme that would be explored across all three plays, each writer running 3–4 exploratory workshops with the ensemble. The group landed on the theme of being stuck; stuck between ideas, between people, and between versions of themselves and who they want to be. The workshops were opportunities to present stimulus and prompts to the ensemble, to improvise and devise in relation to various given circumstances, and to find the unique ways that this ensemble connected to and resonated with the theme. The plays were handed over to the ensemble at draft stage, so that the final polish and nuance could be worked through as part of the rehearsal process, with the writers responding to feedback and incorporating some of the "finds" from the rehearsal room into the scripts.

Time *(Working Title)*

Time (working title) is one of the creative outcomes from the "Verbatim Theatre and Healthy Ageing" practice-led research project, led by Sarah as chief investigator. The project team (which includes Professor Sue Gordon from the College of Nursing and Health Sciences at Flinders University) are researching the lived experience of transitioning into aged care, exploring how that experience can be written meaningfully into performance and documenting the impact that sharing those stories has for both the participants involved and the broader public audience. The project uses a practice-led verbatim theatre methodology to research aged care from the triangulated perspectives of people who are accessing aged care services themselves, their family members and carers, and people working in aged care. Cultural insensitivities, geographic and interpersonal distance from family members, ageism and unsympathetic approaches to communication with patients and families can compound the challenges of the transition into aged care. Change is needed for improved health outcomes in the sector, and key stakeholders acknowledge that this change will only be successful if informed by a comprehensive understanding of the experience of transition – the kind of humanly felt understanding that the arts is excellent at. Stories collected through interviews with each of the three participant groups, as well as community immersion at residential care facilities and storytelling workshops with residents living in care, have informed the creative development of the play *Time*.

> **Highlighted examples – Principles in Practice**
>
> Across this book, we have included examples from a range of other artists' practice, including Alana Valentine, Campion Decent, Claire Christian, Roslyn Oades, Dan Evans, Suzie Miller, Wesley Enoch, Tom Wright, Dylan Bryant, and many more. Sometimes these examples are woven into the chapters, and sometimes we have included highlighted examples – deep dives into an artist's particular approach, their journey with a particular play, or a specific example which highlights the diversity of the field of verbatim theatre practice in Australia. Keep an eye out for these highlighted examples as you read through each chapter.

3 How to Read This Book

As stated in the opening pages of this introduction, we encourage you to jump around to the sections of this book that you're most interested in, but it can also be read chronologically. While the first chapter sets up some crucial theoretical and historical contexts, the remainder of the book travels along a typical path of creation for a community-engaged work grounded in verbatim theatre methodologies. We conclude with a chapter entirely devoted to ethical practice, but of course, ethical practice underscores every discussion we have throughout the book. Every chapter concludes with activities, frequently asked questions, or reflective exercises. These have been written to serve a variety of different readers. You will find exercises here that would be at home in any secondary or tertiary training environment, but are also applicable to professional or emerging artists and practice-led researchers, working in ensembles or individually.

We're excited for you to begin working with these principles, or to deepen your understanding of your current practice.

Works Cited

Alrutz, Megan and Lynne Hoare. *Devising Critically Engaged Theatre with Youth: The Performing Justice Project*. Taylor and Francis Group, 2020.

Burton, David and Janet McDonald. "Performance 'Training' in the Dirt: facilitating belonging in a regional community theatre musical theatre event." *Theatre, Dance and Performance Training* 12(3), 2021, pp. 425–439.

Castagno, Paul. *New Playwriting Strategies, Language and Media in the 21st Century*. Routledge, 2012.
Foxon, Chris and George Turvey. *Being a Playwright, A Career Guide for Writers*. Nick Hern Books, 2018.
Lillie, Jade. "The Relationship is the Project." *The Relationship is the Project*, edited by Jade Lillie, Kate Larsen, Cara Kirkwood and Jacki Brown's, Brow Books, 2020, pp. 159–164.
Mutnick, Deborah. "Critical interventions, The meaning of praxis." *A Boal Companion*, edited by Ja Cohen-Cruz and Mady Schutzman, Routledge, 2006, pp. 33–45.
Peters, Sarah. "The Pedagogy of Pilgrimage on the Camino de Santiago written into performance." *Journal of Public Pedagogies* 4, 2019, pp. 74–81.
Peters, Sarah. "Eternity." *New Writing* 15, 2018, pp. 231–263.
Peters, Sarah. "The Function of Verbatim Theatre Conventions in Three Australian Plays." *Nj: Drama Australia Journal* 41/2, 2017, pp. 117–126.
Peters, Sarah. "The Impact of Participating in a Verbatim Theatre Process." *Social Alternatives* 36/2, 2017, pp. 32–39.
Peters, Sarah. "Acting in Verbatim Theatre: An Australian Case Study." *Australasian Drama Studies* 68, 2016, pp. 143–167.
Schutzman, Mady. "Joker Runs Wild." *A Boal Companion*, edited by Jan Cohen-Cruz and Mady Schutzman, Routledge, 2006, pp. 133–145.
Turner, Cathy and Synne K. Behrndt. *Dramaturgy and Performance*. Palgrave Macmillan, 2008.

1 Histories, Definitions, and Applications

Verbatim theatre can be a contested term, with many artists and academics defining and describing the form in different ways. When Derek Paget coined the phrase "verbatim theatre" in 1987 in an article for *New Theatre Quarterly*, he was documenting what he was seeing take place in theatre practice in Britain at that time rather than giving an absolute and finite definition. Paget describes verbatim theatre as "a form of theatre firmly predicated upon the taping and subsequent transcription of interviews with 'ordinary' people, done in the context of research into a particular region, subject area, issue, event, or combination of these things" (317). Paget's discussion focuses on the *process* of making verbatim theatre, emphasising that working with people in specific communities (communities defined by geography, experience or interest) is central to that process. In this chapter (and across the book as a whole), we are similarly seeking to document what we can see taking place in community-engaged theatre practice that uses verbatim theatre methods, starting with a historical contextualisation and then moving into a reflection on what is happening in a contemporary Australian context. Verbatim practices in Australia have a porous relationship with community-engaged theatre practice, and as we move through the book, we will explore the methodologies used in creating a verbatim performance and how practitioners can apply these methods to various performance projects. Caroline Wake (2010) has suggested that perhaps "we should talk about verbatim theatres in the plural rather than verbatim theatre in the singular" (5) as there are such diverse ways of understanding, making, and talking about verbatim theatre practice. This plurality, porosity, and flexibility is something we seek to emphasise in this chapter.

Our working definition of verbatim theatre is that it is directly informed by people's lived experiences. Our verbatim practice includes a process of sustained immersion within a community and often includes interviews with a community of storytellers. These conversations and experiences are recorded, and the resulting stories are written collaboratively into performance. The language we use is purposeful here, as we shift from referring to an interview, to a conversation, to a story, to a performance. We call this a working definition because we know that as our practice shifts and changes, so too may the words we use to define that practice.

DOI: 10.4324/9781003155706-2

14 *Histories, Definitions, and Applications*

In this chapter, we provide a historical contextualisation for the form of verbatim theatre and community-engaged theatre practice. As two Australian practitioners and scholars, we are also aware of the unique locality of our practice, and we explore what it means to be a practitioner in an Australian context. We briefly discuss the definitions and histories of community-engaged theatre, before shifting into an introduction to the flexibility of verbatim theatre's methods: how interviewing, engaging with communities, and telling stories about actual events can be applied to a diverse array of forms from ethnotheatre to headphone verbatim to reality television. We do this to help provide a context for those attempting to teach verbatim theatre to students, but also so that working artists may draw upon other mediums (from podcasts to documentaries) as forms of inspiration. As Tom Holloway urges in the foreword to his play *Beyond the Neck*:

> read plays or poems or musical manuscripts or novels or look at art or watch films or whatever medium you love because the best way to learn a craft is through the work of others. Read and see these things and when you do, feel liberated to 'steal' from them. Take what you love in them and see how you can make it your own. Let your work be affected by the artists you love (5).

Ethical and reflective ways of working are central to our community-engaged practice. Accordingly, we introduce a very brief discussion of some of the fundamental values and ideas underpinning our approach to verbatim theatre methods here in chapter one before dedicating an entire chapter to the practical and theoretical exploration of ethics in chapter seven. This chapter finishes, as all the chapters do, with a list of reflective questions, exercises, and workshop activities that may be suitable for classroom or individual use.

1.1 Historical Mapping and Contextualisation

What's in a Name?

Derek Paget coined the term "verbatim theatre" in 1987 and these words have since been used to reference a myriad of processes and theatrical products. There is some debate about when verbatim theatre first began, however, Paget explains that forms such as this often exist within a broken tradition: sometimes, methods of creating and performing stories can become more visible in specific socio-political contexts and then be forgotten (2011). This broken lineage is more common for community-engaged forms, rather than styles that are traditionally adopted by the Western canon, such as Realism. This broken tradition begets an assumption that the form is new and innovative rather than deeply embedded in theatre's history. Paget warns that there continue to be "academics who fail to take due account of the history" of verbatim theatre (2008, 135). We want to acknowledge this history and how it has shaped contemporary verbatim theatre. First, we may be more open to accepting a broader philosophical definition of the form if we examine where it arose and better understand the processes and intentions behind its initial development. Second, by interrogating the historical precursors to verbatim theatre, we highlight how the methods and processes used in creating verbatim works are just as integral to understanding the form as its structures and conventions.

Where Did the Idea Come From?

Two separate phenomena enabled verbatim theatre. Firstly, there was a shift in theatrical content post World War One towards an enhanced valuing of lived experiences and authentic community stories, with an explicit interest in the language and rhythm of colloquial speech. "Sturm and Drang, or Storm and Stress, drama of late eighteenth-century Germany" which emphasised the "literal words of the people" (Garde, Mumford and Wake, 9) precipitated this shift. The second more tangible phenomenon was the invention of portable sound recording devices, which allowed for an exact recording of spoken words to be used as "primary source material" (Paget 1987, 317) in the process of developing theatre based on actual events and experiences. Verbatim theatre is often cited as beginning in the 1980s based on this technological development. However, as Gallagher et al. acknowledge, "its impulses can be traced back much further" (28). Two key impulses were 1920s Agitational Propaganda (agitprop) in Russia and Germany, and The Living Newspaper form popularised in the USA in the 1930s during the Federal Theatre Project.

Agitational Propaganda

Agitprop was a vibrant form of political theatre in the 1920s and 1930s, designed for "performance to working-class audiences in non-theatre spaces, ranging from the street to the gathering places of the working people" (Watt 20). Bulletins and local news would be read aloud to townspeople in a square or market, and speakers began to "use speech, song, dance and gymnastics to dramatise [these] texts" (Innes 23). These conventions are still evident in contemporary street theatre and community performance events. Theatre troupes such as those operating under the Blue Blouse Movement (1923–1933), produced a "montage of political facts" (Leach 169) through their performances, using visual and performance literacy to disseminate information to audiences. Erwin Piscator influenced the development of agitprop in Germany. His primary objective was to provide a working-class audience with the opportunity to "politicise itself through the art" (Holderness 106) and to encourage his audiences to believe that they can be changed by their surroundings and can themselves change the surrounding world (116).

Agitprop was political, confrontational, and innovative, with recorded material from life (in the form of newspaper articles, photographs, and radio excerpts) projected into the world of the stage. It valued and validated the everyday experiences of the audience and "exploit[ed] the capacities of the slide projector and film to address topical social issues" (Garde, Mumford, and Wake 11). Through these inclusions and borrowing from "commedia dell'arte festivals, parades and circuses" (Brockett 243), agitprop was a highly accessible community and "common peoples" theatre (Leach 170). It was a unique form of political activism that endeavoured to undermine the oppression of ignorance and used theatrical conventions that, at the time, were considered radical and subversive. Through its dramatisation of news and local events, the phenomenon of valuing lived experience and using theatre to educate and inform was present in agitprop performances. While the political intent may not be as overt, there is a direct thread from the accessible, celebratory, and community-driven ethos evident in early agitprop through to the Queensland Music Festival case studies discussed in this book, particularly concerning the inclusive and community-based methods of practice.

The Federal Theatre Project (Living Newspaper)

The Living Newspaper, popularised in the 1930s during the Federal Theatre Project (FTP) in the USA developed and adapted the agitprop form. It was the first time in US history that "theatre was subsidised by the federal government" (Witham 1). Set up as part of a Works Progress Administration (WPA) program in 1935, its specific goal was "to re-employ theatre artists who were victims of the economic crisis precipitated by the Great Depression" (Witham 2), thereby "keeping artists employed and struggling families entertained" (Garde, Mumford and Wake 11). This meant the production of theatrical classics, development of new works, dance programs, and circuses. The intent was to develop a national theatre to reach a wide audience and represent their stories and experiences on stage (Witham 4). Artistic director Hallie Flanagan described the FTP as fighting "for theatres as an expression of a civilised, informed and rigorous life" (qtd. in Kaufman 2010, 27). Both agitprop and The Living Newspaper incorporated material from real life into the performance. However, rather than projecting recorded material to function as a contrast or juxtaposition to the story, as was common in agitprop (Innes 2), The Living Newspaper wove the material more seamlessly into the dialogue and plot development of the performance. Narration, direct address, and a clear political agenda were also conventions adopted by The Living Newspaper (Barranger 572). Flanagan was "intrigued by what she called 'the entertainment value of the fact'" (Witham 78). This interconnection of "the authentic and the theatrical" (Botham 41), evident in both agitprop and The Living Newspaper, is a core thread binding both forms to verbatim theatre's history. A thread that Barranger (2004), Botham (2009), Paget (1987), and Watt (2009) each independently document linking The Living Newspaper to later documentary and community theatre forms in both the United States and the United Kingdom in the 1950s.

Verbatim Theatre in Australia

Verbatim theatre's development in an Australian context has maintained strong connections to Paget's description of early verbatim theatre, emphasising the language of testimony. This is particularly evident in Australian playwright Alana Valentine's description of her verbatim practice as "close work ... work drawn closely from a source – either in a community or an archive or elsewhere – and informed by the cultural and social dynamics of the world in which we contemporaneously live" (Valentine 2018, 2). Rather than eclipsing the local and community-based stories, there is a genuine diversity within the form, and tension between community and politics often drives the drama. Watt describes this as the "local/global nexus", which "becomes central so that the play is at least potentially about a broader international issue as it is lived at the local level (the global is always local somewhere)" (204). He asserts that the continued connection to the local in an Australian context creates verbatim's sense of authenticity (194). Ros Horin's *Through the Wire* (2004), Roslyn Oades' headphone verbatim plays (*Fast Cars and Tractor Engines*, *Stories of Love and Hate* and *I'm Your Man* 2003–2012), Linden Wilkinson's *Today We're Alive* (2014) and Campion Decent's *The Campaign* (2018) all wrestle with a larger political canvas while maintaining a connection to the stories and language of a community. Garde, Mumford, and Wake's "A Short History of Verbatim Theatre" provides a comprehensive summary of some of the vital verbatim plays developed in Australia since 1990.

Anderson and Wilkinson (2007) discuss the resurgence of verbatim theatre concerning themes of authenticity, empathy, and human connection. They argue that what makes verbatim theatre unique is its "immediacy, [it] demands a focus and works on our imaginations in a unique way" (165) because it is a live encounter with the human experience. They suggest its purpose is to connect with an audience on an emotional and intellectual level, striving to "empathetically inform and empower through authentic story" focused on local living history (156). Verbatim theatre in an Australian context embraces the diversity of the form. It is "a portmanteau term, incorporating a stylistically rich and varied product that owes its origins to spoken text but does not always perform these words literally, as they are spoken" (Anderson and Wilkinson 154). Significantly, this emphasis on spoken experiences includes an agenda of empowerment, of giving "voice to people who might otherwise go voiceless ... and to tell stories that might otherwise go untold" (Wake 2010, 2).

It is possible to apply these definitions of verbatim theatre to international models. However, Australia's international reputation as being culturally "laid-back" could also be applied to verbatim theatre, which generally sees playwrights as less dogmatic about keeping dialogue *exactly* word-for-word. This is in contrast to some international approaches, which favour forensic subservience to transcriptions. Further, as Campion Decent describes, Australian verbatim is often preoccupied with notions of community and belonging. The "Australian character" is very specific for playwrights such as Decent, from their locality to their language. This mirrors the Australian literary obsession with the historical landscape. *Picnic at Hanging Rock*, a novel and film which is generally cited as a key literary work for Australian identity, gave birth to an entire genre of "Australian gothic", where the Australian landscape is pitted against Australian families (in *Picnic* ... a small group of girls mysteriously disappears into Australian bushland). Indeed, Decent's own verbatim work *Embers* deals with the Victorian bushfires, recreating this conflict between people and landscape. For playwrights such as Deborah Mailman and Wesley Enoch (*Seven Stages of Grieving*), or Tom Wright (*Black Diggers*) who are telling First Nations stories, their characters are filled with a sense of loss from the violent colonial disruption of the Australian landscape.

Sarah has written previously about a "Dramaturgy of Belonging" that is present in verbatim theatre, allowing audiences to identify with interview subjects to bring about a sense of unification and community. For playwright Dan Evans, this is uniquely Australian. "It's because we [white Australians] don't belong", he says. "We're looking for something to make sense of our experience of the world". Much of Australian drama, from early outback colonial drama onwards, builds on the idea of characters lost and isolated in a landscape that envelops them. As McCallum notes in his history of Australian playwriting (emphasis added): "Their identity – and by extension the much discussed Australian Identity, or Australian National Character, or Australian Legend – was constructed by talking and performing about this loss and an associated search for a sense of *belonging*" (23–4). In this context, verbatim theatre is uniquely positioned in the Australian theatre landscape to explore themes of community, place, and identity. We posit that a uniquely Australian approach to verbatim theatre, particularly in a community-engaged context, makes a powerful contribution to Australia's literary landscape through the recurring themes of identity, belonging, and reckoning with our place in the world.

Community-Engaged Theatre

Community-engaged practice is written about in a variety of contexts by some wonderful scholars and practitioners. We certainly can't hope to explore the true breadth of community-engaged work in this volume. In order to contain our discussion, much of this book is dedicated to examining the intersection of verbatim theatre methodologies and community-engaged work in practice. In fact, attempting to separate verbatim theatre methodologies from contemporary community-engaged practice can be difficult. A community-engaged practice shares much of its DNA with verbatim theatre in both its history and philosophical intentions. As Jade Lillie makes clear, "community-engaged practice is not an artform. It's not an add-on. It's a way of working: a deep collaboration between practitioners and communities to develop outcomes specific to that relationship, time and place" (9). Community-engaged theatre is also related to a dense family tree of terms surrounding artistic practice with social intent. Community cultural development is perhaps the most apparent antecedent, but applied theatre, community-based theatre, participatory theatre, and socially-engaged art are also related (Goldbard 2006; Ackroyd 2000). All of these forms are generally united in social intentionality (Burton 2021). There is a greater purpose "overshadow[ing] the entertainment function" (Ackroyd 3) of the work. The form's participatory nature is also essential to its definition. As we'll explore throughout this book, the community of participants (or subjects of study that form the research base of a verbatim work) can be almost anyone. Communities of participants may be defined by their geographic location, age, life experiences, political identity or even deliberately chosen for how *contrasting* they are as people.

Outside of artistic practice, community engagement also suggests civic action. Carter and Heim, examining a community-engaged production that utilised verbatim theatre methodologies, discussed the term:

> Community engagement involves interactions between government and citizens for mutual participation in the ambit of policy, programme and service decisions and is central to local government's responsibility to improve civic relationships and progress community well-being through democracy (205).

When applied to artistic practice, this definition makes the inherently political nature of these works undeniable. While productions may not be targeted at "local government" specifically, there is usually an acknowledgment of power structures that impact the participating community in community-engaged works.

Identifying and disrupting these power structures was the life's work of Augusto Boal, perhaps the most influential community-engaged theatre artist of contemporary times. His landmark work, "Theatre of the Oppressed", described his initial experiments in creating a "People's Theatre" in Peru. He saw two ideas as essential. The first was that the "spectator" became empowered in the play's action, becoming an actor. Secondly, he sought to eliminate the idea that character belongs to any individual actor (119). Boal's vision of a democratic theatre aimed to disrupt all power structures, including the illusory separation of audience and artist. Through games and workshops, Boal sought to empower the oppressed. These exercises are described at length in "Games for Actors and Non-Actors", an essential volume for almost anyone interested in community-engaged practice.

Boal, notionally aware of the Federal Theatre Project, the work of Meyerhold, Brecht, and Piscator, was explicitly frustrated by these forms' insistent distinction between product and audience. According to Boal, these forms emphasised and revealed problems, but they did not do enough to empower audiences to find solutions. Boal's theatre, like much of community-engaged practice, calls an audience to a revolution of sorts. In a verbatim theatre context, this may occur through a "dramaturgy of belonging" (Peters 2019), where the audience and the artist become united in a shared identity (and shared opportunity to express identity narratives and make sense of experience) that can be healing and empowering.

The lofty aims of Boal's theatre and community-engaged practice generally can lead to evangelicalism in its practitioners. In looking at applied theatre, Downes issues a warning worth listening to: "the term of applied theatre, has, in recent times, become synonymous with a kind of pure, egalitarian form of theatre which is exclusively beneficial to the participants" (25). There is an astounding amount of scholarship in the field that praises case studies' inherent "worthiness" from anecdotal data given by participants who experienced a perceived positive impact from community-engaged projects. At its least damaging, community-engaged practice that lacks critical discourse can be unfocused and lazy. In more troublesome scenarios, however, practical ethics can disintegrate in the face of an artist insisting that everyone's having a great time. Works such as this book attempt to form a critical discourse around community-engaged practice so that the "inherent worthiness" (Badham 95) is closely examined. We don't do this to spoil the party but to improve it. By becoming more skilled at articulating the aims and ethics of community-engaged practice in various contexts, the practice may evolve and improve.

It is also worth noting an important distinction between this work's authors and artists like Boal. David and Sarah identify themselves primarily as playwrights working in a community-engaged practice (although as we discussed in the introduction, we may occasionally use other words to describe what we do). This category is distinct from Boal and others, who may identify themselves as community-engaged artists who occasionally need to write scripts. Drama teachers, arts therapists, and other community workers are more likely to fall into this latter category with Boal. Sarah and David approach their creative practice from a playwriting and dramaturgical perspective first, which informs the structure and content of this book. Artists working in both of these categories have much to learn from one another.

1.2 Why Use Verbatim Methodologies for Community-Engaged Practice?

The Value to the Artist

Whether you're a professional artist more accustomed to working on extant work, a teacher, or a student, it may appear "simpler" to produce theatrical work that doesn't rely on verbatim methodologies or community-engagement. Of course, works from the "canon", or pre-existing scripts have tremendous social, creative, and pedagogical value. However, for any working theatre artist today, it is foolish to underestimate the value (both economic and artistic) of community-engaged work. Moreover, when we asked practicing playwrights why verbatim theatre was worth the extra hassle, their responses were deep and immediate.

"Yes, it is more work", says Campion Decent, who's written several verbatim-based works for mainstage theatre companies in Australia. "But these projects are really special. And a privilege. I've met people working on these projects that I never would've otherwise". The relative loneliness of being a writer vanishes in community-engaged work. "It's made me more of a selfless maker", reflects Dan Evans, who's worked across the spectrum of theatre, from mainstage "classical" works, to innovative community-engaged experiences.

> You are in servitude of the community. That's the primary difference from narrative based playwriting, which exists in a hierarchy that we've inherited from our English forebears. What this work has taught me is that amazing cultural experiences aren't hierarchical or vertical, they're horizontal. If you can be vulnerable and can meet someone else's vulnerability, then what you'll get is a democratic piece of theatre, that can speak with more sparkling clarity to more people more quickly in a meaningful and robust way. I think it gets right back to what theatre was supposed to do, which is catharsis. It's empathy. Because of that, it can't be dismissed. Love it or hate it, it can't be dismissed. It's irrefutable.

Playwright and teacher Claire Christian makes a similar link to vulnerability and empathy. Independently of Dan, she also spoke of the form's opposition to Modernist theatre, built on hierarchical structures. "Stories matter", she says,

> and historically, old, boring, white men have been telling the stories and deciding whose stories get told. Thankfully, that is shifting. I think this form is a way of disrupting that. We think that stories have to be big or grand to be compelling. But humans are inherently interesting because we have all lived messy, complicated, brilliant, beautiful lives. Being an artist and holding people's stories is a privilege, and it's also something we've been doing for each other since the beginning of time. I think it's important because that's the only thing we have to understand who we are and why the hell we are here.

As director and creative producer Matt Scholten reflects, people often want you to hold their stories, "it's amazing to see how people want to share their story and how they want to talk about what connects them to a topic or to a person or to an event". In these comments, we see some of the spirit of political empowerment that was a key part of community theatre history across the twentieth century in forms such as Agitprop and the Federal Theatre Project. It also underscores the form's relationship with Feminist Theatre Practice, which further informs an ethical code of practice that we discuss in the final chapter.

Quite apart from this spiritual impact on the writer, both authors can attest to the profound skills development that verbatim theatre and community-engaged practice fosters. As working playwrights, no other form permits quite as forensic an examination of language and dialogue. Nor is the assemblage of a dramatic structure ever quite as explicit when the playwright is only allowed to build a work out of pre-existing pieces rather than events they can imagine and bend at will. These skills are applicable to any theatre-making form. Further, perhaps most applicable to almost every artist, the use of interviews as a creative research tool is helpful for all creators and actors. Take, for example, a deliberately non-community-engaged production such as a classical Shakespearean work staged by a state-funded theatre company. Even in this scenario, creators can benefit from fundamental research skills in talking to experts on the themes from the play. The authors believe that verbatim theatre methodologies working in a community-engaged practice framework present profound professional opportunities for working artists worldwide.

Fostering Community Well-Being

The effects of verbatim theatre methodologies on community well-being are measurable and have been proven multiple times. Community-engaged practice and verbatim theatre methodologies can affirm local talents, cultivate respect, enhance feelings of social connectedness, foster equality, engender a sense of place, assist in overall measures of community health and well-being (Hilbers 26–7), and even mirror the work of therapy (Stuart Fisher 2011a, 2011b). Sarah's research in 2019 found that the interviews and community immersion in a verbatim theatre process "provide a context for storytelling that is structured specifically to result in the sharing of identity narratives and the discursive construction of self and sense of belonging" (44). This aligns with Gray et al's earlier findings that performances based on this discursive expression of lived experiences can convey complex life narratives in an empathic way (143), which can have positive impacts on an individual's health, well-being and resilience through participation in the collaborative storytelling project (Gray et al. 2000, Rossiter et al. 2008). Forms of storytelling and performance which value and amplify lived experiences serve to better understand and share the unique histories and contexts of specific times and places, fostering connection and enhancing well-being. The bringing together of multiple people, stories, and experiences through community-engaged practice (and finding a way to hold space for each of these contributions individually while also finding a collective space for the intersection and connection between individuals) is part of the phenomena that leads to enhanced wellbeing. Şimşek explains that when we move beyond individual self-expression and towards "coalitions of stories", we enhance the opportunities for belonging and the impact of those stories on a broader national and international stage (84).

These are big promises, but it's not difficult to imagine when looking at public art outside of the community-engaged framework. Governments and the general public are well aware of public art's massive impact on community well-being. Think about the mass morale boost of a festival event, for example, or the integration of public artworks into parklands and urban spaces. We could even think of the Olympic Opening and Closing Ceremonies as a massive work of community-engaged artistic practice, where community identities and narratives are showcased to the rest of the world. Community-engaged theatre practice attempts to harness much of these same ideas on a much smaller stage but still achieves profound effects on communal health and well-being.

1.3 What Other Theatrical Forms Are "Like" Verbatim Theatre?

As has likely become evident in section 1.1, there is a broad array of nomenclature that has been used to describe performances and theatre making processes which are similar to verbatim theatre. This complex and fluid family tree of forms speaks to how artists, cultures, and societies make creative practice their own, adapting it to suit a variety of audiences, artists, and intentions. We have used "verbatim theatre" as our organising term, however, "theatre of the real" may have served a similar purpose. As Carol Martin asserts, while "there may be no universal agreement on individual terms, there is an emerging consensus that theatre of the real includes documentary theatre, verbatim theatre, reality-based theatre, theatre-of-fact, theatre of witness, tribunal theatre, nonfiction theatre, restored village performances, war and battle re-enactments, and autobiographical theatre" (4). Tom Cantrell suggests the array of definitions and names for forms such as documentary or verbatim theatre may be an attempt to "distinguish the use of found material" (2013, 2) in work. Conversely, Saldaña suggests that the fields of ethnodrama, verbatim theatre and "over 60 other variant terms" (2010, 2) are merely different names for the same process.

We contend that this homogenisation ignores the apparent differences between forms rather than celebrating them. It "rather unhelpfully groups dissimilar devising processes and performance modes together" (L. Taylor 379). As Forsyth and Megson outline, the differences between forms is not a blurring of the same practices "there are points of tension as well as consensus" (2) and this "porosity at boundaries can potentially be celebrated" (Paget 2007, 173) for the innovations and opportunities that one form enables in the other. This porosity is evident in the creative practices used across various forms, such as community immersion, interviewing, maintaining connection with participants, and the creative development of performance. These methods are explored explicitly in chapters two through six, with examples drawn from various case studies to emphasise the porous approach of these methods. In this section we offer a brief introduction to the suite of forms and working methodologies employed in creating work which is porous in style and approach to our working definition of verbatim theatre, and may be considered to broadly fall beneath the umbrella of "Theatre of the Real".

Theatre of the Real

As the name suggests, Theatre of the Real is an identifier which brings together forms of theatre and performance which are connected in some way to reality. In *Theatre of the Real* (2013) Carol Martin describes these performances as claiming a specific relationship with events in the real world (4) and seeks to expand this moniker beyond performances which make use of verbatim and documentary sources to encompass a diverse variety of forms and theatre making processes. Similarly, in her book *Insecurity: Perils and Products of Theatres of the Real* (2019), Jenn Stephenson describes theatre of the real as "theatrical performances, in general, that tap into an international documentary tradition – staging real people, real words, real places – to connect their audiences with that reality" (3). She describes this work as appealing to a desire for authenticity and unmediated realness. A connection to the real – whether that be real people, places, events or experiences – represented through performance, is the organising principle of theatre of the real.

Ethno Theatre, Research-Based Theatre, Documentary Theatre

Ethnotheatre/drama, research-based theatre, and documentary theatre all hold parallels to the process and form of verbatim theatre. Judith Ackroyd and John O'Toole (2010) endeavour to chart the territory of "[e]thnodrama and its close relations" (19), citing documentary theatre and verbatim theatre as existing within this family tree. They demonstrate through an attempt to define each of these forms that labels are transient, "they shift and transmute and combine in different places and spaces" (21). In 2003 Saldaña described ethnotheatre as "employ[ing] traditional craft and artistic techniques of formal theatre production to mount a live performance event of research participants' experiences" (218). The emphasis on participants' personal experience connects the form to verbatim theatre's focus, although they each approach this emphasis from different agendas. Ethnotheatre seeks to research the phenomena of experience clinically to understand it in an educative and tangible sense and present that experience. In contrast, verbatim theatre often explores the emotions, relationships and kinaesthetic qualities of experiences. It can then represent that exploration through metaphor and theatricality. Saldaña describes ethnographers and theatre artists as sharing a common goal: "to create a unique, insightful and engaging text about the human condition" (*Dramatizing Data* 229). This mutual focus on human experience and the common understanding that theatre is an enabling form to explore and analyse that experience is one of the key similarities between verbatim theatre and ethnotheatre.

Mitchell, Jonas-Simpson, and Ivonoffski extend this focus on lived experience to a discussion on research-based theatre, explicitly concerning their project on patients living with dementia titled *I'm Still Here!* (2006). In this project, research-based theatre "proved to be [a] meaningful medium for enhancing understanding of lived experience in different groups and communities" (198). A value underpinning their approach was a sense of responsibility to "giv[e] voice to the experiences" (199) described by their research participants. In part, this responsibility is driven by the belief that sharing lived experience through theatre is an avenue for creating social change. This is reinforced by Beck et al., who outline that "all forms of research-based performances have the potential to expand understandings, engage audiences and provoke new learning experiences" (698). While the critical focus of research-based theatre is primarily on research and education, there is porosity with verbatim and community-engaged projects in the practices and ways of working outlined by Mitchell et al. and Beck et al., such as community immersion, interviews, and continued communication with the community (sometimes referred to as member checking in research practice).

Documentary theatre is a term used to "distinguish the use of found material from plays that are solely the playwright's own invention" (Cantrell 2013, 2). Therefore, performances which use found materials (ranging from archival documents, collected testimonials, and personal artefacts such as diaries and photo albums through to newspapers and websites) in the dramaturgy of their presentation may be considered documentary theatre. In "The Promise of Documentary" Janelle Reinelt investigates definitions, signifiers, and expectations of the documentary, offering:

1 The value of the document is predicated on a realist epistemology, but the experience of the documentary is dependent on phenomenological engagement
2 The documentary is not in the object but in the relationship between the object, its mediators (artists, historians, authors), and its audiences
3 The experience of the documentary is connected to reality but is not transparent, and is in fact constitutive of the reality it seeks (2011, 6)

Reinelt's claims emphasise the relationality of documentary theatre: the relationship between the document/testimony/research and the artists' representation, the relationship between this representation and the audience, and the relationship between the audience and their conjecture/imagined perception of the original document/testimony/research.

Tribunal Theatre, Headphone Verbatim, and Oral Histories

In the UK, verbatim theatre has moved away from a focus on community stories and closer to topical political commentary in the form of tribunal plays (Luckhurst 211). Tribunal theatre uses court transcripts as the core of their dialogue and "demonstrate a shift from the local to the national, and are concerned with miscarriages of justice, the implementation of law, public institutions and issues relating to human rights" (Luckhurst 211). This is evident within the field of works emerging from the UK across the twenty-first century, such as *Guantanomo: Honour Bound to Freedom* (2004), *Bloody Sunday* (2005), *Called to Account* (2007), *Deep Cut* (2008), *Tactical Questioning* (2011), *The Riots* (2011), *Enquirer* (2012), *Home* (2013) and *#BeMoreMartyn* (2018). While the first impulse towards verbatim theatre was a "concern to tell working class histories and stories" (Luckhurst 200), the shift towards tribunal theatre is often a shift away from these communities. The plays "of the last decade deploy ... celebrity voices as much as it does ordinary ones" (212). Paget's 2008 definition of verbatim theatre acknowledges the growing diversity of the form, stating it "originates in interviews, and its scripts utilize in greater or lesser ways recordings of actual words real people have spoken" (130). This definition reflects the continuing development of verbatim theatre in a contemporary context, emphasising the origins of the themes and stories of a verbatim work in the engagement with people and their lived experiences.

Caroline Wake's "Headphone Verbatim Theatre: Methods, Histories, Genres, Theories" traces the development of headphone verbatim (also referred to as recorded delivery in relation to the work of British artist Alecky Blythe), describes the methods of this form, and investigates the reception of this style of storytelling for audiences. Similar to verbatim theatre, headphone verbatim also begins with processes of community immersion and interviewing, however in lieu of transcription the playwright then edits the sound files into the shape of the play. For the actors in rehearsal, there is an audio script in place of a text-based script, and the actors wear headsets or earphones to hear the verbatim recordings. "They then repeat that script as immediately and exactly as possible, including ... every stammer, pause, and repetition. The effect, according to audience members, 'is somewhere between acting, "being", and possession'" (Wake 323). Roslyn Oades is at the forefront of headphone verbatim theatre and immersive audio experiences in Australia. Her work includes *Fast Cars and Tractor Engines* (2005), *Stories of Love and Hate* (2008), and *I'm Your Man* (2012), published together as *Acts of Courage* by Currency Press, as well as *Hello, Goodbye and Happy Birthday* (2014), *Cell 26* (2017), *Sea Stories* (2018) and *The Nightline Project* (2022).

Verbatim theatre has sat adjacent to oral history traditions since its inception (Paget 1987, Summerskill 2021). The two share philosophical and methodological roots in using the form of the interview to capture personal narratives. However, "oral history" productions or projects remove the burden and potential of the title of "theatre" and thus are clear in their aim to capture and show interview data as directly as possible. This technique is used most commonly in archiving witness accounts of historical events. These may then transform into public exhibitions via museums and libraries. Gonzalez (2016) provides an example by citing *The Exodus Greater Manchester Refugee Arts Partnership* project. The project sought to capture the lived experience of asylum seekers. The gathered data eventually became a verbatim theatre show, titled *Exodus Onstage*. Thus, verbatim theatre projects can organically grow out of oral history projects. Overall, aspiring oral historians will likely find valuable knowledge in community-engaged practice and verbatim theatre methodologies, as the forms are interconnected in philosophical values and their emphasis on the interview. Similarly, verbatim theatre and community-engaged artists can learn from oral history scholarship and practice, and we highly recommend Clare Summerskill's *Creating Verbatim Theatre From Oral Histories* in this regard.

Porosity of "Theatre of the Real" with Screen-Based Forms

Verbatim theatre, perhaps more than other theatre styles, struggles to be adapted onto the screen (although there have been attempts, including a 2002 film adaptation of *The Laramie Project*, produced by HBO). This struggle is partly because verbatim theatre is occasionally a direct response to a style that film already does very well: the documentary. More importantly, any adaptation to film inevitably undermines one of verbatim theatre's greatest assets, that of "presence" (Bottoms 2006). Presence is highly valued for community-engaged practice overall, where entire projects depend on a sense of shared storytelling. Audiences and artists unite as one community in dialogue with one another. Direct, unmediated conversation of this sort can never be achieved by traditional film modalities. Still, there are some examples of verbatim theatre methodologies present in film and television. For better or worse, reality television is ubiquitous in our culture and can provide us with a starting point for understanding some aspects of verbatim theatre, especially with young students. There is a clear thematic link, as both forms attempt to exploit the asset of being based in "reality" and are somehow "authentic". But, of course, the version of "reality" both forms represent is intensely mediated (Hill 2019). For students and beginners to the form, reality television can help as a useful lens on two fronts. The first is in the construction of meaning. The second is a more philosophical approach to understanding the connection between verbatim theatre participants and their audience.

Firstly, both reality television and some verbatim theatre typically tell a narrative via at least two modes: a live-action event and a cut-away "confessional" of participants relaying the event in an interview format. Many reality shows (*MasterChef, The Bachelor, Survivor, Keeping Up With The Kardashians, Ru Paul's Drag Race, The Amazing Race*) express their narrative in this way. They frequently eschew the role of a more traditional voice-over narrator or host so that the contestants or participants themselves narrate the action. Verbatim theatre can operate much the same way, where a typical scene might juxtapose direct text from an interview with a physical embodiment (either a literal recreation or something more abstract) of the interviewee's narrative. The collision of these two streams creates a new dramatic meaning. In reality television, interviews are used to support events we watch playing out. In theatre, interviews can serve much the same purpose, but they can also go further. Images, sound, lighting, and other members of the ensemble can deliberately subvert, contradict, illuminate or echo the text of the interview. The only limits are those of the theatrical imagination.

Secondly, reality television, just like verbatim theatre, capitalises on notions of authenticity and community. Take, for example, reality television's constant encouragement for audiences to take to social media and pledge their allegiance to particular contestants. In some competition reality shows, the audience gets a very direct say in who wins the competition. In this way, the audience and the contestant become one community, allowing the contestant to mirror the viewer and vice versa. An audience is drawn to a particular contestant because they see themselves in them. This is especially true for the class demographics of contestants and viewers (Stiernstedt & Jakobsson 2017) and has led some scholars to suggest that reality television is capable of encouraging citizens to critically reflect on the politics of identity (Hill 2019, Lunt 2014, Graham 2017). At its most basic, this is also the aim of verbatim theatre methodologies. By capitalising on notions of what is "real" and "authentic", a viewer is more able to relate to the subject on stage, seeing themselves in the performance and enforcing notions of the community (Peters 2019, Stuart Fisher, 2011a, 2011b).

Verbatim theatre methodologies will rarely operate at the scale of major Hollywood films, although some come close. Director Chloe Zhao spent many months auditioning and immersing herself in communities of regional Americans for her Academy Award-winning film *Nomadland* from 2020. The final product was "scripted", but Zhao appears to have utilised verbatim theatre methodologies in a community-engaged context to help the non-actors retell aspects of their own life stories. *Nomadland* is critically notable in part because it is so unique in its script formulation, casting, editing, and execution. There are very few films like it, but it hints at some of the ways verbatim theatre methodologies share similar processes with film.

1.4 Ethical Practice

Our entire practice is underpinned by an articulation of our ethical values, and while this is the focus of chapter seven, it is worth briefly articulating our approach here in this introductory chapter (just in case some of you marvellous readers are engaging with this book in a linear manner!).

We articulate our ethical approach to community-engaged storytelling as Engaged Verbatim Theatre Praxis. Engaged Verbatim Theatre Praxis is a decision to practice and create theatre inspired by a community's verbal stories in a way that:

1. Values listening to and sharing personal experience and community stories so that people are heard, visible, and empowered through connection, relationship, and community
2. Embraces collaboration, dialogue, and experimentation with theatrical languages and conventions throughout the process of development to create innovative, engaging, and theatrically dynamic performance
3. Challenges normative and oppressive politics and policies, broadening our consciousness and transforming our understanding of the human and non-human world

Understanding the values and intentions underpinning our practice is vital to understand the methodologies we outline in subsequent chapters comprehensively. The theoretical frameworks which inform our approach begins with critical theory's provocation that there are different types of knowledge and different ways of knowing. Notably, within the critical theory framework, learning is contextual and, therefore, changeable. Through an understanding of the context, we can broaden our knowledge of society and self. Critical pedagogy focuses on understanding oppression and social injustice and encouraging others to reflect on their understanding critically. Engagement with other knowledge, ways of knowing, and oppressions occurs through dialogue and sharing experiences. This can be a challenging and sometimes confronting process. Cohen-Cruz provides a model for combining artistic intentions with those of a transformed understanding of social justice issues without compromising either one (12). The shared values of mutuality, dialogue, and everyday lived experience link critical theory and critical pedagogy theories to feminist theatre practice, particularly to our intentions for community-engaged practice that draws on verbatim methodologies operating within an ethic of care. Chapter seven discusses each of these theoretical and ethical concepts in great detail, but we wanted to mention them here as well since they are embedded in the practice to be discussed across the rest of the book.

Across this chapter, we have discussed the history of verbatim theatre, the adaptability of the process and form, and the central philosophical debates surrounding this mode of creating and performing stories. The focus of the remaining chapters shifts towards a detailed engagement with the practical application of verbatim theatre methodologies. These include the initial engagement with a community, guidance around undertaking interviews, and the subsequent exploration of material which will inform the performance, as well as a specific focus on playwriting, rehearsing, and ethical practice. As is exemplified across each chapter, how you choose to apply these methods and approaches will be entirely dependent on your unique context, the community you are engaging with, and your intentions for the performance work.

1.5 Introductory Questions and Exercises

To Begin: a Starting Point for Theatre Artists

As a means of reflecting on verbatim theatre methodologies, it may be helpful to start with these questions:

- What is your experience of verbatim theatre? What are your preconceptions of its possibilities and its limits?
- What similarities and differences can you see between verbatim theatre and other mediums such as documentaries, historical adaptations, nonfiction podcasts and reality television?
- Are there stories that you are connected to that you feel would make a great verbatim play?

- Are you connected to a community of people that don't often have their story shared? Is there a way you can engage with that community?
- What historical stories are you aware of – perhaps through your family or broader community – that you feel need to be captured, archived, or perhaps even theatricalised?

In and Out of the Classroom – Links to Pedagogy

Verbatim theatre has found its way into the Australian Drama Curriculum for secondary students in recent years. In universities, verbatim theatre frequently appears as a form of study inside community-engaged practice units. This book addresses teachers and students in these fields of study, but it is worth pausing on verbatim theatre methodology's broader appeal to pedagogy overall.

Implicit within any community-engaged practice is a rigorous approach to "active listening", which we discuss in chapter three. Then, in chapters four and five, we discuss how artists and students might begin to transcribe, edit and transform this data into a creative product. In this, a tremendous amount of responsibility rests on the individual artist or student. In essence, they are creating their versions of another's story and learning how to articulate it. As Orr and Shreeve (2017), point out, this is "identity work", where "students are working out new forms of identity as knowledge, practices, beliefs and values are presented through engagement in learning" (81). This "becoming" process has positive and negative aspects, but it is crucial for any arts student. Further, "language is crucial to an identity of becoming" (82), and verbatim theatre methodologies demand students examine language and community/contextual vernacular in forensic detail.

For the authors of this book, who have engaged in countless workshops and classrooms with students from all ages and backgrounds, the greatest gift of verbatim theatre methodologies inside a community-engaged practice, is the empowerment of individual students to become arbiters of their collected stories. It differs significantly from other arts practices where a student creates work from within themselves. Instead, the task to first listen and hold space for another person's story gives the student a sense of responsibility and care, particularly if facilitated in a matter with an emphasis on ethical practice. As a creative practice, it can "plant seeds of change or moments of perspective-building" (Alrutz and Hoare 27), and give students "a chance to produce equitable spaces in which to work, in which they can be "me and not me", thereby meeting the alterity in themselves and encountering themselves as others" (Nicholson 213). Through holding another's story, they must shape their own. Thus, they engage in an "identity of becoming" that fosters critical pedagogy and an ability to articulate their artistry better.

More broadly, verbatim theatre methodologies and community-engaged practice typically have pedagogy embedded within them, even when activities are taking place outside of a formalised educational setting. Community-engaged practice, and verbatim theatre, typically draw upon marginalised communities or those whose stories are not regularly heard (Stuart Fisher, 2011a, 2011b). While the playwright or supervising artistic team may come from within this community of study, they are often sourced elsewhere. This separation between the community of study and the community of practice creates a collision that all must navigate. The collision is further complicated by the introduction of other communities, which may be brought in to provide additional stories or creative support. They may be present to provide production support (such as lighting and sound) or address organisational concerns (sponsors and stakeholders requirements). At the centre is the playwright, director, or creative team. For the successful and sensitive navigation of these stakeholders, the artist is called upon to enact a broad range of intrapersonal skills that are challenging and invaluable. Educational theorist Etienne Wenger provides helpful language in describing these artists as "social artists" capable of facilitating "open learning spaces" that invite a "learning citizenship" (2). Indeed, in community-engaged practice, students don't usually learn the most from the "teacher" (playwright/director) but from each other. The teacher must merely facilitate the space where such collisions can occur. This "peer-learning", which is also essential to any higher education arts curriculum (Orr and Shreeve 2017), is the engine that drives community-based practice, fuelled by verbatim theatre methodologies.

Principles in Practice

Playwright and author Claire Christian frequently relies on verbatim theatre methodologies in her work with young people, particularly when facilitating them in a group-devised process to make new work. She usually begins by asking participants to respond anonymously to provided stimuli. This material is then used to stimulate new improvisations or writing from the group. For Claire, this process is about, "the empowerment of young artists to use their own voices and their own content". She continues:

> When they're emerging, it's about them identifying what kind of artists they want to be and what they want to say. Devising is a really great way to clarify that for some of them. I love watching those kids who will inevitably be makers. Something wakes up for them and they go, 'I have agency over the stories I tell and whose stories are often not told'. And that of course happens with verbatim theatre, so often it showcases the voices that aren't often represented. It resonates with students who identify with that.

Using Reality Television to Discuss Verbatim Theatre

This is an exercise that can work in a classroom setting for secondary or tertiary students. Professional or amateur artists may also find it interesting or inspiring. This may serve as an introduction to the genre of verbatim theatre, or as a way to deepen students' understanding. It may be particularly helpful in bridging the experience between interviewing and editing verbatim data.

Begin by sourcing a reality television program. It is usually best if it is a competition reality program. Other, lifestyle-focussed or makeover programs (such as the *Real Housewives* series, *Keeping Up With The Kardashians* or *Grand Designs*) are still generally usable, but are inherently less dramaturgically useful than competition programs.

For this session, focus on a particular segment of an episode that includes a beginning, middle, and end. This may be a particular challenge that the contestants undertake. The exercise involves you examining the footage forensically, so usually, just ten or fifteen minutes of an episode is more than enough.

Watch the segment through once. Ask students to discuss or note the following:

- What was the beginning of the story beat? Is there a clearly identifiable inciting incident? What triggered the central dramatic tension or conflict?
- What were moments of tension in the narrative of this segment?
- Was there a climax? Or a resolution?

Now, watch the segment again. This time, ask students to observe *who* is telling the story and *how*. In most reality programs, the narrative thread is split across many modes and narrators. Ask students to list them. There are likely to be at least three:

- The footage of the event playing out, edited for time and tension
- A host, either narrating in the voice-over or appearing with contestants
- Retrospective one-on-one interviews with contestants, narrating the action after the event

Before watching for a third and final time, ask students to draw a table that they will use to "map" the narrative unfolding. In each column of the table, write down one of the modes or narrators that were listed in the second viewing. In each row of the table, list five to ten clear "beats" in the story.

On the final viewing, ask students to roughly track which of the narrators is used for each story beat. Depending on the segment you've chosen, you may need to slow this viewing down, stopping every minute or so. Once the activity is completed, reflect and discuss what students found.

- The narrators likely had different personalities. We can presume that all contestants were filmed after the event and asked to narrate their experience. Why did editors choose specific narrators at specific times?

- How often do editors cut away from the action to a narrator? Why?
- How much editing has happened of the actual event? Why?
- What role does the host or narrator play?
- Who reminds the audience of the task and the stakes? Which narrator best heightens tension?

There are many links to verbatim theatre that can be explored in this exercise. Different modalities of narration have different effects. Importantly, competition reality television has incredibly clear dramaturgical boundaries that assist in the narrative. There is a challenge that must be completed. The winner receives a prize or an advantage in the larger competition. The loser's very existence in the competition is likely at stake. Verbatim theatre data rarely presents its stakes quite as clearly, but a playwright can be assisted in at least entertaining a more simplistic view. What is at stake? Where does the tension or conflict come from?

There is also worthy discussion in exploring the dramatic difference between *seeing* the actual footage of the event, versus the recounting of it in later interviews. Sometimes, a contestant will experience a moment of great emotion in the interview. Editors usually gravitate towards this, at times building an entire segment around a contestant shedding a tear in an interview. Other times, editors and producers may stumble across "gold" when filming an event live, and leave such moments relatively unadorned by editing or cutaways. Discuss with your students what verbatim theatre can lose or gain by using both of these modes. How would the segment have differed if narrative beats were told by different narrators?

Using Podcasts to Discuss Verbatim Theatre

While reality television provides important lessons in dramaturgy and narrative modes, podcasts are closer to the experience of experimenting with audio data and interviews. While it's possible to mirror the reality television exercise above with podcasts, we'd also encourage you to use podcasts as a potential "script" that students can experiment with in class. Try listening to a segment of any of the below pieces, and asking students to "stage" the segment for a theatrical audience. This can be done through lip-syncing, or through accessing a transcription of the podcast and asking students to treat it as a play script.

Again, this will elicit a slew of questions for discussion:

- What is lost and gained in the translation from audio to theatrical?
- If you could, are there pieces of the script you would edit because some of the story-telling can be achieved through a visual medium only?
- What work in the staging *affirms* the dramatic meaning of the podcast? Can you make staging decisions that deliberately *subvert* the dramatic meaning of the podcast? when does this feel satirical? When does it feel *unethical*?

34 *Histories, Definitions, and Applications*

Check out some of the below podcasts for help:

- *Radiolab* produced by WNYC is a non-fiction podcast that explores a whole range of topics. It is most well known for its incredibly high production value. This is about as theatrical as podcasts get: lush soundtracks and sound effects galore. In verbatim theatre workshops, we recommend the episode "Playing God", produced in 2016
- The *TED Radio Hour* is produced by NPR. It takes TED talks and talks to the people behind them. This podcast often attempts to explain incredibly complicated ideas in compelling ways. In verbatim theatre workshops, we recommend the episode "Peering into Space", produced in 2013
- *Where Should We Begin?* presented by Esther Perel is an intimate glimpse into couples therapy. Each episode centres around a one-time counselling session with a couple, presided over by renown therapist Esther Perel. The episodes are frequently unsuitable for secondary students. For tertiary students and professionals, however, they're an alluring piece of inspiration. Perel edits her episodes down to fit an hour, but there are long stretches of discussion that are completely uninterrupted. The discussions will often fall apart on stage and become – potentially – boring. Challenging workshop participants to stage, edit or re-imagine the session can be a helpful way of discussing staging verbatim theatre

Using Agitprop and Living Newspaper to Understand Political Performance

As discussed, agitprop and the Living Newspaper are forerunners to community-engaged and verbatim theatre performance. Agitprop and Living Newspaper scripts can be incredibly difficult to find. This is because they are historical documents, and finding a suitable English translation that is also somehow relevant to twenty-first century high school or university students can be impossible. Instead, we suggest using some of the conventions of agitprop to introduce your students to political performance. Your students may already be familiar with political performance, particularly if they've studied Bertolt Brecht. However, if your students have only been primarily exposed to musical theatre, realism, or contemporary commercial theatre then the true expanse of what is available in political theatre may come as a surprise.

It is easiest to begin by sourcing some news articles. You can set your students a particular challenge by making the topic of the news articles especially dry or technical. An easier path is to deliberately seek out stories that resonate with students. This may be about a particular music artist or celebrity, video game culture, or any issue that is particularly relevant to young people. A bold teacher may use a school newsletter, or a school's principal's speech (trickier territory for the teacher, but will ensure a high-quality result!). Once you've sourced your articles you can encourage your students to set out on a miniature verbatim theatre process. They must edit the information they've been given into a script and stage it. This can be the focus of a single lesson's work or the

Histories, Definitions, and Applications 35

focus of an entire semester. Essentially, there is very little difference between this and most Living Newspapers' performances.

Separate to this, or at some point during the process, it is helpful to introduce some of the key elements of agitprop and political performance. These include:

- Repetition
- Chorus work to emphasise key ideas or phrases
- Simple skits that demonstrate a point
- Use of projection of videos and images to communicate ideas
- Satirical representation of real people to subvert authority
- Use of songs and jingles

Using the above elements, students should be encouraged to remix the source material to communicate their opinion about the issue at hand.

All of these elements are frequently used in verbatim theatre. In completing this exercise, students have essentially experimented with both agitprop and the Living Newspaper forms.

The Beginning of the Journey: Understanding your *Community*

If you are particularly studious, you may be reading this book from front to back. If so, then you're at the beginning of a big journey. Before embarking on an artistic process that will see you immersed in a community and studying it intensely, it is worth examining your own biases, prejudices, and background. Verbatim theatre's historical roots are in political performance, and community-engaged practice is most known for giving voice to oppressed groups. In order to do this properly, a high degree of self-awareness is paramount. Too many community-engaged projects can become about a singular artist seeking to "save" a community, thereby aggrandising themselves. Exploitation and poverty pornography are the most extreme (but not uncommon) results of community-engaged artists who have not studied themselves (and their true intentions) properly.

This exercise is helpful for anyone at any level of experience, and can bring about provocative conversation and valuable self-reflection.

It is worth first making explicit your own community. Where *you* come from. We often fail to see what is special or unique about ourselves because we dismiss it as "normal" or "boring". But in examining yourself you may find that you already have access to communities and stories that are worth celebrating. This was the case for Sarah when she embarked on her work *bald heads & blue stars*, which focussed on women with alopecia.

Take a piece of paper and note:

- Your gender identity – are you a part of communities that identify themselves strongly with this gender identity?

36 *Histories, Definitions, and Applications*

- Your ethnic background – how has your relationship with race and culture shaped who you are? And do you connect this with any of the communities in your life?
- Your age – what generation are you a part of? Do you have strong feelings about this generation?
- The income of your household – has it always been like this? Do you identify as a particular class? What insights or access does your class give you?
- Your explicit communities – are you a part of a church group? A sports club? A parents group? A playgroup?

In conjunction with the above questions, a helpful classroom exercise can be a "privilege walk". It is difficult to trace the lineage of this exercise, as it has now been the subject of viral internet videos, professional development seminars, and many classrooms. Its popularity hints at its potential for profundity. Searching online for examples of the "privilege walk" will net you many results. We've provided just a few suggestions or prompts here, but we encourage you to expand the list to suit your needs (and consider carefully what you're asking students to disclose by responding to these questions).

Ask students to stand in a line in the middle of the room. Students will be asked to take one step back or forward depending on the prompt.

- Take one step forward if you're right handed
- Take one step forward if you grew up with more than thirty books in your home
- Take one step back if you've ever been forced to skip a meal because you couldn't afford food
- Take one step back if you would have anxiety about calling the police in a distressing situation
- Take one step forward if either of your parents attended university
- Take one step back if you feel pressure to apply cosmetics before leaving the house
- Take one step back if a member of your family is currently in prison
- Take one step forward if you feel good about the way people who look like you are portrayed in the media

Leave plenty of time for discussion after this exercise. In linking to community-engaged practice, it is important that we recognise our own communities before we ask to be a guest in others.

Principles in Practice

Suzie Miller reflects that sometimes the starting point for a play can be "just one thing that catches your eye or your attention, that somehow sticks and keeps asking you questions". She describes that experience happening for her when writing *Cross Sections,* a play set in Kings Cross which introduces audiences to a variety of characters living in Sydney's red light district. Miller recalls the moment

> a young rent boy client was left by the side of the road bleeding after being hit by a runaway cab. I remember the look on the 21-year-old homeless guy's face. After all he had been through – assaulted countless times, childhood abuse, beaten up by people in authority – and yet here he was, so shocked by this latest lack of humanity "how could he leave me there to die like a dog by the side of the road?"
>
> He was weeping more about that than his significant injuries. It made me just contemplate how he could still have had such faith that he was shocked by that, and also to ask why the cabbie would have driven off? Why did he see this young man as not worth stopping for, and don't we all at some level allow street kids to be invisible?

1.6 Further Reading

Below is a list of major international verbatim works that would be suitable for reading as an introduction to the format:

- *The Laramie Project* by Moises Kaufman and the members of the Tectonic Theatre Project, published by Knopf US, 2014
- *Twilight: Los Angeles*, 1992 by Anna Deveare Smith, published by Random House US, 1994
- *Talking to Terrorists* by Robin Soans, published by Oberon Books, 2012
- *Permanent Way* by David Hare, published by Faber Plays, 2005
- *Home* by Nadia Fall, published by Nick Hearn Books, 2015
- *The Exonerated* by Jessica Blank and Erik Jensen, published by Farrar, Strauss and Giroux, 2003

Australian examples of verbatim works (or works informed by Verbatim theatre methodologies) include:

- *Aftershocks* by Paul Brown, published by Currency Press, 1993
- *Embers* by Campion Decent, published by Playlab Theatre, 2008
- *The Campaign* by Campion Decent, published by Playlab Theatre, 2018
- *Gaybies* by Dean Bryant, published by Playlab Theatre, 2017
- *Black Diggers* by Tom Wright, published by Playlab Theatre, 2014
- *Seven Stages of Grieving* by Wesley Enoch and Deborah Mailman, published by Playlab Theatre 2020
- *Driving into Walls* by Suzi Miller, published by Playlab Theatre, 2013

- *Talking to Brick Walls* by Claire Christian and the Empire Youth Arts Ensemble, published by Playlab Theatre, 2015
- *Bogga* by Rob Pensalfini, published by Playlab Theatre, 2017
- *Bukal* by Andrea James with Henrietta Marie, published by Playlab Theatre, 2018
- *Cribbie* by Michael and Margarey Forde, published by Playlab Theatre, 2009
- *The Long Way Home* by Daniel Keene, published by Playlab Theatre, 2014

An example of Oral Histories would be *Titanic*, written by Owen McCafferty, which collected the testimonies of survivors from the Titanic for its hundredth anniversary. You can find a published version by Faber and Faber.

There are many examples of Tribunal Plays. Tricycle Theatre Collective have collected many of theirs into a single volume: "The Tricycle: Collected Tribunal Plays 1994–2012", published by Oberon Books.

Some of the case studies we use for this book are published by Playlab Press, including *St. Mary's In Exile* and *April's Fool*, available online via Australian Plays Transform, including *Eternity, Blister, and twelve2twentyfive,* and a DVD of *bald heads & blue stars* is available through the Australia Alopecia Foundation website.

Finding examples of agitprop can be difficult. If you do find scripts, the quality of the English translation can sometimes be dubious. In addition, by its very nature agitprop is so *local* and timely that finding scripts that still have any meaning outside their original context is near impossible. However, some do exist and can be useful in classrooms as very quick, easy ways to formulate performances. A good place to start may be "Agitprop to Theatre Workshop: Political Playscripts 1930–1950" by Ewan Maccoll and Howard Goorney, published by Palgrave Macmillan, 1988.

Augusto Boal's works are very handy and a necessary accompaniment to almost any community-engagement arts practitioner. We highly recommend the use of *Games for Actors and Non-Actors.*

Works Cited

Ackroyd, Judith and John O'Toole. *Performing Research: Tensions, Triumphs and Trade-offs of Ethnodrama.* Trentham Books Limited, 2010.

Ackroyd, J. "Applied Theatre: Problems and Possibilities." *Applied Theatre Researcher* 1(1), 2000, pp. 1–13.

Alrutz, Megan and Lynne Hoare. *Devising Critically Engaged Theatre with Youth: The Performing Justice Project.* Taylor and Francis Group, Proquest Ebook Central, 2020.

Anderson, Michael and Linden Wilkinson. "A Resurgence of Verbatim Theatre: Authenticity Empathy and Transformation." *Australasian Drama Studies* 50, 2007, pp. 153–169.

Badham, M. "The Turn to Community: Exploring the Political and Relational in the Arts." *Journal of Arts & Communities* 5(2), 2014, pp. 93–104.

Barranger, Milly. *Understanding Plays*. 3rd edition, Pearson Education, 2004.
Beck, Jaime, et al. "Delineating a Spectrum of Research-Based Theatre." *Qualitative Inquiry* 17, 2011, pp. 687–700.
Botham, Paola. "Witnesses in The Public Sphere: Bloody Sunday and the Redefinition of Political Theatre." *Political Performances, Theory and Practice*, edited by Susan Haedlicke, et al., Editions Rodopi, 2009, pp. 35–53.
Bottoms, S. "Putting the Document into Documentary." *The Drama Review* 50(3), 2006, pp. 56–68.
Brockett, Oscar. *The Essential Theatre*. 4th edition. Holt, Rinehart and Winston, 1988.
Burton, David. *Playwriting methodologies in Community-Engaged Theatre Practice*. Queensland University of Technology, 2021, doctoral thesis
Cantrell, Tom. *Acting in Documentary Theatre*. Palgrave MacMillan, 2013.
Cantrell, Tom. "Playing for Real in Max Stafford-Clarke's Talking to Terrorists." *Studies in Theatre and Performance* 31.2, 2011, pp. 167–180.
Carter, D. and C. Heim. "Community engagement or community conversation? 'Boomtown', a large-scale, regional outdoor community theatrical event." *Australasian Drama Studies* 66, 2015. pp. 202–204.
Cohen-Cruz, Jan. *Engaging Performance, Theatre as Call and Response*. Routledge, 2010.
Decent, Campion. *Embers*. Playlab, 2008.
Downes, B. *From Life, to Page, to Stage: Exploring Theatrical Artistry, Community and Storytelling with Margery and Micahel Forde*. Australian Catholic University, 2013, PhD Thesis.
Flanagan, Hallie. *Arena: The History of the Federal Theatre*. University of California, 1940.
Gallagher, Kathleen, Anne Wessels, and Yaman Ntelioglou. "Verbatim Theatre and Social Research: Turning Towards the Stories of Others." *Theatre Research in Canada* 33.1, 2012, pp. 24–43.
Garde, Ulrike, Meg Mumford, and Caroline Wake. "A Short History of Verbatim Theatre." *Verbatim: Staging Memory and Community*, edited by Paul Brown, Currency Press, 2010, pp. 9–17.
Goldbard, A. *New Creative Community: The Art of Cultural Development*. New Village Press. 2006.
Gonzalez, A.A. "Historia oral, memoria colectiva y comunidad en el teatro del mundo: El caso del teartro verbatim." *Signa* 25, 2016, pp. 273–296.
Graham, S. "The X Factor and Reality Television: Beyond Good and Evil." *Popular Music* 36(1), 2017, pp. 6–20.
Gray, Ross, et al. "The Use of Research-based Theatre in a Project Related to Metastatic Breast Cancer." *Health Expectations* 3, 2000, pp. 137–144.
Hilbers, J. "The Challenges and Opportunities of Community Celebrations that Value Diversity and Foster Unity: Beyond 'Spaghetti and Polka'." *Journal of Arts and Communities* 3(1), 2011, pp. 23–37.
Hill, A. *Media Experiences*. Routledge, 2019.
Holderness, Graham. *The Politics of Theatre and Drama*. Macmillan, 1992.
Innes, Christopher. *Erwin Piscator's Political Theatre: The Development of Modern German Drama*. Cambridge University Press, 1972.
Kaufman, Moisés. "Anatomy of an Experiment." *American Theatre* (July/August), 2010, pp. 27–30.
Leach, Robert. *Revolutionary Theatre*. Routledge, 1994.

Lillie, Jade. "The Relationships is the Project." *The Relationship is the Project*, edited by Jade Lillie, Kate Larsen, Cara Kirkwood and Jax Jacki Brown's, Brow Books, Victoria, 2020, pp. 159–164.

Luckhurst, Mary. "Verbatim Theatre, Media Relations and Ethics." *A Concise Companion to Contemporary British and Irish Drama*, edited by Nadine Holdsworth and Mary Luckhurst, Blackwell Publishing, 2008, pp. 200–222.

Lunt, Peter. "Reality Television, Public Service and Public Live: A Critical Theory Per-spective." *A Companion to Reality Television*, edited by Laurie Ouellette, Wiley. Blackwell, 2014, pp. 501–515.

Martin, Carol. *Theatre of the Real*. Palgrave Macmillan, 2013.

McCallum, J. *Belonging: Australian Playwriting in the Twentieth Century*. Currency, Syndey, 2005.

Mitchell, Gail, Christine Jonas-Simpson and Vrenia Ivonoffski. "Research-Based Theatre: The Making of I'm Still Here!" *Nursing Science Quarterly* 19.3, 2006, pp. 198–206.

Nicholson, Helen. *Theatre, Education and Performance*. Bloomsbury Publishing, 2011.

Orr, S. and Shreeve, A. *Art and Design Pedagogy in Higher Education: Knowledge, Values and Ambiguity in the Creative Curriculum*. Routledge, 2017.

Paget, Derek. "'Acting with Facts': Actors Performing the Real in British Theatre and Television since 1990. A Preliminary Report on a New Research Project." *Studies in Documentary Film* ½, 2007, pp. 165–176.

Paget, Derek. "New Documentarism on Stage: Documentary Theatre in New Times." *Zeitschrift fur Anglistik und Amerikanistik* 56.2, 2008, pp. 129–141.

Paget, Derek. "Verbatim Theatre: Oral History and Documentary Techniques." *New Theatre Quarterly* 3.12, 1987, pp. 317–336.

Peters, Sarah. "Verbatim Theatre and a Dramaturgy of Belonging." *Australasian Drama Studies* 74, 2019, pp. 39–63.

Reinelt, Janelle. "The Promise of Documentary." *Get Real: Documentary Theatre Past and Present*, edited by Alison Forsyth and Chris Megson, Palgrave Macmillan, 2011, pp. 6–23.

Rossiter, Kate, et al. "Staging Data: Theatre as a Tool for Analysis and Knowledge Transfer in Health Research." *Social Science and Medicine* 66, 2008. pp. 130–146.

Saldaña, Johnny. "Dramatizing Data: A Primer." *Qualitative Inquiry* 9, 2003, pp. 218–235.

Saldaña, Johnny. "The Backstage and Offstage Stories of Ethnodrama: A Review of Ackroyd and O'Toole's Performing Research." *International Journal of Education and the Arts* 11.5, 2010, pp. 1–9.

Şimşek, B. "Digital Storytelling for Women's Well-being in Turkey." *Digital Storytelling*, edited by Dunford and Jenkins, 2017.

Stiernstedt, F., and P. Jakobsson. "Watching Reality from a Distance: Class, Genre and Reality Television." *Media, Culture & Society* 39(5), 2017, pp. 697–714.

Stuart Fisher, Amanda. "'That's Who I'd Be, If I Could Sing': Reflections on a Verbatim Project with Mothers of Sexually Abused Children." *Studies in Theatre and Performance* 21.2, 2011a, pp. 193–208.

Stuart Fisher, Amanda. "Trauma, Authenticity and the Limits of Verbatim." *Performance Research: A Journal of the Performing Arts* 16.1, 2011b, pp. 112–122.

Summerskill, Clare. *Creating Verbatim Theatre from Oral Histories*. Routledge, 2021.

Taylor, Lib. "Voice, Body and the Transmission of the Real in Documentary Theatre." *Contemporary Theatre Review* 23.3, 2013, pp. 368–379.

Valentine, Alana (2018) *Bowerbird: The Art of Making Theatre Drawn from Life*. Currency Press, 2018.
Wake, Caroline. "Headphone Verbatim Theatre: Methods, Histories, Genres, Theories." *New Theatre Quarterly* 29.4, 2013, pp. 321–335.
Wake, Caroline. "Towards a Working Definition of Verbatim Theatre." *Verbatim: Staging Memory and Community*. Currency Press, 2010, pp. 2–5.
Watt, David. "Local Knowledges, Memories, and Community: From Oral History to Performance." *Political Performances, Theory and Practice*, edited by Susan Haedicke, et al. Editions Rodopi, 2009, pp. 189–212.
Wenger, E. "Social Learning Capability: Four Essays on Innovation and Learning in Social Systems." *Social Innovation, Sociedade e Trabalho*. 2009. Booklets 12 – separate supplement, MTSS/GEP & EQUAL
Witham, Barry. *The Federal Theatre Project: A Case Study*. Cambridge University Press, 2003.

2 Community Immersion

Community Immersion – spending time in the community you are working with – is the first phase of a verbatim theatre process and an integral component of ethical practice. It is an opportunity for the creative team to get to know the community and the community to get to know the creative team. In this chapter, we define our approach to community immersion and outline some of the critical intentions and values of this initial phase of a verbatim theatre process. Finally, we provide examples of the range and diversity of community immersion strategies we have applied in our practice across multiple case studies.

2.1 Definition of Community Immersion

Developing relationships with members of the community means engaging in two-way dialogue. On a macro level, Jan Cohen-Cruz outlines a theory of practice called "engaged performance" and describes it as a dialogue between the social call of a community and the cultural response of an artist. She says when working with a community, the process and project must benefit the people whose lives inform the project, and not "just promote the artist" (Cohen-Cruz 2010, 2). An iterative process of call and response – an ongoing conversation between the creative team and the community across the project's life – creates a collaborative engagement that builds relationships and trust for all involved. Similarly, in her edited book, *The Relationship is the Project,* Jade Lillie describes community-engaged practice as "a deep collaboration between practitioners and communities to develop outcomes specific to that relationship, time and place" (Lillie et al. 2020, 9). Cohen-Cruz and Lillie's description of engagement as mutual, responsive, and connected to place applies to various art forms and processes. We suggest community immersion and the associated strategies of this practice are ways we enact meaningful community engagement in verbatim theatre.

Community immersion is a process of collaborating with and getting to know the community who are at the heart of a verbatim theatre project. You might know that community well (and be a member of the community yourself!), or you might be an outsider to that community invited in or asking for access. Regardless, our definition of community immersion brings our values and intentions as artists into tight focus. Before committing yourself to community immersion, it's essential to be mindful of your intent and the values preceding your intent. Without this clarity, you can encounter ethically murky waters as your project develops. For example, your project may be perceived (correctly or not) as only a vehicle to promote your work, or the immersion itself may manifest as a one-sided conversation, excluding critical voices and invisible knowledge.

Principles in Practice

Campion Decent describes working with "intermediaries" as part of his approach when working with communities. In *Embers,* this was Les Hume, a local rural recovery support worker and ex-fire officer who was assigned to work with Campion as they conducted over 75 interviews in relation to the 2003 bushfire event in North East Victoria. In his work on *The Campaign,* Campion reflects that "without the blessing of Rodney Croome and Nick Toonan we wouldn't have got that project off the ground. And it really needed their support ... you can understand it, people like Rodney who have been through a lot over the years with the media, when someone comes in and says, "I'd like to do a play about that campaign you did', you know, they're gonna go, 'oh, hang on, who are you? Where are you coming from?' all that. So you've got to win their trust". In the development of his latest verbatim work, *Unprecedented,* Campion collaborated with the First Nations producer at HotHouse Theatre as an intermediary in order to ensure an ethical approach to representing First Nation characters and experiences. These intermediaries provide a bridge between Campion and the communities he is working with, providing opportunities for relationships – and trust – to be built as part of the project.

Values

Values precede intentions and inform the artistic impulse of any work, whether based on verbatim methodology or not. This is more than a simple esoteric or hypothetical discussion. Instead, it is essential for every artist, operating at any level, to be clear and transparent about their values before beginning community immersion. Community immersion is exciting, seductive work. Without clarity around one's intent and values before starting, the artist can become lost in a rising tide of stories and data. It's important to be clear from the start of a project to ensure dramaturgical robustness and ethical standing.

For us, our values around verbatim theatre arise from its historical roots in feminist theatre practice; community-engaged practice that is highly collaborative and made manifest in a variety of theatre forms. Many of these forms are non-linear, and while some can be captured in the term "verbatim theatre", they have also been preceded by forms by Erwin Piscator, Bertolt Brecht, and Augusto Boal. Our work as artists intersects with our role as teachers, where we practice critical pedagogy. Critical pedagogy, arising from educational practitioners such as Paulo Friere and Henry Giroux, holds space for transformation by "asking new questions and indicating new connections" (Doyle 1993, 5). In this, we leverage the inherently political nature of schooling to examine cultural spaces and facilitate conversations across political identities critically.

These values are the foundation upon which we can launch community immersion. Our feminist theatre practice experience, for example, immediately infers that we are not simply playwrights with a vision to impose upon a community. Instead, we are one collaborative partner that seeks to open a two-way dialogue with the community. Importantly these values not only inflect upon the *beginning* of a process (usually marked by a period of community immersion) but are also refracted throughout an entire process of making, right through "opening night" to a project's evaluative measures.

Principles in Practice

Verbatim theatre methodologies are the bedrock for Queensland theatre-maker, playwright, and educator, Claire Christian. Claire trained and worked as a high school teacher before beginning her professional playwriting career, and still works consistently in the tertiary education sector, where she is frequently asked to facilitate a "devising" process where students create new work. In these situations, Claire applies verbatim theatre methodologies to the performers themselves. In this way, the ensemble of performers becomes the community of study *as well as* the performers in the eventual performance product. She frequently uses anonymous submissions as a way of establishing trust, vulnerability, and authenticity among young artists.

In one example, Claire used Duncan MacMillan's play *Every Brilliant Thing* as stimulus. She then asked students to anonymously submit a list of things that they were grateful for or they considered "brilliant". She then asked students to write a list of things that they were *not* grateful for. "It was a strategy to build authenticity and honesty in the class," Claire reflects. "But part of it is also a strategy to keep participants safe. So they can be vulnerable and honest, but don't have to share directly." This tension, between vulnerability and safety, is a key value for Claire's devising process with young people. Beginning with these simple exercises allowed for a direct demonstration of her values, and the values she wishes to imbue in the classroom.

Intentions

What is community immersion aiming to achieve? While it can look and feel a little different in every project, it is a process that enables the creative team to:

- Develop relationships with members of the community
- Actively engage in and support community events and projects
- Build awareness of the creative project within the community
- Better understand how to tell stories with and about that community in a meaningful way

Derek Paget emphasises that community-engaged theatre focuses on a particular community and the stories, tensions, and ideas they want to explore (2010, 175). Meaningful community immersion intends to better understand the specific stories, places, people, and events of that community so that any resulting performances are coming from a place of integrity and informed authenticity of that community's experience. It serves the quality and richness of the work. It also enables the creative team to better publicise the project, ensuring the community's breadth of participation and involvement. Our approach to community immersion is also informed by an ethics of care (Hankivsky 2004). As such it is a mechanism through which the creative team can provide service and sustained connection across the project's duration. If a community is going to trust you with their stories, you need to be worthy of that trust. A playwright must take their chosen community of study with them as the project progresses, preparing them for how they might experience the project and consider accessibility to the project. As the first phase of a community-engaged project, immersion is a responsibility of the creative team and requires sensitivity and time.

Principles in Practice

One element of Alana Valentine's community relationship building and immersion process is to create what she refers to as a "chain of connection"; interviewing someone who is already connected to someone else you have interviewed, and then asking them to recommend someone else, and so on. This chain of connection means that you might be able to more easily build the relationship – "if they trust that person they may be more disposed to trust you" – and it also means that "if the interviewee might experience flashbacks or bad memories because of your discussion, it is both ethical and responsible to know that they have someone they can call if they need to debrief" (Valentine, 59). Valentine emphasises that

> we are not trained counsellors. We are not trained to deal with the people whose memories and pains we are rifling through. It may be at their invitation and you may think, well they're adults and they can make that decision for themselves. But we have to be strategically responsible even to people who think they will be fine. And probably will be fine. Indeed, most people benefit from telling you their story. Sometimes you are the first person they have spoken to about their past pain and they find it liberating; the telling can help them to heal. I have seen that happen to a large number of interviewees and it helps me to keep going (Valentine 2018, 59–60).

Strategies and Practices

With these intentions for community immersion in mind, what can it look like in practice? There are a variety of strategies and practices that we and other creatives using verbatim theatre methods have used as part of community immersion. Not all of these will be right for every project, and you might focus on only one or two depending on the community you are working with and the story you are telling.

Contacting Peak Bodies, Media Outlets, and Support Services Connected to the Community

There may be a peak body associated with your community, or local media outlets and service organisations that can help facilitate your connection with the community. For example, in the *bald heads & blue stars* project, the Australia Alopecia Areata Foundation was a key organisation that Sarah worked with in the initial stages of her community immersion. The AAAF have a strong connection to their members and are a trusted source of support and information. By accessing the alopecia community through the AAAF, this trust and validity was extended to Sarah's project and she was able to access a much wider cross section of the alopecia community then she could have done on her own. Connecting with a peak body in this way not only helps to facilitate access to a community, but can also help promote creative work, building audience numbers and arts engagement in a broader population.

Working with media outlets and support services familiar to the community you are engaging with helps connect your project with a local audience. When Australian playwright and screenwriter Linden Wilkinson began work for her play *A Day in December* (which details a deadly train accident near the Blue Mountains in 1999), she advertised the project in the Blue Mountains Gazette (2010). Using a media outlet familiar with the community prompted locals to volunteer for the project and share their experiences of the tragic event. In the *twelve2twentyfive* project, Sarah collaborated with counsellors and psychologists in Toowoomba and the Darling Downs to conduct interviews so that when young people who accessed mental health support participated in the project it was with someone they knew and who could bring their training and experience to the conversation if needed. For *St. Mary's In Exile,* David began by immersing himself in the group of rebel Catholics who still practiced weekly illegal "Eucharist" in inner-Brisbane. David attended several masses and meetings, eventually also coming to understand the administrative relationship the community had with a social justice not-for-profit organisation called *Micah Projects.* Coming to understand the importance and history of the Micah Projects organisation greatly informed the final work, but it also gave nuanced insight into the history of the *St. Mary's In Exile* community.

Principles in Practice

Valentine reflects on the importance of working with reputable organisations connected to the subject of verbatim works. When working with adult survivors of child abuse, Valentine

> worked with a reputable organisation, ASCA (Adults Surviving Child Abuse, now the Blue Knot Foundation) and some interviewees found out about my project through their website. I also went to ASCA workshops for health professionals, where I met therapists and doctors and asked them to recommend any patients they thought might be 'ready' to speak about their ordeal ... I maintained my contact with the Blue Knot Foundation long after the public event took place, in fact I am still working with them. I make a professional commitment when I work in a community to develop a trust relationship, and invest time and self and work (Valentine, 61).

Engaging in Activities that Serve the Goals of that Community

Community immersion can also be an act of service. The creative team can attend and participate in community events, help raise awareness and visibility of the community and its goals through news and social media outlets, and simply listen to the breadth and depth of stories of that community regardless of whether they are informing the final creative work or not.

For the Queensland Music Festival project *The Mount Isa Blast,* David committed to a period of community immersion in the small outback town in Central Queensland. As it was a musical project that would utilise local talents, the production needed local musicians. A local rock band, Bulldust, wanted the chance to perform. Attending a Bulldust gig in a busy pub on a Saturday night was a rich community immersion experience. Asking the band to perform in daylight in a neutral setting would've allowed the creative team to meet and assess their talents, but witnessing the musicians in full flight was invaluable. So too was immersion in the culture of a Saturday night in Mount Isa. A large contingent of coal miners, who would've otherwise likely been alienated by potential involvement in an "arts" project, was open to discussion after a first casual chat and a beer in the pub, with "Bulldust" playing AC/DC in the background.

Having Conversations with the Community

This is the most well-known verbatim theatre method; interviewing community members and recording their stories to inform the development of the creative work. It is such a vital component of the process that we have dedicated an entire chapter to it in this book. Yet this method is just one in a myriad of approaches designed to prompt conversation (sometimes recorded, sometimes not), which help the creative team understand which stories are meaningful to that community. It also educates the artists on *how to tell* those stories in a meaningful way. Any activity that prompts a conversation – exchanging emails, writing letters, having coffee or sharing a meal – can be a great way to immerse yourself in the community.

The community immersion for *Blister* meant Sarah walked the Camino de Santiago – an 800km pilgrimage in northern Spain – and had thousands of conversations with fellow walkers across this month-long immersion. The only material trace of these conversations were Sarah's daily journal entries, yet this month spent conversing (and walking) profoundly informed the play and the authenticity of the representation of the Camino experience.

The community immersion for the *Queensland Music Festival Signature Community Events* meant David was embedded in regional Queensland communities, part-time, for many months. Every single interaction was potential fuel for the final production, including conversations with hotel staff, waiters serving breakfast and dinner, teachers, police, and many more. These conversations were rarely recorded, but much like Sarah and *Blister*, David religiously committed to writing details of conversations down when appropriate.

Principles in Practice

Much of Dan Evans' work with The Good Room (a Queensland based performance collective) involves the use of anonymous submissions made by participants in online forums. However, as part of the development of *Let's Be Friends Furever* (2021), Dan met with dog-owners to hear them speak about their love for their pets. Dan reflects on the difference in vulnerability when stories are shared in the anonymous online space compared to being "in the room";

> vulnerability is hard, vulnerability with another human in the room is more difficult ... as a maker I learned that authenticity is so closely linked with vulnerability, and there's a continuum there. And I just think that's really interesting. And you can't fake authenticity, and you can't fake vulnerability, but the methods of eliciting that vulnerability is different when you don't get to meet the person.
>
> In his experience, people might be more willing to be vulnerable about the description and detail of their experiences when describing them anonymously online, but when they
>
> removed the screen and sat in front of people and asked them about their dog in what became much more like a documentary sort of format – that was all the feels ... you're sitting and you're living an experience with someone right in front of you ... And there's a beauty to that. There's a beauty to being anonymous, and there's a beauty to someone being there and sharing your story. And then everyone witnessing their story with you.

Providing Creative Service to the Community

Sharing your creative skills can be a wonderful way to nurture relationships and give back to the community. This might come in the form of offering arts-based workshops, facilitating professional development activities for members of the community, mentoring emerging creatives, and involving the community to varying degrees in the resulting performance. Alana Valentine's community immersion for *Comin Home Soon* (2012) began as a request to conduct writing workshops with the Indigenous inmates at Goulburn Correctional Centre, working with the inmates to write stories about their experiences. This then led to speaking with children of incarcerated parents and the correctional centre officers (qtd. in Goulburn Regional Art Gallery 7), all of which informed the playwriting process.

For many works involving young people, such as the *Queensland Music Festival Signature Community Events*, David typically offers free creative workshops in high schools, designed to respond to specific curriculum needs. These workshops serve a dual purpose. They genuinely service the community, while also allowing David to understand the implicit culture of a given classroom, including inside jokes, their self-perception, and the perception of their town. All of this is invaluable insight for the final work. In addition, the school and drama classroom become allies to the production. For the QMF works, this could eventually mean assistance in securing rehearsal space for the final production.

Principles in Practice

In 2011, Claire Christian was part of a state-funded effort to work with young people in the Lockyer Valley after a devastating flood. Everyone, including Claire, presumed they would be creating a work about the flood. But in talking with the young people, it became clear that they didn't want to talk about the flood. Claire says, "and they were sick of it. They wanted to talk about why their crushes don't like them, or why their parents grounded them, and all the chaos of being a teenager. So we made a work about that".

This is an example of effective community immersion. Even though initial funding for the project was built on the idea of "flood support", Claire listened when the community articulated what it really wanted, and this then became the focus of the project.

Maintaining Connection with the Community

Community immersion is not just something that occurs at the beginning of a project. It is an ongoing, sustained, durational aspect of community-engaged practice. You can maintain connections by sharing drafts of the creative work with the participants, providing updates on progress, holding play readings and feedback sessions, and following up with the community after the public sharing of new works. If your community immersion meant participating in and supporting community events, this might continue beyond the creative project. At a bare minimum, maintaining a connection is relatively easy within social media. A simple Facebook group can ensure people stay connected and informed regarding the project's progress.

Principles in Practice

Claire Christian applied Verbatim Theatre Methodologies to her work, even when writing a novel. For *It's Been A Pleasure, Noni Blake*, Claire reached out to her followers on social media. She asked for responses from female-identifying people about what gives them pleasure.

> There are chunks of that data, verbatim responses from participants, that are in the book. So much of how I ended up thinking about the book came from those responses. They were these simplistic answers: I would wear more lipstick, I would try riding a motorbike, I would have sex outside, I would leave my husband. Those answers informed the entire project.

> Many years on from that initial survey, Claire maintains a connection to the original survey and her social media followers. The novel has gone on to be adapted into a screenplay, and is now a theatrical work. She informs her social media followers at each step, consistently engaging in a conversation with them about the pursuit of pleasure.

Ensuring Accessibility to the Project and Preparing Participants for Being Involved

Every industry has its own language, and the arts are no exception. We use words and phrases specific to our practice that are not accessible by those outside of the field. An integral part of community immersion is adapting or translating elements of that practice so that everyone can understand it. Suppose you haven't been to the theatre very often or have never read a playscript. In that case, it can be challenging to imagine how a conversation with the creative team may inform what's on stage. Being sent a draft of the script may not paint a clear picture of the actual final performance. Individuals might give you their permission to be interviewed or recorded without really understanding how those stories might be used. This is the difference between consent and *informed* consent.

It is vital to make your process accessible to the community. Explain that using their stories "verbatim" may mean that sometimes they are used word for word (it is sometimes best to do this both in person and in writing). Sometimes, the stories they share may be amalgamated with others who have shared similar stories. These stories may coalesce into a single, fictional (but informed by reality) character. Explain that they might recognise themselves in the play, or they might not (depending on your approach).

Similarly, seeing yourself reimagined through theatre and performance can be a wonderful, confronting, exhilarating, and overwhelming experience. Consider how you might prepare the community to witness their stories and how you might organise opportunities for reflection and share post-performance. Caroline Wake explores some of the possible impacts of interviewing and performing traumatic stories from a community. She cautions that the interview and sharing process can inadvertently re-injure participants either because "they have never told their story or because they have told it too many times" (Wake 2013, 104). Beyond the interview, she discusses concerns over agency. "Double silencing" (where a person and their story may not be included in the final performance) is troublesome for many verbatim playwrights (104). Depending on the context and identity of the community and the focus of the creative work, preparing participants for the potential impact, both challenging and empowering, is something to be considered as part of the community immersion process.

Before diving into four detailed case studies of community immersion from the author's own practice, the following Principles in Practice detail the many and varied ways that playwright Campion Decent and Director Matt Scholten connected to and maintained relationships with the community at the heart of their production of *The Campaign*.

> **Principles in Practice**
>
> *The Campaign*, written by Campion Decent and Directed by Matt Scholten, is based on testimony, parliamentary transcripts, and media reports relating to arrests made in Tasmania in 1988 when the Tasmanian Gay Law Reform Group held a stall with petitions to decriminalise sexual activity between consenting adults at the Salamanca market. These arrests prompted a campaign which ultimately led to a repeal of these laws in 1997. Matt describes visiting Hobart in 2015 for the touring production of *Mother* (written by Daniel Keene and starring Noni Hazlehurst), and heading down to the Salamanca market on a Saturday morning;
>
>> there was a plaque that commemorates the site where the first arrests of the Tasmanian Gay and Lesbian Law Reform group had happened, and there's also this beautiful piece of public art work a bit further down ... and I just burst into tears ... I had this completely emotional reaction to this piece of artwork which was a commemoration of this really amazing event, which I knew nothing about.
>
> That evening Matt attended the book launch of Rodney Croome's *From This Day Forward: Marriage Equality in Australia,* and spoke with Rodney to thank him for his activism;
>
>> I said 'thank you so much for what you've done ... I'm sure someone's already done a play or a film or something about this work'. and he said, 'Oh you know, no'. I said, 'I can't believe that'. And he said, 'well, because it's a queer story, because it's Tasmania. No one cares'. And I said, 'Well, I care. I would like to do something' and he said, 'Look, people have asked me or said that to me in the past, and nothing has ever come. So I guess I'll', you know, this is classic Rodney he said that 'I guess I'll either hear from you or I won't'. And I was absolutely determined to do it ... I explained to Rodney that the only way we could do it is if we had his endorsement, and if he would be prepared to help us connect with people. He basically said to me, 'okay, get your pen out. Start writing down these numbers and people's names'. And I still have that piece of paper somewhere. I just scrawled. Like, I think about 30 names of people and their phone numbers.

Matt met with Campion Decent who agreed to come on board the project as playwright, and through the support of Playwriting Australia's *Duologue* program, the Tasmanian Theatre Company, Blue Cow Theatre, and Matt's company If theatre, the project was underway. One of Blue Cow Theatre's founders, Robert Jarman, was also one of the original campaigners who had been arrested in 1988. He became part of the project both as a member of the community being interviewed and as an actor in the play who played a younger version of himself as well as a variety of other people.

Matt and Campion were both present for the interviews, Matt reflects;

> it was just a really lovely collaboration between he and I, and I'll always be grateful to him for that … I got to be with him while he did the interviews and I learned a lot from him about being a professional in terms of interviewing and protocols about doing verbatim interviews and permissions and consent and things like that. And it was also hugely beneficial for me as the director, because I had met pretty much all the people who appeared in the play. So when I was working with the actors I was able to kind of give them extra detail.

During the creative development members of the interviewing community (such as Rodney Croome, Nick Toonan, and Lee-Gwen Booth) zoomed in with the cast and were involved in the development process. Matt recalls one day during the development; "As Rodney was leaving he said 'can you come out with me to the car?', and I thought 'Oh God, what's going to happen', and he said 'you don't need to have my permission anymore. You have permission now to take this. I trust you'. And that was a remarkable thing to have, and I thank him still for that".

The play premiered on the anniversary of the first arrest in 1988.

> And then I'll never forget, sitting in the Peacock Theatre at the Salamanca Arts Centre, right, literally opposite where the store was where they were all first arrested. Physically, that you had to cross that threshold, those cobblestones to get into a theatre. The end of the play changed in two ways. We got to have Todd Harper's beautiful story about going to pride march with his nephew. And the end of the play the last lines of the play are Todd talking about the experience of bringing his nephew to pride in Hobart in 2017. And how amazing it was because Todd had been spat on at previous pride events and locked in fridges and really demonized as a young fella. And the last lines of the play are Todd saying 'It was beautiful'. And we realized that Todd was talking about being at pride with his nephew, but also looking back at the story that despite everything that happened to him it was beautiful.

> Campion and I sat together on opening night. We had pretty much all the real people who are onstage in the audience. So the real activists watching actors play them. And it was a really, it was a really heavy night for that reason, because the actors were obviously aware of it too. And Campion and I put ourselves in the corner so we could actually turn and look at the real people. We had them in front of us. So I had an opportunity to sit with my friend, the playwright, and hold hands with him through the whole play. And to be able to watch the actors do their beautiful work in front of us, but to be able to turn like this and just watch maybe 30 people and to see them, each time their voice came back to them through the mouths of an actor, through the body and the voice and the gestures of an actor, to see them laugh and cry and cheer was just incredible.
>
> I said to Campion, 'I'd love the play to end with us going out. I want to end the play with us going out to Salamanca place' and so what Campion did was he wrote an ending where the actors kick open the side door of the theatre, and marched out singing and dancing to *Born this way*. And they kicked open the doors and danced out into the street. And the activists got up and walked across the stage and danced out there with them.
>
> I remember thinking, if I don't get to do another play ever, I'm glad that I did this one.

2.2 Case Studies of Community Immersion

bald heads & blue stars *Case Study*

Snapshot of Community Immersion Strategies

- Attending support group meetings
- Contributing to awareness of the community (newspaper and online articles)
- Collaborating with a peak body for that community
- Radio interviews
- Providing service
- Relationship building both via email and in person

The Story of the Community Immersion Process

The alopecia community was the focus for the *bald heads & blue stars* project, and more specifically, women with alopecia living in Queensland (one of Australia's eastern states). Alopecia is an autoimmune condition that results in varying degrees of hair loss, and the *bald heads & blue stars* project explores the female experience of alopecia. What does it mean to have alopecia? How does this influence and inform your sense of self and identity, the way you express and present yourself to others, and the way you navigate the world?

Sarah has had alopecia since she was three years old (so in some ways, that is when the immersion in the alopecia community began!), however, it was in 2012 when Sarah connected with the Australia Alopecia Areata Foundation (AAAF) that the community immersion process for *bald heads & blue stars* formally began.

In 2012 Sarah attended an alopecia support group meeting. She contributed a story to the AAAF website as her first foray into officially introducing herself to this geographically diverse community and helping in their endeavour to raise awareness of alopecia. She began raising awareness about the verbatim theatre project by contacting the President of the AAAF via email and asking if they could send out a brief blurb about the project to their database of members, along with information about how the community could get in touch with Sarah (via a uniquely created email address specifically for this project). A week later, Sarah continued to build momentum and publicised the project through her local newspaper, *The Toowoomba Chronicle,* which resulted in her headshot on the front page. This article and image helped validate her membership of the alopecia community and demonstrated her commitment to one of the critical goals of the AAAF; to "inform the public and create awareness of Alopecia Areata" (www.aaaf.org.au). *The Toowoomba Chronicle* also made a short film about the project. This video and article were shared across their online network, resulting in replies from women on the Sunshine Coast (Australia), the USA, and Canada.

Sarah contacted her local radio station (ABC Southern QLD) and was invited to promote the project on their breakfast program. This led to being involved in one of the radio station's ongoing programs. Sarah subsequently had monthly interviews from April 2013 to the inaugural season of *bald heads & blue stars* in August 2014. This enabled Sarah to continue her service to, and support of, the alopecia community's awareness efforts, along with continuing to attend support group meetings for the community and volunteering as a social media administrator for the Queensland AAAF Facebook page.

As potential participants began getting in contact, Sarah started developing individual relationships. This process of community immersion occurred predominantly via email. The initial round of email responses varied in both length and intent. Some were short indications of interest, such as, "Fellow female alopecia baldy here:) what chu wana [sic] know for your play?", through to providing lengthy details about their age, location, experience with alopecia, extensive contact details, and in some cases, even photographs. Many also conveyed how they responded to seeing the newspaper article or reading about Sarah's story; "[y]our photo is on my fridge. Today I feel less lonely and a little bit stronger". By promoting the project to the general community and immersing herself in the alopecia community, Sarah reached a more extensive network of participants and created moments of connection, culminating in 15 volunteer participants for the *bald heads & blue stars* project.

56 Community Immersion

Integral to developing individual relationships with each of the participants was continued communication across the project duration. The 15 women who participated in this project were sent a draft of the script and invited to provide feedback and suggestions. They were kept in the loop as planning and rehearsal began for the performance season. The AAAF organised a dinner on the night that many of the women were attending the performance. The AAAF also funded the filming of the play and a DVD recording of the performance is available for purchase through their website. Sarah remains connected to the organisation and still keeps in touch with some of the project participants.

Personal Impact of Community Immersion

The community immersion process can also be personally challenging – particularly in this project where Sarah was a member of the focus community and the playwright. Sarah reflected on how being on the front page of the local paper made her feel as though "I had 'outed' myself as some sort of alopecia role model, which impacts the creative process and my role in it. I am navigating the roles of 'role model', 'artist', 'academic'". Positioning herself within the alopecia community with these three roles and within her hometown community had consequences for Sarah personally that she had not anticipated. Sarah was recognised in public either by the photo or the radio interviews and as she had positioned herself in the media as someone who was completely confident in her balding body, it was challenging when she was having a self-described "bad hair day". Doing the ABC interviews and *The Toowoomba Chronicle* article gave Sarah insight into what the participants in her verbatim project might experience throughout the process. There were some inaccuracies in the newspaper article – they had misrepresented some of the facts of Sarah's experience in their translation from the interview to the article – and Sarah experienced firsthand what it might feel like to receive back a story that was not an accurate depiction of her experience. This personal experience led Sarah to spend a lot of time explaining to her participants how their stories might be used in the performance (word for word, sometimes amalgamated with other stories, sometimes used to inspire the writing of a fictional scene), and to allow them to read a draft of the play and request any changes to be made to elements of the script.

St Mary's In Exile

Snapshot of Community Immersion Strategies

- Attending weekly gatherings
- 'Traditional' research: books, articles, blog posts, documentary film and Catholic law
- Accessibility ensured through newsletter call-outs
- Relationship building in person and via email

The Story of the Community Immersion Process

St. Mary's In Exile (2016) told the true story of two Brisbane Catholic priests who were effectively ex-communicated from the Roman Catholic Church for politically progressive practices. At the apex of national media attention in 2009, the priests led their congregation of hundreds away from St. Mary's South Brisbane to an office building down the road. They still gather weekly in that office building and practice their version of a Catholic mass, calling themselves 'St. Mary's In Exile'. The play was commissioned by Queensland Theatre Company in 2015 and written by David Burton.

Several factors about this particular community made immersion easy. Firstly, the community itself wasn't opposed to artistic collaboration, and saw the opportunity of working with a playwright commissioned by the state theatre company as a way to continue to spread their political message. Secondly, their weekly gatherings became an ideal touchstone for becoming immersed the community's unique culture, beliefs, and stories. Gaining trust in these weekly meetings meant further access was then provided to the community's impressive e-mail and online network, a dense but engaged list of contacts from around the world. This aspect of community immersion meant David could learn very quickly about the community and start to build vital relationships.

Before interviews began, while simultaneously becoming acquainted with the online and in-person community of *St. Mary's In Exile,* David was able to draw upon a wealth of pre-existing media content that had been created about the community. This included many articles, podcasts, blog posts, a book, and a documentary film. Importantly, this also illuminated several key people who were no longer within the community or had been established (at least in the media) as antagonistic to the community's aims. Given the inherently political nature of the story, it became essential to understand *their* communal culture in addition to the central *St. Mary's In Exile* players. While reaching out to people for interviews within the community was simple enough due to their online network and weekly newsletter, finding those outside the community was a patient process that relied on personal networking to establish trust. David sharing his values and intentions helped to ease this process. In this case, David wasn't looking to create a piece of theatre with clear heroes and villains. Those potentially fearful of coming forward were relieved by the notion that David wasn't writing a piece of theatre set out to defame the Catholic Church. David was more interested in the complex nature of belief and spirituality to the personal and the political. Articulating this gained David access to several essential voices that may have otherwise been out of reach, such as the Archbishop of the Brisbane Diocese and several practising Catholic priests.

Personal Impact of Community Immersion

Once David began interviews, he instinctively felt drawn to the stories of Peter and Terry, the two priests who had walked away from the Roman

Catholic Church. Their conversations were long and sprawling, and at times deeply personal. Both men disclosed vulnerable information to David on the record, uncovering parts of the *St. Mary's In Exile* story that had not previously been covered in the press. The personal impact of this was not properly felt until David was in rehearsal grappling with the play's final drafts. Taking the trust that Peter and Terry had given him seriously meant closing down rich narrative possibilities. In the end, the play moved away from a strict verbatim presentation and was replaced by a performed drama, but much of the dialogue from participants was sourced from verbatim research. Even after a successful season and a satisfied Terry and Peter, David is still uncertain whether he made the right calls in serving the community that had given him his trust. In practice, this meant sleepless nights as the play was being drafted and complex creative negotiations internally.

Peter and Terry had access to most script drafts, although they later admitted they found it much easier to understand the work once it was staged. The community itself was invited to an initial reading of the play script. This was an overall positive for the community, but it resulted in an overwhelming wave of contradictory feedback for David.

Eternity

Snapshot of Community Immersion Strategies

- Workshops
- Letter writing
- Playreadings
- Participants as performers

The Story of the Community Immersion Process

Eternity was a commissioned work through the University of Southern Queensland (USQ) to be written for and with the first year acting cohort in 2017 (who became the focus community for the project). Initially, this project was designed to be an adaptation of Thornton Wilder's *Our Town*, however, it quickly evolved into an exploration of belonging, memory, and growing up in regional Queensland, with a particular focus on difficult conversations; the ones we have, want to have, and might not ever be able to have. Sarah had recently completed her PhD studies at USQ, and while not a direct member of the focus community (who were all young people aged 17–19 years), she had grown up in the rural community of Roma (in southwest Queensland) and had embodied experience living in a similar context to that of the focus community. In this project, the participants were intended to be the performers of the resulting work.

Community immersion in this project began with Sarah facilitating a series of workshops. These workshops were designed to both provide an insight to the creative development and playwriting process for the cohort, as well as an opportunity to workshop ideas, play with stimulus, and generate material for the play. In the first workshop, Sarah facilitated a devising activity which involved objects as stimulus. A random assortment of objects was placed around the workshop space and the class was invited to explore these objects–interact with them if possible, inspect them, observe them, and listen to them. Watch their peers interact with them. Pay attention to the objects' detail and specificity. After a few minutes, they were asked to find the object that most resonated with them and form groups around the objects.

In their object groups they were asked to imagine that this object was found in a time capsule. A community of people chose this object to signify something important about who they were, what they wanted to be remembered for, and how they lived. The groups were tasked with imagining and devising the capsule commitment ceremony that would have been performed at the time the object was buried in the time capsule. They were asked to consider: who is the community that this object belonged to? How would they choose to perform the capsule commitment ceremony? What would they say or do at this ceremony about this object? Performing these scenes gave Sarah an insight into the cohort; their interests, values, humour, sense of ritual, belonging, and tradition.

Sarah was then invited to one of the first year cohort's lessons where they each performed the monologue they had performed at their auditions the year prior. This was an opportunity for Sarah to meet each of the students in the group and see them perform something that they had specifically chosen. After seeing their monologues Sarah wrote each young person a letter, responding to their monologue and posing two questions based on some of the themes that had come out of the first workshop: a) what are you most afraid of? and b) how would you like to be remembered?

This process of facilitating workshops and writing letters back and forth between Sarah and the cohort became an iterative process across the next three months of the project. The second workshop focused on developing specific characters and tensions, and the group explored the difficult conversations they didn't get to see enough in the stories they consumed. More letters back and forth. The workshops in this community immersion process acted as creative service to the community with the students learning about creative development and playwrighting processes. In contrast, the letters were moments of conversation, moments of vulnerability, insight, and personal sharing. They served as spaces where stories and ideas that couldn't be shared in the group community context could still find a place in the world of the play. Sarah facilitated a playreading of the work in progress which began with reading a letter to the assembled audience. In addition to the verbal feedback provided at the end of the reading, the audience was invited to also contribute a letter in response.

Personal Impact of Community Immersion

Committing to community immersion in your practice means committing your time. In this case study, individual letter writing and reading took a considerable amount of time, yet it was just as crucial to the building and strengthening of relationships and community understanding as interviews in other projects.

The Time Is Now *(A Youth Theatre Project)*

Snapshot of Community Immersion Strategies

- Weekly drama workshops focussed on ensemble building
- Online spaces constructed for ongoing conversation
- Play-building processes

The Story of the Community Immersion Process

The Time Is Now was a production with a unique set of circumstances, but in essence, followed a youth-driven play-building process that will be very familiar to youth drama practitioners. This field is replete with knowledge in its own right but has frequent cross-over into verbatim theatre methodology. In *The Time Is Now* and other youth-centred arts experiences, the concept of community "immersion" is isolated within a set time and place. Spontaneous and organic connection can be more difficult to orchestrate in a school setting, for example, when the facilitating artist is simultaneously a care provider operating within a very specific role as well as being an artist in their own right. *The Time Is Now* represents an example of how community immersion strategies can be applied in the youth and education sector.

The Time Is Now was produced by La Boite Theatre Company in 2021. A company of ten young performers, ranging in age between 12 and 19, were auditioned and selected. From here, "three co-creators" were contracted: David Burton, Ari Palani, and Aleea Monsour. The brief was to build an original seventy-minute devised non-linear performance centred around political speeches the performers had written on topics of interest to them. Time was (ironically, given the play's title) extremely limited, with just two months until opening night. Most rehearsals were spaced a week apart, taking place for four hours after a school day. On school holidays, and the fortnight immediately preceding opening night, more intensive rehearsals allowed for greater sustained momentum.

In this circumstance, the community was *imposed*. Beyond their age, the students had little in common with each other. In fact, they had been deliberately chosen in part because of their diversity. The facilitators leaned on much of the community-engaged facilitation research and techniques spearheaded by Augusto Boal to create "rehearsals" that involved games and activities designed to help devise original material, improve ensemble, and skill-share in performance craft. In between rehearsals, participants could connect on Facebook, in a group set up by the facilitators. But this was rarely active. Instead, participants found their own way to connect independent of the facilitators, setting up message streams on TikTok and Snapchat where they could build their sense of connection to one another away from the eyes of adults.

As a playwright, David worked with his co-creators to learn about the young people at great speed. This meant any small interaction was noted and shared when the students were in rehearsal. Words and slang they used were noted. Organic power dynamics were made explicit in conversations between the co-creators after rehearsal (a shared dinner between the co-creators became one of the most important creative practices, in order to share information and reflections with one another).

For this process, community immersion and playwriting, and rehearsing all happened simultaneously. In a more traditional process, while there may be some overlap, these would happen sequentially. The community, so to speak, wasn't able to articulate itself as a community until there was a script already written. In this instance, the script became a reification of the community immersion process, where all participants, not just co-creators, were immersing themselves into an unknown, liminal, and nascent community: their own ensemble as performers.

Personal Impact of Community Immersion

As any youth arts worker knows, working with young people in a compressed timeframe is a daunting task. However, the power of youth community immersion is very special, and for *The Time Is Now* the co-creators were able to work with the young people to build an energised, affectionate, and reliable ensemble. The power of a creative team here is not to be underestimated. It's no accident, perhaps, that a lot of verbatim theatre involves working in writing "teams". Even in cases that involve individual playwrights, it's often the conversations that happen "in the margins" of a project with other creators, whether they be research assistants, producers, directors or actors, that can be illuminating and supportive. For *The Time Is Now*, the co-creators worked together to build community through immersive activities.

2.3 Practical Activities/Reflective Tasks

Frequently Asked Questions

Community immersion sounds expensive, or like I need producing partners. What if I'm operating by myself?

Community immersion can occur at varying scales. At its most expensive, it may involve travelling to a different location and taking up residence inside a community. High-profile examples of this include the 2020 film *Nomadland*, where director Chloe Zhao took her film crew into Arizona, Nebraska, and surrounds to embed themselves in the community that was the subject of their film. Of course, not all of us have such options available to us, but technology offers some solutions.

Social media can become a crucial tool for any artist looking to immerse themselves in a particular community. Availing yourself of online groups, and participating in message boards and group forums, can help in establishing meaningful online connections with important stakeholders. Of course, this is only one instrument, and would ideally exist as the foundation upon which you reach out for phone conversations or online meetings. Talking in person – even if it's just on the phone or online – will always help to support greater connection.

What do I need to consider as especially important when I am part of the community I am also immersing myself in?

As Sarah reflected on her experience with *bald heads & blue stars*, working with a community that you are a part of can be incredibly liberating and complex. In all regards, it takes a great deal of self-knowledge and self-care for an artist to negotiate this process. If the issue feels too "hot", or if it's something you're still actively grappling with in a clinical or therapeutic setting, then diving headfirst into an arts project may not be ideal. Waiting until you are ready, or at least feel more prepared and robust, is rarely a bad thing.

On the other hand, being a part of the community that you're immersing yourself in brings a certain amount of implicit worth to your project. Trust may be easier to establish. You may already have an extensive knowledge of concerns that are pertinent to the community. Some of this knowledge will be invisible to you, you won't have conscious awareness of your embodied knowledge. Making that embodied knowledge conscious will be essential for your artistic process, especially if your eventual audience will also not be from the community you're focussing on.

What do I need to consider as especially important when I am not a part of the community I am immersing myself in?

We will talk more about the sensitivities around appropriation throughout this book, and in particular in the final chapter on ethics. It's firstly important to note that being external to a community does not automatically invalidate you working with them. Some communities require more sensitivity than others. A metropolitan-based artist working in a regional community, for example, needs to exercise sensitivity. But that sensitivity is not as complex or delicate as a white artist working with a community from another culture.

In their excellent book *Writing The Other: A Practical Approach,* Nisi Shawl and Cynthia Ward lay out different roles artists can take when writing about other communities (Shawl and Ward, 2011). You can be a tourist – in which the community makes room for you, and you offer some compensation back to the community for that opening. In the case of community-engagement, this can take many forms. You may offer skill-building workshops that run parallel to your workshop. You may offer paid work opportunities. Or you may be amplifying a particular political message that is important for that community. You can also be an invader – an artist who rudely enters a community and takes whatever isn't nailed down. The third is as an invited guest, where a relationship is grown over time and built on authentic trust and shared mutual interests. Obviously community immersion advocates for the third. This may mean taking care to involve community stakeholders at a leadership level of your artistic practice. Can you provide a budget for a community consultant? Is it appropriate to invite a dramaturg or co-writer to the project? In Australia, it's important to meet with any First Nations stakeholders regularly and make sure their consultation is authentically valued in your artistic process.

How is community immersion different from interviews?

Every project is different, and in some cases, the "interview" stage of a process may overlap significantly with a community immersion process. In almost all cases, however, it's best not to go into interviews blindly. Establishing some kind of foundational knowledge in the community is necessary to make sure your interviews are efficient, and work to build trust with the community at the centre of your project. As described above, these techniques can range from reading books and blogs on your community of choice, to actually travelling and residing with them.

Reflective Questions in Community Immersion

Simply immersing yourself in a community with any of the techniques listed above is a first step. But value is truly gained when a rigorous reflective process is applied. For Sarah and David working on solo projects, often means journaling. On other projects where the writer is part of a larger team, it's often the most-meeting meals or car trips that the true learning takes place. A reflective discussion, either with yourself or others, is essential.

Here's a suggestion of some reflective questions that may reveal critical information about the community:

- What are the power structures that are evident within the community? Who has power? Who doesn't?
- Who are the voices that are invisible with your current methods of immersion? How can you contact them?
- What demographics are especially present or absent in the community as you see it? What's the average age? Gender? Class? Race?
- What has elicited a strong emotional response from you so far? Why?
- How are you influencing how the community behaves around you?
- How can the resources available to you be shared among the community in a meaningful way? How can your purposes intertwine?
- Can you identify a list of key community stakeholders who may be able to open up other parts of the community to you? How can you make sure to spend time with them and make sure they feel valued?

Works Cited

Cohen-Cruz, Jan. *Engaging Performance, Theatre as Call and Response.* Routledge, 2010.

Doyle, Clar. "The Need for Critical Pedagogy." *Raising Curtains on Education: Drama As a Site for Critical Pedagogy*. Bergin and Garvey, 1993, pp. 1–19.

Goulburn Regional Art Gallery. *Comin Home Soon*. Goulburn Regional Art Gallery, Goulburn, 2012.

Hankivsky, Olena. *Social Policy and the Ethic of Care*. UBC Press, 2004.

Lillie, Jade, Kate Larsen, Cara Kirkwood and Jax Jacki Brown. *The Relationship is the Project: Working with Communities*. Brow Books, 2020.

Paget, Derek. "Acts of Commitment: Activist Arts, the Rehearsed Reading and Documentary Theatre." *New Theatre Quarterly*, 2010, pp. 173–193.

Shawl, Nisi and Cynthia Ward. *Writing the Other: A Practical Approach*. Aqueduct Press, 2011.

Valentine, Alana. *Bowerbird: The Art of making theatre drawn from life*. Currency Press, Sydney, 2018.

Wake, Caroline. "To Witness Mimesis: The Politics, Ethics, and Aesthetics of Testimonial Theatre in Through the wire." *Modern Drama* 56.1, 2013, pp. 102–125.

Wilkinson, Linden. "'A Day in December'." *Performing Research: Tensions, Triumphs and Trade-offs of Ethnodrama*, edited by Judith Ackroyd and John O'Toole, Trentham Books, 2010 pp. 123–144.

3 Interviewing and Listening for Aesthetics

Conducting interviews is one of the key ways that stories and lived experiences are shared and documented in a verbatim theatre process. In a symposium report on "Verbatim Practices in Contemporary Theatre" Chris Megson outlines that while verbatim practitioners are embracing a more diverse range of methodologies informed by "feminist and postcolonial discourses, and shaped by new technologies" (Megson 2006, 530) the practice of interviewing within the verbatim process has remained integral. In this chapter we position and define the interview as part of a creative practice – sometimes even a performative practice – and explore the aesthetic skills and artistry involved in the listening and responding which takes place in a verbatim interview. We call this Listening for Aesthetics and outline this framework for understanding your role in a verbatim interview throughout the chapter. The stories shared in a verbatim interview can provide the cornerstones of the resulting performance work, so the site of the interview and your work as the interviewer needs to be as conducive as possible to generating, receiving, and responding to those stories – and this chapter is here to guide you through!

> **Principles in Practice**
>
> Navigating the administrative and logistical burden of building interviews in a classroom environment can be tricky, but not impossible, to accomplish. We provide some suggestions in Section 3.7: Negotiating Interviews in a Classroom Environment. However, it is possible for students to still experience the tangible "realness" of interviews, even if they don't conduct interviews themselves. Using a script that is already published is useful. Claire Christian has had the experience of working with school students working on a verbatim script she had created collaboratively with *another* group of young people, *Talking to Brick Walls*. Even though six years separated the original production from the new one, the sense of responsibility to care for the voices was still felt by the students involved. As an educator, Claire reflects on the value of verbatim material in the classroom:

DOI: 10.4324/9781003155706-4

66 *Interviewing and Listening for Aesthetics*

> For young artists it makes them recognize the importance of what they're saying. This experience was real for someone. So what are you going to do as an actor to give that the emotional integrity and weight and honesty that it deserves? That really clocks on for a lot of young artists to go: I have a responsibility to tell this story.

3.1 The Verbatim Interview

What is the verbatim interview, and how does it differ from other styles of interview? While other research methodologies assist and support the playwriting process, in traditional verbatim theatre, interviews are the centrepiece and the intent of the interview is to generate stories that can be translated through the dramatic languages and into performance. This favouring of a single creative practice (or research method) in the verbatim process means the art of interviewing is worthy of intense scrutiny.

As discussed in previous chapters, verbatim theatre grew out of broader documentary theatre traditions, and lines of comparison can be drawn to other "non-fiction" entertainment from practices as diverse as factual podcasts to reality television. All of these forms share verbatim theatre's attention to interviewing, leveraging the "authenticity" of real voices to tell a story or carry a message. To a certain extent, an interview is: a conversation between two or more people used to source data. But verbatim theatre's process of making renders the interview potentially problematic. Other forms of entertainment (such as television journalism) will edit an interview – and certainly, this editing can be ethically spurious, or work at undoing the intended meaning of the interviewee. Still, the inherent authenticity of the data is given legitimacy through the use of the speaker's voice. No one can argue against the fact that the interviewee *said those exact words.*

In theatre, however, we further manipulate the data. A playwright edits and curates the interview, an actor finds their own interpretation, a director adds staging, and a host of technical artistry is applied, all in service of applying meaning. Often stories from an interview are used to inform the development of an otherwise fictional character and narrative, rather than used exactly word for word, further separating the source of the interview from the artistic outcome. To ensure that stories are captured ethically, authentically, and respectfully, playwrights need to be clear with their interviewees about how the stories/data/material generated in the interview will be used in the development of performance. We refer to this as a process of informed consent, which means providing great clarity to the interviewees about your intent as an artist and how you might use their words – and doing everything you can to ensure this intent is being communicated clearly – so that the interviewee is legitimately informed and can choose whether or not they consent to be involved. (We go through this process in great detail in chapter seven.) Stating your role as an artist and your intent to create a performance piece informed by the stories shared with you in an interview are key elements of the informed consent process.

Declaring your role as an artist helps to position the interview as a creative and performative practice. Della Pollock asserts that the interview should be "[u]nderstood as performance" (Pollock 2005, 3) and Derek Paget suggests that every phase of the verbatim theatre process is informed by an "awareness of theatricality" (324). What then is your "role" in this creative and performative space? To provide the prompts which allow you to listen for the aesthetics of your interviewee's story. Sometimes these prompts occur through the role of a formal interviewer, sometimes you may be a storyteller yourself, and at others, you will take on the role of an engaged audience member to your interviewee's story. Oscillating between these three roles (which are outlined further in the next section) can assist in establishing a respectful relationship with the interviewee *and* in generating theatrically dynamic stories.

It could be argued that the desire for clarity marks the verbatim theatre interview closer to an act of research than of artistic making. This is an important distinction and one which some playwrights may debate. While there is pressure for journalists and documentary filmmakers to approach each interview with a sense of objectivity, we argue that this pressure – while still present for the playwright – is more diffuse because of the shared understanding of "artistic license". It is vital, however, that a playwright still remains open in an interview and to truly listen. Approaching an interview with an artistic vision already cemented negates the need for an interview at all. Part of the joy of making verbatim theatre is to allow yourself to be surprised by the stories you hear, to learn from them, and to improvise and collaborate *with* them. In this way, verbatim theatre is not the delivery of a vision from an auteur playwright, but a conversation between the playwright, audience, and interviewee, and it's *this* unique relationship that often renders verbatim theatre as community-engaged.

Principles in Practice

In an article for *Storyline* in 2013, Australian playwright Suzie Miller described the process of writing her play *Transparency*, and how the interviews she conducted as part of the research shifted, influenced, and informed the final direction of the piece. *Transparency* explores the theme of rehabilitation for those convicted as violent juvenile offenders. Miller reflects;

> Hours were spent in a very dark place contemplating the opposite of what I had held as an unquestionable belief. Was it possible that someone could be born evil? I then began the research. I read

> everything there was to read about child killers, and was, dare I say, grateful for the fact that my assumptions of then being children from horrific situations seemed to be true. Show a child violence and they learn how to be violent. Then I spoke to the families of people who has lost a child in such circumstances and read factual police accounts. This rocked me to my core, sent me to a place of such confusion and hell, they the play just had to be written.
>
> (Miller, 81)

3.2 Listening for Aesthetics

In Sarah's early research into verbatim interview processes, she coined the term "Listening for Aesthetics" which draws upon the work of oral historian Jacquelyn Hall, researchers Deirdre Heddon and Della Pollock, and the experience of several playwrights including David Burton. Listening for Aesthetics in a verbatim interview can be broadly divided into three essential components:

1 Paying attention to the dramatic action of a participant's story
2 Responding in an improvised manner to these stories
3 Applying strategies to assist in generating story

In parallel to all of these actions, the interviewer is listening to the actualised context of the interviewee, and holding space to listen to the context of creative possibilities.

It is important to note that Aesthetic Listening is a term widely employed in educational contexts, particularly in the development of emerging literary skills in young children (Korkmaz 2019). It's also a term that has been adapted into music education and appreciation (Reese 1983) where students are encouraged to listen *to* aesthetics and develop their aesthetic awareness and appreciation. All of these ideas stem from an understanding of the value of aesthetics, a term largely popularised by philosopher Frank Sibley, as a means of describing the principles which underpin art or beauty. In other words, aesthetic listening is largely an *emotional* and *human* process, which relies on a very human and intuitive response to what is being listened to. The verbatim theatre artist is engaging in aesthetic listening as they emotionally receive the stories of the communities they work with, however, as they are also listening with a very clear intent to create in response to that listening, they are also listening *for* aesthetics. Listening *to* focuses on hearing and receiving, listening *for* balances this receiving with the intent for creation.

Paying Attention to the Dramatic Action of a Participant's Story

This suggests that the interviewer is hunting for narrative. It's common for some questions to be necessarily simple and factual. You may need to establish some clear facts with an interviewee about their placement in the site of interest. A verbatim piece around a natural disaster, for example, might begin with questions which would quickly establish the interviewee's geographic location and summarise their overall relationship to the event. But from there we need *dramatic action*. This implicates the elements of drama, taught as a fundamental introduction to drama in most secondary school classrooms: "situation and roles directed by focus, driven by tension, made explicit in time and location, through the media of language and movement, to create mood and symbol, which together create dramatic meaning" (Haseman and O'Toole 2017). That's a lot of elements to think about at first, but in practice, this is simply the act of encouraging natural storytelling from your interviewee. Most people are gifted at storytelling, and when encouraged will find themselves in anecdotes that contain tension, clear roles, and a developing set of stakes. Any artist who has had previous experience with qualitative data gathering – whether as an oral historian, journalist, or documentarian – will be on familiar ground here in developing "narrative-generating questions" (Hopf 2004).

Here are some examples of narrative-generating questions. In this instance, we've maintained our connection to research surrounding a natural disaster, but you could easily replace this with your own incident of interest.

- Take me back to the day when the storm hit. Where were you just before things started getting serious?
- I've heard that you had a particularly tough time in securing your insurance claim. Can you walk me through that story?
- What are your clearest memories around the immediate aftermath? What do you most remember about those first few hours?
- Tell me about how the people around you were reacting to the situation.

Responding in an Improvised Manner to These Stories

This is essential! Given that we are playing with narrative, we are limited in how many questions we can realistically prepare. Sticking to a prepared list of questions limits our capability to respond to the interviewee. Many people rush through storytelling at first, purely because they are not used to someone sitting in rapt attention to their story for an extended period of time. Some people provide a long list of events without pausing to engage in the emotion of a story. If you're comfortable, you can encourage them to go into more detail or ask to explore their feelings. It's hard to give clear examples of what this looks like because ideally, these improvised questions come from a *very authentic place* in you. If you are shocked, you're allowed to be shocked. If you want to laugh, you're allowed to laugh. If someone breaks down in tears, you're allowed to say, "I'm so sorry that happened, that must've been awful. I don't know what to say".

Here's an example of a simple exchange between an interviewer and an interviewee. The first question is planned by the interviewer, but the rest are improvised. The interviewer isn't doing anything particularly special here, rather they are just listening and responding authentically.

INTERVIEWER: Take me back to the day when the storm hit. Where were you just before things started getting serious?

INTERVIEWEE: I remember that clearly actually. I woke up and got the news on the TV, and I wasn't quite sure how serious it was going to be, but we realised pretty quick that we were in a bit of danger.

INTERVIEWER: So just walk me through that morning - hearing it on the TV. What time of day was it when you got up? Who else was in the house? Just give me details.

INTERVIEWEE: Right, well. I got up and it was about eight I guess. I'd slept in a bit because I'd had a few beers the night before. We were celebrating my daughter's formal together, it was this great night. And I got up and I ... I shaved I think. Now I'm wondering if it was the radio or my phone or ... actually my daughter came and got me. My daughter came and got me and I had shaving cream on my face still. And she said, "come and look on the news, they're talking about our town". And she was all excited and I ran out and there it was, yeah, on the news. And we just watched it, and I still had shaving cream on my face and a razor blade in my hand. And those winds ... I mean even then it was clear those winds were going to batter us. I think we kept going with our morning but not long after that my mate rang.

INTERVIEWER: What did you feel?

INTERVIEWEE: At that time? Um. A bit of, what's the word, trepidation, I guess. Like, you're not quite sure. And they moved on from it pretty quick on the news and you sort of go, "all right, I'll get back on with my day". But then I got my phone call from my mate, Graham and he said "have you looked at the sky this morning?" And I walked outside and saw these clouds. And that's when I got scared.

INTERVIEWER: What did the clouds look like?

INTERVIEWEE: Big. Bloody big. And grey. And ... you know before hail you get that like, faint tinge of green? Well, these guys were green *all over*. And black. It was like night time, it was just ... yeah.

One question, with several improvised provocations from the interviewer, and we manage to capture all of the elements of drama – even managing a bit of poetic symbology with the interviewee's description of the clouds. Without the improvised questions, we would have potentially cut out this rich piece of the story, all before the storm had even begun.

Listening for Aesthetics is a performance and includes an active/responsive element. Listening is a visible act, "in the listening process there are elements of reflection, interpretation, and understanding which are visible in the confirmation and feedback" (Fredrikson 1173) to the storyteller and is not a passive process. Through active listening, the interviewer is reproducing or affirming the meaning of the storyteller and in dialogic listening, they are coproducing stories and knowledge in mutuality. Within the Listening for Aesthetics framework the playwright is actively translating the story through the dramatic languages in their mind during the interview, and this thought process then influences how they respond.

Applying Strategies to Assist in Generating Story

This is a further cementing of the two steps described above. It is best to recall the basic elements of drama: explore time, character or tension. Time can take us before, after, or into a specific event. Characters may illuminate additional relationships, or assist in building a larger web of contacts for more interviews. Tension, of course, is key, and any hint of tension or conflict can be teased out. For interviewers and interviewees this can be confronting if done improperly. There's no need to be assertive. Applying a soft curiosity often wields the most honest responses.

Here are some examples of questions that can help reveal tension and conflict in a story:

- I've realised from other research that this may be a sensitive topic, but I was wondering about your thoughts on …
- When you were telling that story it seemed like this particular moment was a point of tension. Could you talk about that more?
- I want to make sure I get your side of the story crystal clear. Can you talk to me more about …

We'll be discussing ethics in a later chapter but it's essentially up to the individual interviewer as to how much they "push" an interviewee for a response. However, it's critical to keep the goal of listening for aesthetics in mind. Pushing past an interviewee's comfort zone will rarely gain rich narrative data. On the other hand, an on-the-record "I don't want to talk about that" can create a powerful moment on stage. In verbatim theatre, what is *unsaid* can often be just as impactful for an audience, and leave plenty of room for an actor to play.

Sometimes the strategies you apply to generate a story involve oscillating between several roles: "a traditional interviewer, a mutual storyteller to help prompt and encourage the sharing of experience, and playing the role of engaged audience member to the interviewee's story" (Peters 40). Learning to intuitively swing between these roles is primarily learned through experience and observation, however, we have gathered up some tips and tricks to get you started:

Traditional Interviewer

Performing the role of a traditional interviewer can confer a degree of credibility to the process and also facilitates the formalities of the ethical components of interviewing practice.

- Thoroughly prepare a broad-ranging list of questions (but simultaneously be prepared to let go of this plan and follow the path the interview takes)
- Bring along any information sheets and consent forms to talk through with the interviewee (don't assume that they will have had the chance to read these thoroughly in advance)
- Read over any written communication (texts, emails, etc) you've had with the interviewee prior to the meeting. This can often serve as a reminder about any questions or concerns they've had, as well as information they have shared which might be useful to refer to when first meeting them
- Talk through the informed consent process, making it explicit and clear how you intend to use the stories gathered through the interview
- Clearly let the interviewee know when the recorder is being turned on and when it is being turned off
- Returning to a more formal interviewer role at the conclusion of the interview can help mark a clear "end" to the conversation

Mutual Storyteller

At times the interview can be similar to a conversation, with both parties sharing stories and commentary on the topics or events discussed. The practice of mutual storytelling can help develop the relationship with the interviewee and encourage a greater depth in the content and emotion of the stories shared.

- While the interview should primarily be a space for the interviewee to tell their stories, sometimes it is useful for you to share a short anecdote of your own that may be relevant to the theme/event you are exploring. This can sometimes serve to demonstrate that you genuinely do understand what the interviewee is talking about
- Sharing a short anecdote can also provide a "model" for telling a story, and this example might be useful to the interviewee when considering how to tell their own stories
- In the same way that it can be useful to use photos or objects as prompts in an interview, sharing a short story or experience yourself can serve as a type of "metaphorical object" that the interviewee can respond to, build upon, resist, feel validated by or perhaps even serve as a memory prompt

- Mutual storytelling can generate greater familiarity between the creative team and the interviewee, and this can sometimes lead to the sharing of more dynamic and engaging stories

Engaged Audience Member

In her work on theatre audiences, Susan Bennett states that the primary condition of an audience is that they recognise themselves as such. By positioning yourself as an engaged audience member to the story (or performance!) of the interviewee you become a "tangibly active creator of the theatrical event" (10) prompting the interviewees through your responses and reactions to provide extra detail, to reiterate certain moments, to rush through or dwell on particular feelings or experiences. There are a few ways to make sure you're doing everything possible to be an engaged audience member for your interviewee:

- Whenever possible, be physically present for the interview. Lennart Fredrikson explains that the phenomena of presence can be understood in two ways: "being there" and "being with" (1170). While being with means being available and "at the disposal of the other person" (1171), being there is "not only a physical presence, it also encompasses communication and understanding" (1171). Fredrikson describes being there as an action, that presence in this category is an active phenomenon, and that being there, physically being in the same space as another person, provides support, comfort, encouragement, and reassurance (1171), all conducive to generating dynamic stories. Of course, sometimes interviews can only happen online and over the phone. This often can't be helped, but it's important to understand that this will affect the data
- Be empathetic to the experience of the interviewee, responding to their feelings and non-verbal cues. An audience member is a "psychological participant and empathetic collaborator ... ready to find meaning and significance in the events taking place on stage" (Gaylord qtd. in Bennett 148) – be open to the story being shared with you. Radio or television journalists will often be trained out of giving auditory replies when interviewing (little sounds like "mmm" or "I see" that show an interviewee you're listening), but in a verbatim theatre context, these small signs of humanity are crucial, and make an interview feel more like a conversation

While much of the remainder of this book will largely be focused on the translation of gathered data into a theatrical work, it is important to reflect on how we might imagine our gathered data being used at the outset. The research field emphasises the interview as a "dialogic encounter" (Stuart Fisher 2011), which is then repeated in the performance space, most often through the use of direct address. Direct address, where a character breaks the "fourth wall" of the theatre space and speaks to the audience, is a common trait of verbatim theatre

74 *Interviewing and Listening for Aesthetics*

(more common than the use of in-person interviews). Through direct address, an actor or character invites the audience to "hear voices that address them directly as if they were part not just of the original interview but of a profoundly human conversation ... [A] kind of proximity is achieved by means of this closeness to the fact of the interview" (Paget 2010). Thus, in the final translation, the verbatim theatre process circles back to where it began: one person listening, the other sharing a story or message about themselves.

3.3 The Importance of Interviewing

It is certainly possible to build a piece of verbatim theatre without interviewing anyone. In these instances, data is typically sourced from external sources (news articles, social media, or documents in the public domain), from online surveys or through sustained and lengthy community immersion. Sourcing stories from external sources and online surveys can be attractive to teachers in particular, as the logistical burden of organising students to interview community members can be daunting. They can be equally alluring to emerging artists, or those who find the thought of interviewing strangers a nerve-wracking task. In the concluding section of this chapter, we'll address these points specifically, and talk about solutions for data-gathering that don't include in-person interviews. First, however, it's important to understand what is lost if in-person interviews are sacrificed.

Principles in Practice

Of course, data needn't come from interviews exclusively and may come from a diverse group. When Claire Christian gathered stories on virginity for her *Virginity Mologues* project, she welcomed anonymous online submissions, hand-written letters, and one-on-one interviews. "For a lot of people," she notes, "one-on-one interviews were important, because they wanted to be kept completely anonymous, and they didn't want to have the experience of having it written down anywhere."

While it would be a mistake to call any tenets of verbatim theatre exclusively traditional or pure, certainly the in-person interview is most conventionally described as the cornerstone of verbatim theatre. Using other kinds of data, it could be argued, more likely situates the work in broader documentary or political theatre styles. This is only undesirable if it's the practitioner's intention to commit to a whole-hearted verbatim theatre experience. This is particularly true in the classroom, where teachers may find it easier for students to draw upon pre-existing data. This inevitably neuters the very deliberate messiness of verbatim theatre-making. The pressure one feels in an interview, the responsibility one feels in curating and editing another's story, and the creative freedom and challenge that comes from staging it are intentionally and powerfully risky, confronting, and liberating.

> **Principles in Practice**
>
> Queensland playwright Dan Evans has had a wide scope of experience with interviews and surveys in developing work with his collaborator Amy Ingram for their company, The Good Room. The Good Room first created a triptych of works built on online, anonymous submissions in response to a theme (regret, love, and forgiveness). Many years later, The Good Room returned to this model of theatre-making with a show about owning dogs, but this time, Dan and Amy conducted interviews in person. Dan reflected on the differences in the data:
>
>> People are so much more willing to be vulnerable, when they know that they won't be connected to what they are offering. So when the offering is anonymous, the vulnerability increases. When they're in front of you giving their story ... way more time is required. And sometimes you don't even get it. If you do get it, it's fleeting and it sparkles in front of you.
>>
>> There was one amazing story with a dog owner. We did the whole interview, like forty minutes, and I was wrapping it up. And then he said: 'Yeah ... this dog. It's amazing, you know, um ... . and I lost a child recently. And, yeah ...' And he went somewhere. And he hugged the dog really tight and then he looked back to me and smiled.
>>
>> But the time he took to get there, and not even to fully expose that piece of his heart, but it was a really beautiful exchange. Vulnerability with another human in the room is more difficult. But it's perhaps more rewarding as a maker because you like, touch the flesh and be in the room and breathing, when it happens.
>
> Here, Dan provides an excellent example of how different mediums of data-gathering affect the texture of the interview itself.

The more compelling argument for including in-person interviews, however, quite apart from an intellectual act of theatre form conservation, is the benefits it supplies for all participants, including the audience. The verbatim theatre process most often includes core features of belonging such as "identity narratives, people making sense of their experiences and discursively identifying their sense of self and how they belong in their community" (Peters 40). Peters' research linked this dramaturgy of belonging as a "direct result of the practice of community immersion and interviewing in a verbatim theatre process" (41). The concept of belonging is essential here, where, in the act of committing to a sincere conversation with an interviewee, an interviewer's sense of empathy towards the subject inevitably increases, and this is then amplified through the act of staging their story.

The idea that sincere conversations with a narrative focus spreads empathy certainly isn't new. In fact, it's at the forefront of contemporary sociological research, particularly in attempts to heal political divides. Popular sociologist researcher Brene Brown has created a framework for these conversations, which she describes as "rumbles" (2018), and their core definition has many correlations to Listening for Aesthetics as described in the previous section:

> A rumble is a discussion, conversation, or meeting defined by a commitment to lean into vulnerability, to stay curious and generous, to stick with the messy middle of problem identification and solving ... and, as psychologist Harriet Lerner teaches, to listen with the same passion with which we want to be heard.
>
> (Brown 2021)

Without conversation, we are prone then to injure our ability to empathise. This is especially important to consider in a community-engaged context, and quickly reveal the history of these forms are implicitly political and challenging. These tools become especially important in the contemporary context of intensifying political polarization. The value of conversation and empathy in bridging political ideology is the focus of much of sociologist Arlie Russell Horchschild: "Our polarization, and the increasing reality that we simply don't know each other, makes it too easy to settle for dislike and contempt" (2016). Conversations as an antidote to a divisive and anxious society is the entire premise of projects such as "Civil Conversations Project" (On Being 2021), where entrepreneurs, poets, monks, nuns, and researchers meet to discuss and provide resources on "social healing". Most recently, the "Me Too" movement is largely credited as an exercise in story-sharing in a global context to enact healing for survivors of sexual harassment and assault (Strayed 2017).

In this context, the power and value of the type of conversations that verbatim theatre hosts becomes especially important, and extremely valuable in a classroom setting. While it's far from a cohesive solution to the social anxieties of our time, verbatim theatre does create a creative open space where the art of civil conversation can be facilitated and taught. For young people especially, it provides opportunities to practice conversation and empathy. Unsurprisingly, social anxiety is on the rise and especially prevalent in young people across the globe (Jefferies and Ungar 2017). In our experience, however, classroom teachers are often asked to teach the tenets of verbatim theatre without being given the resources to effectively manage an interview process. We hope to ameliorate some of that risk by providing alternative solutions in the section at the end of this chapter.

> **Principles in practice**
>
> Verbatim theatre often deals with sensitive topics, and immersing oneself in a community bound by trauma or fear can come at a high emotional cost for the playwright. David and Sarah have experienced this across their careers, as has Campion Decent, whose early work included the stories of people living with HIV/AIDS, or those who had lost their properties or livelihoods to bushfires in *Embers*. The thought that he may need some mental health maintenance throughout these processes hadn't occurred to him until a team member brought them up. Having a partner in the experience (a dramaturge, assistance or a director) was invaluable for Campion. For *Embers*, he would drive with a collaborator for several hours after a day of interviews. "We would talk it out," Campion says. "What I learned through that process was you really need to have a colleague, a buddy, to talk it out with."

3.4 Danger Zones and Ethical Conundrums

Verbatim interviews can, of course, go very wrong. Leffler (2012) argues that verbatim interviews can be disempowering for the storyteller, especially in contexts where an interview is misrepresented as a kind of therapeutic dramaturgy. Instead, it could be reminiscent of a Christian discourse of confession (348), particularly if the promotion of the need to tell a story "becomes an imperative from without rather than a self-directed action" (350). This discourse of confession is designed to admit a perceived "wrongness" about one's character or behaviour (351) and is therefore a negative positioning of the storyteller. He argues that the verbatim interview establishes the framework for a self-deprecating discourse, disempowering the storyteller. This is further problematised in contexts where the playwright and interviewee have complex power dynamics involving age, gender, ethnicity or a prior relationship. At its worst, verbatim theatre can exploit the stories of the "marginalized and vulnerable ... [and be] used to authenticate the plays that theatre makers wish to construct" (Stuart Fisher 94). It is familiar territory to many working artists, who are often commissioned to deliver a community theatre project by an organisation that has a "predetermined artistic or political agenda" (Kelly and Coleman 54).

Conversely, not all interviews are automatically sites of disempowerment for the storyteller. Playwright Robin Soans (qtd. in Jeffers 2006) states that "people are not only willing, they're absolutely desperate to talk" (7), and argues that when people know their words may be used in performance they are eager to engage in the process. This is certainly true for us. The strongest antidote to our own potential nerves about interviewing strangers has been eased by the pride and delight most people express in even being asked to share their story. It is rare, after all, that anyone has the undivided attention of a listener for an extended period of time.

Overall, however, these ethical concerns are to be constantly negotiated, not dismissed entirely. Given the inherent risk of verbatim conversations, as explored above, all storytellers and interviewees should be strictly voluntary. It is up to the playwright to give as much space to the interviewee as possible to excuse themselves from the process without penalty. Before interviewing, it should be made clear to all participants (ideally in writing), that their words will be recorded and used for creative purposes, including being potentially used in a very public setting. The playwright's ultimate right to *not* include the data in a theatrical outcome should also be stated explicitly. Some playwrights offer the interviewee a 24 or 48 hour "cooling off period", in which they may contact the playwright and retract their data. Generally speaking, we advise the use of a letter of consent. Our methods and discussions of ethics take place in greater depth in chapter seven.

3.5 Interviewing Case Study Examples

Examples from **April's Fool** *by David Burton*

April's Fool was written by David in 2009, and centred on the tragic death of a nineteen year old man, Kristjan Terauds. Initial interviews began just six months after his death. David began with Kristjan's parents, instinctually interviewing them separately to one another. At first David was intimidated by the sensitivity of the topic being discussed but found two eager conversation partners in Kristjan's parents. Given the closeness of the tragedy, emotion was often very intense, and David surrendered to the lengthy and intimate conversations. In all, David ended up with around twelve hours of interview data from those two interviewees alone. It was an overwhelming amount of data, but the conversations with Kristjan's parents found the dramaturgical spine of the eventual final script. David hasn't since encountered this kind of detail and intensity in other interviews. The cost of getting such valuable and rich data from Kristjan's parents was its enormous volume to sort through. Since that time, David attempts to keep most interviews under an hour, unless the interviewee is particularly central or has a complicated relationship to the topic at hand.

The nature of the conversational process meant not all paths were fruitful. A particularly strong memory comes from one of David's conversations with Kristjan's father (confusingly also named David). In the conversation, the interviewee was detailing the events of Kristjan's final few days in hospital, as he lay unconscious. As the interviewer, David had very recently talked to Kristjan's mother about this same period of time. Kristjan's parents responded in incredibly different ways to their grief, and the playwright felt this was rich ground. The father was talking about a desire to "host" the endless stream of guests that were visiting Kristjan's bedside. He talked about wanting to "hold it together", to joke with and console many of Kristjan's young friends. As an interviewer, David was interested in how this behaviour might be especially masculine, as it was starkly different to Kristjan's mother's reaction at the time. He asked, "why do you think you responded like that?" The interviewee shrugged. He genuinely had no idea. "Why do you think others didn't respond similarly?" Again, the interviewee shrugged. "I wasn't really thinking about it". The interviewer pushed a third time, this time more explicit, and less bound in the narrative: "do you think there's something particularly masculine in the way you reacted?" Looking back now, David is ashamed of the question as an interviewer. While not outright disrespectful, it reveals his position as a playwright attempting to think about themes or political meanings, rather than simply being engaged and present with the interviewee. Again, the interviewee shrugged, and sniffed away at his tears. "I don't know, it's just the way I behaved".

In retrospect, it's clear the interviewee wasn't in a place to reflect or intellectually muse on their process of grief. At the time, they were only six months away from the tragedy, so their grief was still very active. Even if the interviewee had managed to articulate a profound dissection of masculine grief, it wouldn't have likely ended up in the script, as it would've taken away from the narrative gravity of the work overall. Listening back over the interview, David felt negative about his questioning. But over a decade on, it's easier to understand that in a handful of hours of improvised interviewing and conversation, there are going to be some points that don't flow. On reflection, the points of data that became the most useful were those when David would forget any other role other than the listener, and simply engage with the narrative as it unfolded. In this, he played the part of the future audience of the work, who would similarly be pushed along by the narrative of the story.

Examples from Time *by Sarah Peters*

Time is based on interviews with three groups of people; people accessing aged care services, their family members or carers, and people providing aged care services. When Sarah first did the call out inviting people to get in touch with her to be involved in the project, the first responses were all from family members or people working in aged care. The interviews with people who were themselves accessing aged care services didn't take place until a longer period of community immersion occurred with a residential care home. Sarah spent time at the home, initially interviewing staff on her first visit, and then spent time participating in activities with the residents such as chair exercise classes. She then facilitated some storytelling workshops with the residents, and it was only after this period of time that interviews took place. These interviews took place either in the resident's individual rooms or in one instance in the dining room over lunch. The different locations really changed the frame of the interview. When entering a residents room, this is the one space in the building that is really their own – it is like walking into someone's home and made even more intimate by the fact that furniture in the rooms is scarce, and generally, the only spot to sit on is the bed.

Despite already establishing familiarity at the home, Sarah tried to remain mindful of how potentially intrusive her visit to the resident's room might be, making sure to ask (more than once) if she could sit in a certain place, or move to look at a photo on the wall or continue the interview, making sure to give opportunities for the interview to come to a close at any time. During one interview, a staff member came to deliver some morning tea, and after a short moment, a nurse then came to check on the resident. Sarah suggested that perhaps she should leave, but the resident grabbed onto Sarah's shirt and assured her that she should stay and that she really enjoyed having visitors. A similar interaction took place in a later interview with a different resident, who asked Sarah to touch her fingers (the resident had peripheral neuropathy, and she felt like her hands had the texture of an old wheat bag). Sarah did, and the resident then held onto her hand for the remainder of the interview. In a different context, having the interviewee pull at your shirt or want to hold your hand might be cause for concern and require the establishment (or reminder) of boundaries. In this context, where both residents had shared that they wish they had more visitors and missed their families, where they had both talked through the physical impact that ageing has had on their bodies (their mobility, their connection to others, their sense of self) and where Sarah was sitting in what was ostensibly their bedrooms, on their beds – the physical touch was an assurance that both residents were happy to participate in the interview and have Sarah present in their rooms.

3.6 Frequently Asked Questions about Interviewing

How Many Interviews Should I Do?

Your total number of interviews will be dependent on the event or theme you are focussing on, the total time you have allocated to your project, and the accessibility of your interviewees. Campion Descent has described writing verbatim plays sourced from sixty, three hundred and zero interviews. Suzie Miller wrote the sixty minute play *Driving into Walls* based on over 500 interviews with young people aged 13–18 in West Australia. All are possible and valid. Most traditional verbatim plays, such as *The Laramie Project*, feature an exhaustive interview process, with many dozens of interviews over many months (and, in the case of *The Laramie Project* specifically, a team of interviewers). But smaller projects may feature interviews with only half a dozen people. For Campion's verbatim theatre work that involved zero in-person interviews, he collected all of his data from pre-existing documents in the public domain (news articles, legal documents, and public speeches and interviews with people holding public office).

Every playwright struggles with the point their *research* or interview process crosses into a *creation* process. There may be overlap between the two, and of course, you can always interview more people if you discover a gap in your script. When precisely you start your writing process is largely an intuitive decision. Generally speaking, however, we advise it's important to avoid the temptation of deciding what your play is too early. Making decisions early creates the risk of closing yourself off to further interview data. The opposing problem is having too much data, and this is concerning also. A playwright can become paralysed in the face of a wall of interviews. Our advice on this front is to stop, or at least pause, interviews once you begin to feel this paralysis creeping in.

How Long Should an Interview Be?

Again, this is largely an intuitive decision. At a practical level, you need to be aware of the sheer volume of data you're gathering. If every interview you encounter is several hours long, your job of editing and managing the resulting data pool will be overwhelming. Some contacts may only require a short twenty-minute discussion. This is particularly true if you're concentrating on a particular theme, as opposed to a specific story or event. Some interviewees will be especially critical and sensitive and will require a large commitment of time.

Where Should I Interview People?

A neutral, quiet space is preferable, but not always achievable. The most effective interviews undertaken by David have been in dressing rooms of an empty theatre, or spare offices that have been provided by a theatre company. Other spaces are of course perfectly satisfactory, but you may be surprised by how much the choice of location can affect interview data. Public spaces, such as cafes, mean a lack of intimacy, but if this is where your interviewee feels most comfortable meeting you then it is the best option. Securing a quiet space so that a recorder can clearly hear their voice can be tricky. Interviewing people in their homes is, again, perfectly sound. This can be useful in providing a full picture of your interviewee's life. Depending on the sensitivity of your conversation, however, you may be interrupted by children, pets, phone calls, or other distractions. You should also keep your own personal safety in mind when organising locations to meet people for interviews.

What If Someone Doesn't Want to Talk? What If No One Wants to Talk?

If you've communicated your objective clearly and responsibly, and someone is unwilling to talk, then there's little you can do. Our advice is not to insist. A verbatim interview done under pressure doesn't result in high-quality data. If the interviewee is particularly critical, you can include their refusal to be interviewed within the script itself, just like any journalist would: "we reached out to Mr. Smith, but he declined to comment".

As previously discussed, it is rare to find yourself in a situation where *no one* wants to talk. Most people, in our experience, are eager to have their voice be heard. If you find that once you've reached out to people, your uptake is low or non-existent, you may need to consider how you're phrasing your intention. Are you giving people the opportunity to be empowered in sharing their voice? Are you coming to them without an agenda? Are the people you're reaching out to genuinely interested in your theme or topic?

What Happens If I Miss Someone and They Come to Me When I've Completed the Script?

Sadly, this happens almost every time. It's impossible for you to reach out to everyone. You can only offer apologies to this individual and encourage them to see the show regardless. Most of the time, people's discomfort with being excluded is eased once they see the show. If you've done your job properly, they are likely to see a piece of their story reflected in the interviews you collected regardless.

In the instance where you're tackling a large topic that could potentially involve hundreds of interviewees, opportunities for audience members or other community participants to share their stories can be provided as an adjacent outcome to eventual production. A website where people can post their story, or even an installation in the foyer of the theatre, has all been used as ways to encourage story sharing to continue beyond a performance.

Can I Get into Legal Trouble If Someone Gets Upset with How I've Used Their Interview Data?

If it is found that you have defamed someone or treated them unfairly in your script, then the short answer to this question is: yes, you could. When you have the resources, you would ideally ask (or have your commissioning theatre company hire) a lawyer to examine the final draft of a script to highlight any areas of concern.

Most of the time, however, you are more free to use creative license more often than you think. Particularly if the interviewee has signed a letter of consent (explained in the final chapter of this book), then all parties understand that the interview data can be used by you with artistic freedom. In the spirit of verbatim theatre, it is rare for any one person or organisation to be labelled a distinct "villain", or for a script to go so far as to emphasise a particular person and damage their reputation. A verbatim theatre's strength is often in showing the multiple sides to any one story. If, as a playwright, you are drawn to a version of the narrative that presents a clear moral binary and presents some of your interviewees as clear antagonists, then you may no longer be in the field of strict verbatim theatre. You can disguise their identities, make their submissions anonymous, or transition to a script that fictionalises events that are "based on a true story".

How Should I Record My Data?

A reliable digital recording is ideal. Unless you want to use the recording for broadcast later, a phone will usually be fine. There are hundreds of apps available that can upload your data straight to a cloud server. If you're committed to a project, investment in a digital recorder can be a wise investment.

Whatever system you choose, make sure you are completely comfortable with how it works before committing to your first interview. Always pack spare batteries, memory cards, and have contingency plans at your disposal should anything go awry. Once the interview is complete, commit to a consistent process of uploading or copying the data so that you know it is safe. Never delete data without first making sure you have a copy, unless you're intentionally destroying data.

3.7 Negotiating Interviews in a Classroom Environment

For secondary and tertiary schools, committing to an interview process can be a heavy administrative load. We've often been asked to teach verbatim theatre processes to teachers and students alike. From our experience, we recommend some of the following options to ameliorate risk and logistical load.

- In the first instance, consider running interviews inside the school. Students may interview other students, staff, or support services. The topic of the interview may focus on a particular event (an athletics carnival for example), or a theme (interviewing seniors and juniors about their first day at school, for example)
- If you're committed to teaching verbatim theatre annually, you may be able to set up a relationship with a local community organisation. Your school is most likely already connected to a support organisation that has access to a community of participants. These may include aged care, refugee and migrant services, local churches, or local hobby clubs. If you're able, organising your students to go to one of their local meetings is ideal. Alternatively, inviting them to come to the school at a specific time mean the students can operate within their comfort zone
- If you have too many students for too few interviewees or have trouble trusting some students, then getting students to interview in pairs or small groups is perfectly acceptable
- You may only target one or two key interviews, and conduct these as a whole class, where invited guests are welcomed to the classroom, and students can take turns asking questions. You may then supplement this data with online surveys, or any other publicly available material

3.8 Practical Activities

Running Practice Interviews

This is a quick and simple way to begin to rehearse the interview process. This exercise can be done hastily, over half an hour, or it can stretch out to be an entire day. It depends on what your goals are, and the focus of your participants. Participants should get into groups of three. Randomly assign a person "A", "B" and "C". Person A will begin as the interviewer. Person B will begin as an interviewee. Person C will begin as a scribe.

Make a decision as to how committed your scribe will be. They may be able to record on their phone if they have the time later to transcribe the data and examine it. Alternatively (and more commonly for the sake of convenience), scribes can simply be advised to stand by at the ready with a pen and paper or a computer. When they hear something interesting – an anecdote, a phrase or anything that grabs them – the scribe can make a note of it, taking down as much detail as they can. Once the interview has concluded, the scribe can go back over their notes and have some time to fill them out with more detail. As this is a "dummy" run, exact transcription isn't necessary or practical.

The focus of the exercise should be on the interaction between the interviewer and the interviewee. The interviewer is given four basic "narrative-generating questions" that they may use to trigger a conversation where they would further improvise questions and generate discussion.

Here are some suggested questions:

- What is one of your favourite things about your family?
- What's something about your family that you find difficult that you wouldn't mind sharing?
- What do you really enjoy about school/your workplace?
- What's something about your school/workplace that you find difficult that you wouldn't mind sharing?

Instruct interviewers in listening to the interviewees, and hunting for clues that would help them spin out a narrative. Scribes also play the part of an important third party here, who may be able to notice nuances in the exchange between interviewer and interviewee that can assist both parties in reflection. If rushed for time, you may give as little as ten minutes for the interview to take place. If your participants are more mature, and you have more time, you may want to give as much as half an hour or forty-five minutes.

As an instructor, you may want to pause interviews to make some vital observations. Teenage students may initially start out interviews by lounging, for example, or doing whatever they can to avoid making actual eye contact. Otherwise, let the interviews take place, and then leave plenty of space for the scribes to catch up, noting stories or moments of particular value or interest. Allow time for reflection and discussion as well. How did the interviewers feel? Did they have much success in finding the story? Did the interviewees feel safe to share? Did they feel listened to?

If time permits, rotate roles in the groups so that everyone has a turn at each role. Again, time permitting, you may use these initial, rough pieces of data to begin a quick exercise in editing and staging verbatim work. In your reflective discussion, it's useful to use the interview as the anchor here. What happened in the interview that then allowed the work to be staged in a particular way?

Studying Great Interviewers

It can be difficult to find a veteran verbatim theatre practitioner to mentor you in the art of interviewing. However, finding a plethora of excellent interviewers is not. Studying YouTube clips and podcasts of interviewers you admire can be extremely helpful in developing your own approach, especially when you look for the tenets of Listening for Aesthetics as outlined in this chapter. While absolutely different from verbatim theatre, interviews for entertainment (whether using video or audio), are still looking for a narrative. In the list below are a host of different interviewers. You will notice very few similarities between them, other than they are very authentic to themselves (the interviewer doesn't try to "disappear", in fact, they are an active partner in the conversation), and they are hunting for story.

We haven't included late-night talk show hosts here for a very specific reason. Talk show hosts are gifted entertainers and can be worth examining in some instances, but the vast majority of their interviews are highly vetted by publicists and done with a great deal of preparation. This means they aren't improvised, and so lack the spontaneous connections (and disconnections) that occur in verbatim theatre interviews. We have also excluded political journalists from the list below. They are often expert listeners and can use the interviewee's own words against them. However, again, this is not always the goal of a verbatim theatre practitioner, particularly in a community-engaged context.

The list below focuses on some of the most popular interviewers that dominate podcast charts. The interviewer clearly prepares extensively (often with a team), but also remains open to conversational detours, and is constantly hunting for a story.

- *On Being* with Krista Tippett
- *WTF* with Marc Maron
- *Fresh Air* with Teri Gross
- *Armchair Expert* with Dax Shepherd and Monica Padman
- *Conversations* with Richard Fidler
- *The Griefcast* with Cariad Lloyd
- *How I Built This* with Guy Raz
- *Unlocking Us* with Brene Brown

Works Cited

Bennett, Susan. *Theatre Audiences: A Theory of Production and Reception*. Routledge, London, 1990.

Brown, Brene. *Dare to Lead*. Random House UK, 2018.

Brown, Brene. "Let's Rumble." *Brene Brown.com*. 2021, https://brenebrown.com/blog/2019/05/01/lets-rumble/.

Fredriksson, Lennart. "Modes of Relating in a Caring Conversation: A Research Synthesis on Presence, Touch and Listening." *Journal of Advanced Nursing*, 1999, pp. 1167–1176.

Haseman, Brad and John O'Toole. *Dramawise Re-imagined*. Currency Press, 2017.

Hopf, C. "5.2 Qualitative Interviews: An Overview." *A Companion to Qualitative Research*, edited by U. Flick, K. Ernst, and I. Steinke, Sage Publications, 2004.

Hochschild, Arle Russell. *Strangers in their Own Land: Anger and Mourning on the American Right*. New Press, 2016.

Jeffers, Alison "Refugee Perspectives: The Practice and Ethics of Verbatim Theatre and Refugee Stories." *Platform* 1(1), 2006, pp. 1–17.

Jefferies, P. and M. Ungar. "Social Anxiety in Young People: A Prevalence Study in Seven Countries." *PLoS ONE* 15(9), 2017, pp. 1–18.

Kelly, Kathryn, and Emily Coleman. "Community Engagement in Independent Performance-making in Australia: A Case Study." *Social Alternatives* 38(1), 2019, pp. 53–65.

Korkmaz, Selma. "Evaluation of Aesthetic Listening Skills of Pre-school Children." *Journal for Eductors, Teachers and Trainers* 10(2), 2019, pp. 115–126.

Leffler, Elliot. "Replacing the Sofa with the Spotlight: Interrogating the Therapeutic Value of Personal Testimony within Community-based Theatre". *Research in Drama Education* 17(3), 2012. pp. 357–353.

Megson, Chris. "Backpages 6.4: Verbatim Practices in Contemporary Theatre: Symposium Report." *Contemporary Theatre Review* 16(4), 2006, pp. 529–532.

Miller, Suzie. "Adrift: The Story of Writing Transparency." *Storyline* 33, 2013, pp. 78–83

On Being. "Civil Conversations & Social Healing." *Onbeing.org*, 2021. https://onbeing.org/civil-conversations-project/

Paget, Derek. "Acts of Commitment: Activist Arts, the Rehearsed Reading and Documentary Theatre." *New Theatre Quarterly*, 2010, p. 188.

Peters, Sarah. "Verbatim Theatre and a Dramaturgy of Belonging." *Australasian Drama Studies* 74, 2019, pp. 39–63.

Pollock, Della. "Introduction: Remembering." *Remembering Oral History and Performance*, edited by Della Pollock, Palgrave MacMillan, New York, 2005. pp. 1–17.

Reese, Sam. "Teaching Aesthetic Listening." *Music Educators Journal* 69(7), 1983, pp. 36–38.

Strayed, Cheryl. "The Power of 'Me Too'." *Onbeing.org*, 2017. https://onbeing.org/blog/cheryl-strayed-the-power-of-me-too/

Stuart Fisher, Amanda. "'That's Who I'd Be, If I Could Sing': Reflections on a Verbatim Project with Mothers of Sexually Abused Children." *Studies in Theatre and Performance* 21.2, 2011, pp. 193–208.

4 Transcription, Exploration, and Community-Engaged Workshopping

You've done your interviews, spent time immersed in a community, and had conversations and cups of tea. Depending on your project and your approach, you might already know what the story is going to be. You might know where you want to start and what you want to say. If that's the case, you can probably skip straight to Chapter Five where we focus on writing. If you're not yet sure what the focus of your script/performance is, but you have gathered stories and documented experiences and are interested in collaborating with others in the initial stage of the creative development process, then this chapter is for you. We'll look at some of the different ways artists transcribe and organise their collected materials, strategies for exploring what you've gathered, and practical suggestions for collaborative creative development. This is all designed to get you thinking widely about how you are going to communicate something to your audience and find your "way in" to the writing process.

Before we dive in, it's useful to know how people in the academic field have referred to what happens post-interview in a verbatim-inspired process. Sarah wrote about this in an article for Drama Australia Journal in 2017, exploring the myriad of terms used to describe how verbatim material is written into performance. These include "compression" and "shaping" (Luckhurst 2008, 207), "editing" and "juxtaposing" (Bottoms 2006, 59), "framing" (Jeffers 2006, 14), and describing the verbatim as being "distilled" (Anderson and Wilkinson 2007, 154). Each of these terms conveys a sense of how a writer may use verbatim material. They predominantly focus on the theme of reduction and the process of minimalizing verbatim material into a cohesive narrative.

There is no doubt that transforming hours of conversations and stories into an hour or two of performance absolutely requires reduction and editing. Sometimes though, you might first need to embark on a process of exploration and expansion in order to really engage with the complex fabric of the stories you have collected. We want to encourage you to think broadly across all of the means of dramatic communication available to you, to

DOI: 10.4324/9781003155706-5

88 *Transcription, Exploration, and Community-Engaged Workshopping*

advocate active experimentation with dramatic languages, and to share some of our experiences transcribing, documenting, and exploring stories.

4.1 Transcribing Interviews

Artists have individualised practices when it comes to the transcription process. Some artists describe transcribing recordings in their entirety, such as Linden Wilkinson for *A Day in December* (2010). Wilkinson's transcription process included every "nuance of language and every emotional colouration" and these "hesitations, repetitions, laughter and tears all became clues for actors in performance" (126). Other playwrights describe listening to the recordings and only making note of the time and content of particular stories that are meaningful to them. There's no way to sugarcoat it – transcribing interviews is a time-consuming task. Depending on your preferred way of working you might choose to use transcription software to do the first rough draft of the transcription for you (notes and recommendations on software can be found in the final section of this chapter), or if you have funding available (and consent from your participants/interviewees) you can pay transcription companies to turn your recorded interviews into words on a page. Or you might choose to listen to the recordings and transcribe them yourself. There is no right or "better" way, but it's important to keep in mind that decisions made in this phase of the process can have a significant impact on the shape and content of the resulting creative work.

Some questions to consider before transcribing:

- Am I going to transcribe the full recording?
- Am I going to transcribe only the sections or stories that seem creatively dynamic or interesting?
- Am I going to transcribe as faithfully as possible, documenting all the false starts, ums, ahs and half sentences?
- Am I going to take notes on tone of voice and mood along with the transcription?
- What did I tell the interviewee I was going to do with the recording and transcription?
- Am I going to send the transcribed interview back to the interviewee for review?

That's quite a lot to think about! Here are a few things you might want to consider to help inform your decisions:

- If you are interested in the *way* people express themselves and communicate then you might be drawn towards a full and faithful transcription,

where there are also notes on the tone and mood. You could use software to do the initial transcription for you, and then listen to the interview yourself, correcting any errors in the transcribed document and making your own annotations and notes as you go
- If you are interested in focusing on the content and narrative of the interview material – on the characters and relationships and tensions – then you might be drawn to the option of only transcribing the "interesting" bits of the interview. This is another point in the process where your unique creative vision will come into play, as you decide which stories to make note of and which stories to leave out

You can also consider what format or template you might use to help organise your interview transcriptions. If you're transcribing them yourself in a style similar to a script, you might find that typing out the names is too onerous and using initials is easier. You might do away with individual identifiers all together, and use regular font for one speaker and italicised font for the other, using the shortcut keys on the keyboard. When transcribing interviews for *bald heads & blue stars,* Sarah used a template in order to keep track of the interview details. In this template below, you'll see that there is also a column titled "creative impulse". Sarah uses the term impulse here in reference to Peter Abbs' description of the five phases of art making and how this begins with an impulse: an idea, a flash of energy a "stirring of the psyche" (199) desiring expression. Sarah used this column to document the ideas and imagined moments that came to mind when listening back to the interviews and transcribing the stories and added to the column when later reading back over the transcribed material. Including it in the template means the creative idea sits right next to the section of the interview which stimulated the impulse.

Rich Brown writes about the work of Moisés Kaufman and Tectonic Theatre Project (*The Laramie Project* is one of Kaufman and Tectonics' most famous verbatim plays) investigating their practice of Moment Work. In this approach, collaborators develop moments – short sequences of performance that vary in length but can include text, movement, lighting, and costume – and then present these to their colleagues in a workshop setting for exploration. These short performance moments sometimes become stimulus for further development, although it is the process of engaging with each idea to see what it may yield in a collaborative space that is valued by the company. A moment "can be as simple as a single gesture or breath or as complex as an entire scene" (Brown 51). Sarah's creative impulse column reflects this description of moments, as rather than only being ideas for text or dialogue they draw on the full breadth of the dramatic languages and provide a starting point for future collaborative workshopping.

90   *Transcription, Exploration, and Community-Engaged Workshopping*

Interview Details	
Interview No.	
Date of interview	
Participants	
Location	
Duration	
Notes	
Interview Transcript	
Creative impulse	Transcript

bald heads & blue stars transcription template example.

In *bald heads & blue stars* Sarah started out transcribing full interviews and then shifted to only transcribing specific stories and moments. In *twelve2twentyfive* the interview transcripts were sent back to the psychologists and clients for review, so the full interview was transcribed in this project (however no notes on tone or manner of delivery were made). As Sarah wasn't present for those interviews she first listened to the recordings in their entirety and then began the process of transcribing. There's a lot of stopping, starting, rewinding, and relistening that happens in the transcription process, so Sarah wanted to hear the full interview in "real time" before hearing it in a more abstract way. For the *Time* project, Sarah conducted all of the interviews and was lucky to work with a research assistant who completed all of the transcriptions. Since Sarah was present for the interviews she didn't feel the same need to listen to the recordings as she did for the *twelve2twentyfive* project.

When writing *April's Fool* and *St. Mary's In Exile*, David found the recorded files of his interviews to be the most valuable documentation possible. The actual transcription process ended up being secondary to David's impulse, which was to simply saturate himself in the audio recordings. David would effectively spend months with the data, listening back to interviews while he was walking, doing the dishes, or driving in the car. These would inevitably inspire ideas for scene construction or characterisation, and David would jot these down on any spare piece of paper he could find, or keep a note file in his phone. This process was messy and unorganised, but it allowed David to move through the work organically. These notes would eventually reach a critical mass, where entire scenes were coalescing in his mind. At this point, David would make full use of a stack of index cards and a large wall. He would give each interview its own index card, noting the time codes for key moments in the interview. From there, he created a separate pile of index cards, each one describing a moment or scene in a finished draft of the play itself. He was able to then cross-reference the specific interview moments, and how they would fit into each scene. This resulted in an "outline" for a script, that David then began to write, transcribing the specific interview moments he knew he wanted, often in the order that he desired.

Principles in Practice

Australian playwright Campion Decent prefers the laborious task of transcribing entire interviews himself, as he sees numerous virtues in the experience.

> I want to hear the voices again. I want to spend six hours transcribing a one hour interview and go back and go back and go back. It's really important that you have a real understanding of the DNA of that interview.

Reading back over interview transcripts can be an odd experience. When tone, pace, and volume are removed from words their meaning can come across quite differently than how they were intended when spoken. Lines said in jest (through laughter or with a playful tone) can appear quite direct and sometimes even rude when printed on the page. This is something to keep in mind when making decisions about what you will transcribe, and about who will have access to the transcriptions. In our projects, we tend to restrict access to the transcripts to the people who were present in the interview, and a small circle of creative collaborators. Whatever you choose to do, make sure you are transparent about your choices with the community of participants.

Principles in Practice

This is a good time to remember that in Headphone Verbatim there often isn't a transcription process. Playwrights and makers will often edit the sound recordings directly, and these recordings are then played through headphones to the actors as they rehearse and perform. In Roslyn Oades *The Nightline* (2022), the actor as mediator is removed, and audiences take a seat at a table for one, pick up the handset of the rotary dial phone, and listen directly to the recordings in an intimate performance for one. Described as "a listening club designed for insomniacs, night owls, lonely-hearts and dreamers", over 700 anonymous voice messages were recorded between midnight and 6 am to inform this work, and "in the spirit of creative nonfiction, this work draws on field recordings, phone messages, composition, and site-responsive design to create an evocative theatrical audio experience."[1]

Caroline Wake explains that one of the qualities of headphone verbatim and audio-based works which engage her is the way that it "models, enacts, and enables listening for its audiences". She argues that "listening, both as a practice and discourse, might reframe headphone verbatim, and verbatim theatre more broadly, as a form that does not so much 'give voice' as 'grant an audience'" (2013, 321). *The Nightline* is an excellent example of this, which not only gives voice to the stories of the night owls in our society but also grants those stories an audience through the privilege of listening.

4.2 Documenting Community Immersion

If your community-engaged process doesn't involve interviews you might like to think about other ways of documenting stories and ideas. This documentation can take a variety of forms but will generally respond to the following prompts, which cover both the documentation of experience and the initial response to and reflection on that experience:

- What was shared or experienced
- How was it shared or experienced
- Why is it meaningful?
- How can you imagine it in performance?

This might take place through a written or audio-recorded journal reflection, a series of photos with notes or captions, the collection of documents, materials or souvenirs, or a video diary. Documenting your community immersion can be useful for remembering the feelings and facts of a place or experience and for keeping track of your creative ideas as they develop. It can serve as a useful prompt for creative development and playwriting. We've included a variety of examples from our projects to demonstrate just how diverse the forms of documentation can be.

Journals

While walking the Camino de Santiago (which informed the play *Blister*) Sarah kept a daily journal where she documented her experiences. Part of Sarah's process of reading back over these journal entries involved summarizing key moments or themes on separate index cards for each day of the pilgrimage (similar to David's approach when listening to interviews). The two pages of journaling from the day Sarah arrived at St Jean Pied de Port to begin what would end up being over 1030 kilometres of walking, were condensed into a few lines: a note about having to learn the culture of "The Way", and an idea for the central character Rosie to think about what she would do differently next time.

David is envious of Sarah's organisational ability and commitment to regular journaling, but has never been able to replicate it! David tends to document everything, but in a variety of mediums and without a consistent approach. His original notes for projects such as *April's Fool* and the early Queensland Music Festival Signature Community events were haphazard, usually amounting to a tangled web of bullet points, often spread across multiple notebooks. Some of the pages of these notebooks would find themselves on index cards that David used in the transcription process (see paragraph above).

Over the years, however, David's note-taking has become more digital. These days, any basic model smartphone also serves as a quick note-taking device, a dictaphone, and a camera. When handwriting journals or notes David's now made the habit of taking a quick photo of the page for safe-keeping. He's also found audio note-taking especially helpful. It's also simple enough to set up your device so that all of these files are automatically up-loaded to a central cloud server (such as Google Drive). This at least means that all notes and journals are located in one spot, and are automatically time-stamped. In so doing, David builds a useful archive that can make the physical writing process substantially simpler. For both Sarah and David, the physical act of writing the draft script of a play is often minimal, as the hard work has been offset by extensive documenting of the entire artistic journey. By the time it comes to actually write the play, detailed outlines have often naturally coalesced or emerged across the immersion, engagement, and documentation process.

Collected Materials and Artefacts

In the development for *Eternity* Sarah and the community of participants wrote letters to each other in response to questions and provocations given in workshops. These letters were often personal, detailed, and specific to each of the individuals in the project. In this project, the intention was to engage with the community to draw on lived experiences and authentic means of expression, but not to make depictions of that community directly. After reading the letters from participants Sarah wrote summaries of the content, reflecting on the main themes that were raised, the tensions, contexts or relationships described, and key phrases and quotes used.

While your project may not share something as specific as letter-writing, in community-engaged work material is often abundant from sources other than interviews. The whole starting point of David's *April's Fool* was a journal kept by one of the central family that was the subject of the play. In large-scale community-engaged work that David undertook with Queensland Music Festival, featuring casts of hundreds, David wasn't always able to be present at every single workshop. Instead, small teams of workshop facilitators would collect responses from participants. These would take the form of bullet-pointed documents, or short videos displaying improvisations or responses to provocations, or audio clips. All of these artefacts would find their way to David, and he would work with the workshop facilitators to filter the data gathered.

In many youth workshops, it is relatively simple to emerge with a nest of artefacts that may not be strictly traditional "verbatim" material but have been used by community-engaged practitioners for many decades. These may be original artworks, improvised scenes or songs, or photos of a whiteboard crowded with notes and thoughts. These artefacts, as mentioned above, can often be used as an addendum to in-person interviews, and assist in noting a wider context for the themes of your work.

4.3 Collaborative Creative Development

There is no community-engaged theatre without some degree of collaboration. It is important to establish from the outset (and perhaps revisit and rethink from time to time) the nature of your collaboration on each project. Sometimes projects are collaboratively authored and everyone involved has a say in the direction of the creative work. Sometimes you might invite others to collaborate with you through workshops, developments or feedback, but it is very clear that you are still the playwright and have final creative control. As Turner states, having "communication about communicating, may be an essential part of facilitating a productive dialogue" (117). For a collaboration to go well, having clear and transparent conversations about how the collaboration will work, what the intentions and ground rules of the collaboration are, what timeline and level of commitment is required, and how feedback will be provided can all be vital to ensuring a successful process. In this brief section, we explore just a few ways that collaboration may work inside this stage of a project.

Voicing Stories and Formal Creative Developments

Reading gathered stories aloud with other people is a wonderful way to explore what resonates with you. This is quite different from reading the stories yourself in your own mind, or even reading out loud to yourself. While this can give you a more nuanced insight into the story, reading it to others (or better yet, having them read it to you) provides the basic tenets of performance – something being communicated to someone else – and this performance frame changes the way you hear and receive the story. The person reading it is putting their own voice onto the story, and they are starting a process of interpretation and meaning-making as they decide what pace to read at, where to place a vocal emphasis, when to pause, etc. This enables you as the writer to hear the story anew, not in the voice of the person who originally told the story and not in your own voice, but in a third new way.

If you have transcribed interview material you may want to begin by looking for themes across these and grouping all of the stories relating to a particular theme together. Then bring all of the stories related to one theme together with a group of creative collaborators, and read the stories aloud. You may consider this an initial focus group or early developmental laboratory for your work. This voicing of the stories will likely lead to discussions about the content of each story, which aspects in the narratives connect with or challenge your readers, and how these different stories might work together to convey something to an audience about the experience being shared. Consider who you could bring together to do the voicing of the stories, and how different groups of people would bring a different insight to the work. A group of theatre makers will likely give a different perspective than a group formed from the community who were initially interviewed.

Sarah used the process of voicing stories in the writing of *bald heads & blue stars,* running workshops with undergraduate theatre students as part of the creative development process. She found this a really useful way to see whether or not stories that were about a very specific thing – in this case, the female experience of hair loss – would be interesting and engaging for people who had no knowledge of the experience. Across the workshops, the theatre students discussed being emotionally affected by the stories of the women interviewed, and through their reflections and discussion it became apparent how people without alopecia might connect with these stories. They described how the lack of control the women had over what was happening to them resonated across many experiences, along with feelings of not belonging, not feeling "normal", and how people learn to navigate great changes in their lives. This provided a thoughtful insight and provided some dramaturgical direction for the playwriting process as the theatre students personal reflections indicated which stories may hold wider resonance for an audience.

Voicing stories was also an approach used in the creative development of *Time,* and in this project, Sarah worked with three professional actors across two workshops. The workshop began with a check in, with each participant sharing their name, pronouns, and something they cherished about their personal creative practice, and letting the group know if there was anything we could do or should know in order for their involvement in the workshop to go well (in relation to access, mobility, etc). This was followed by some simple physical warmups, including some stretching and two short drama games. The goals for the creative development included hearing the stories anew, being open to inspiration, imagining how the stories might be performed, and giving our collective creative attention to the story, community, themes, and lived experiences of the project for a few hours. The group took turns reading stories from the interviews out loud, discussing what felt true or resonant, what they wanted to know more about, and what they cared about.

Later in the workshop, the actors were given complete transcripts and a highlighter and tasked with shaping a monologue from this material in 20 minutes. They then had 10 minutes to consider how they might "perform" that monologue before everyone shared their work with each other. Each of these opportunities to hear other people's voices on the stories generated creative ideas and theatrical impulses for the next writing stage of *Time*.

For both *April's Fool* and *St. Mary's In Exile*, David had the benefit of creating the works in partnership with professional theatre companies. As such, creative developments with professional actors were common. These were usually one to three day affairs, reading very early drafts of the script (which tended to be bloated with too much interview material), or raw interview data itself. A dedicated dramaturge and a director were usually also present. A full day of development would usually look like this:

- An initial reading of the script followed by a short break
- Either an informal discussion or asking creatives to respond to very specific queries from the writer
- A second reading of the work
- A conversation between director, playwright, and dramaturg on next steps for the following draft

Every playwright ends up discovering what their ideal creative development "day" would look like. For David, a full day that includes two readings is often too overwhelming. An initial read-through and discussion is usually enough to fuel changes for another draft. Ideally, David has twenty-four hours to make changes, before gathering with everyone again to read a new, hastily revised version of the script. Many playwrights prefer a more immersive approach however, taking a full week with other creatives to simultaneously examine drafts of the scripts, ideas for scenes not yet written, raw interview data, and even begin to build prototypes of set, costume, and technical design.

The budget required for such a time-intensive exercise is sadly more of a factor than many would like. However, the principle of these developments can be replicated among friends and independent artists. Simply giving time in your transcription process to read over early collections of data or muse over initial ideas for scenes can be extremely valuable. (To this day, both David and Sarah host informal events for a close network of trusted professionals where they toss around early ideas for new work, usually over a meal.)

The voicing stories approach might also help you decide which sections of the gathered material are already theatrically compelling or dynamic on their own, and which sections might be able to be combined or woven together in order to best serve your overarching story. At times the people you ask to read those stories will not be able to help contribute their own ideas, and their ideas may not necessarily be right for you, but they will likely provoke some element of inspiration even if it helps you articulate what narrative paths you don't want to pursue.

> **Principles in Practice**
>
> For some projects, the form of the final work may already be known at the time of the script's creation. In the development for Claire Christian's *The Virginity Monologues*, Claire knew she would have access to four actors. Knowing this magic number, she worked backward, deciding each actor would have three monologues each, for a total of a dozen. This question became one of the driving forces in editing her data: "What are the twelve themes or stories that need to be represented to accurately reflect the submissions we've received?" This limitation allowed Claire to focus tightly on the data and build the structure of the work.

Devising through Discussion

Devising is when you create a performance without starting from a pre-written script. It means thinking dramaturgically about how meaning is communicated in performance through different combinations of dramatic and theatrical languages. This experimentation with the building blocks of performance (role, relationship, movement, mood, story, sound, design, etc) often occurs in a physical and practical way in a devising process, however, it is also possible to talk through and brainstorm theatrical moments, verbally illustrating and describing how moments of performance might capture and convey a moment of the story. This approach of devising through discussion is a strategy you can use when first exploring your gathered material and is another collaborative starting point to the writing process.

Devising through discussion can extend the work done through voicing stories to highlight the points of connection between stories. It also begins the process of verbally illustrating their translation into performance. Ideas can be developed in the dialogue between your group of collaborators, riffing from and building into each other's ideas of how the stories from the gathered material might be made manifest in performance.

The practice aligns with Turner's description of "dialogic listening" (110), a concept Turner borrows from communications theory to describe an element of collaborative writing practice. Dialogic listening "highlights the productive and mutual qualities of communication between people" (110). One of the key strategies of dialogic listening is to mutually discuss metaphors, to encourage "each other to share and build on these metaphors" (115), so that collectively you are creating something familiar as a point of connection to something that might be outside the realm of your own experience. The dialogic listening of devising through discussion can be a useful way to explore your gathered material in preparation for writing and to discover metaphors, symbols, and ways into the story which serve as points of connection for your audience.

> **Principles in practice**
>
> Working as playwright and director simultaneously, Queensland theatremaker Dan Evans shared with us his process of creating *I Should've Drunk More Champagne* with his collaborator Amy Ingram. The piece was crowd-sourced from online surveys asking for submissions on the theme of regret. At first, members of the creative team would review all the submissions individually. Then, in an initial creative development, the team word "sort" the several hundred submissions along a spectrum of "heavy" to "light". Importantly, this spectrum was defined in response to the data itself. For their next work, *I Want To Know What Love Is*, the team decided to sort data into the arc of a relationship: flirting, falling in love, fighting, breaking up, and moving on. From there, he continues,
>
> > we start to look at themes, images and recurring words. This idea of space or the universe kept coming up in people's submissions. There were a few submissions that mentioned the colour orange ... . and then we set about responding to those submissions in a devised way. So, 'here's submission number 76 Amy, go away and respond to it, create a theatrical image that responds to it'.
>
> Through this method, the sorting of the data merges into the writing of the script, and the assembling of the final show, seamlessly.

When writing *Blister* Sarah had quite a few monologues for the main character Rosie scattered across the play, and also included two characters who served as Rosie's inner voices. In earlier drafts for the play these inner voices only appeared periodically at key moments, however, through a devising discussion with the cast in the lead-up to the premiere of the play, the idea to weave these characters more consistently throughout the play was offered. The cast and director verbally workshopped the idea, devising a moment of performance through discussion which used the original monologue as stimulus. Sarah then re-wrote this section of the text, incorporating this offer.

Here is the original moment of performance which has Rosie delivering a monologue in direct address to the audience, shifting at times between reliving the experience "in the moment" and reflecting on the experience in the past tense.

ROSIE: The worst day, 15 days in. The snotty-sick-rain day.

In the morning we're staring out at the drizzly mist and I could feel a little tickle in the back of my throat. We walk and talk, and there's mud but it's ok, and my throat is feeling sore, but it's ok.

Then the rain sets in. My boots, which had stayed water proof up till now, began to leak and soon my socks were soaked. Wet squelching with every step. Within the space of two hours the sickness had enveloped me. I was wet through, trudging in the rain. No point reaching for the soggy tissues making a wad in my pockets. Snot running down my face which I – and this is probably embarrassing but I didn't even care – wiped across the arm of my rain coat and figured the rain would deal with it.

Beyond caring.

Greg told me later that he saw me reach a small crest ahead of him and that I turned back for a moment. Turned back – then continued on. He said that was his first clue that I wasn't just a little sick – the fact that I didn't wait for them. I had blinkers on, there was nothing outside the meter square I was walking in.

I was staring at the path when I began to wonder why the rain was bouncing off the ground. Since when did rain bounce?

Oh. Hail. Good.

No trees, no cover, no choice but to continue, with the hail pinging a steady rhythm against my pack.

Few kilometres later and I could finally see the town ahead of me. The only thing standing between me and a I-hope-to-God-they-have-hot-water shower is a path a foot deep in freezing water.

I'd have laughed if I'd had the energy.

My Camino family wordlessly let me have the first shower. My body was blotchy and red, no feeling in my thighs. Half the contents of my bag damp and cold, barring one jumper and half the sleeping bag. I huddled, shaking on the edge of my bed, wrapped in the dry end of the sleeping bag and unable to stop the chattering of my teeth.

I'm not good at asking for help. And by this point I was completely incapable of formulating a coherent sentence.

Tissues appeared beside me. Pain meds passed over with a bottle of water. Cold and flu tablets pressed into my palm. A whispered promise that someone had asked the owners if we could please have soup with our dinner.

In this moment I loved them all.

Shift. The wind builds to a gale. A door slams and Saskia and Paul enter.

The full story of this snotty-sick-rain-day is conveyed in the monologue and told in only Rosie's voice. The devising through discussion in this example was not related to the content of what would be told in the play, but rather in relation to the style and conventions. The creative development process for *Blister* allowed Sarah to work through which conventions best suited the tone and mood of the play, and the decision was made to "lean in" to the characters who played the inner voices and have them more involved across the script. This convention allows there to be more interaction and theatrically dynamic "in the moment" recreations of the experience of the snotty-sick-rain-day. In this revised version you'll see how all of the key elements of the story remain the same, but this time Rosie's inner voices are on the road with her, experiencing the rain and the hail together.

ROSIE: The worst day? 15 days in. The snotty-sick-rain day.

Shift

    I'm staring out at the drizzly mist in the morning and I can feel a little tickle in the back of my throat. We walk and talk

V1: There's mud
ROSIE: But it's ok
V2: Throat is feeling a little sore,
ROSIE: But it's ok.
V1: Then the rain sets in.
ROSIE: My boots, which have stayed waterproof up till now, begin to leak and soon …
V1: I can feel it
ROSIE: My socks were soaked. Wet squelching with every step. Within the space of two hours the sickness had enveloped me.
V2: Wet through, trudging in the rain. Fun.
ROSIE: Snot running down my face
V1: No point reaching for the soggy tissues making a wad in your pocket.

Rosie wipes the snot with her arm.

ROSIE: I don't even care.
    I reach a small crest and look back.
V2: It's Greg, and Henry
V1: You could wait for them
V2: Or just keep going
ROSIE: Just keep going. I can't.
    My blinkers are on, nothing exists outside of the meter square I'm walking in.
    Then the rain starts to bounce off the ground in front of me. Since when did rain bounce?
ALL: Oh. Hail. Good.
V1: No trees,
V2: No cover,

ROSIE:	No choice but to continue, with the hail pinging a steady rhythm against my pack.
	My head is a raging fever, and I think
V2:	"I could just crawl into a whole and die"
ROSIE:	And that would be ok.
	I arrive, and the last thing I want is to be around people or have to talk. I have nothing to give, and just want to hide away somewhere.

V1 and V2 become Greg and Judy. They help Rosie

GREG:	We'll just take this off *(pack)*
JUDY:	Wrap yourself in this *(blanket)*
GREG:	Here we go (untying her laces and removing her boots)
JUDY:	I got these from Kate, take them both *(tablets with water)*
GREG:	Henry's already asked and there's chicken soup with dinner
JUDY:	Here you are – no you keep the pack *(tissues)*
GREG:	I'll pop these by the door *(the shoes)*
JUDY:	Tuck that right round *(the blanket)*. There you go.

Greg and Judy exit.

ROSIE: In this moment I love them all.

Shift. The wind builds to a gale. A door slams and Saskia and Paul enter.

The collaborative moments of workshopping afforded through voicing stories and devising through discussions allow writers the opportunity to experiment with ideas, hear stories anew in different contexts, and consider how the same content might be differently communicated.

Creative developments and group devising require humility, and can often bring up difficult truths for the playwright. In the very first drafts for *St. Mary's In Exile*, David relied on a lot of gathered verbatim material. The story centred around two priests and their congregation. David had envisioned a dramatic arc that would see the priests lead their congregation away from the Catholic Church at the end of act one. Act two would reflect on their journey beyond this point. A creative development with actors, a director, and a dramaturg allowed for an initial "voicing stories" phase. This version of the work was read aloud to many people who were interviewed. David was overwhelmed with feedback from many points, but a common theme emerged: the first act was gripping, and the second act was problematic. A week later, David sat one-on-one with dramaturge Louise Gough. She gently proffered essentially ditching the second act and stretching the narrative of the first act out longer. After his experience in the week's creative development, talking over scenes and characters with a range of creatives, David knew this was the right move. It meant ditching fifty pages of script and essentially shrugging off hours of gathered interview material. It stung, but it was the right move when considering the dramaturgy and the intended audience for this particular piece.

A playwright working in a collaborative environment must remain highly tuned to their inner voice and attempt to be critical of the feedback that comes towards them. Not all radical changes are inherently wrong or right. It is ultimately up to the playwright to decide if they are resisting change because it's painful, or if it's because it is not the best path forward (or of course, it could be both!). In verbatim and community-engaged works in particular, questions of ethics can often play a central role in these decisions, which we talk about at length in chapter seven.

Principles in Practice

When presenting work back to a community, Campion Decent emphasises the need to deliver this in the form of a reading, rather than a script. Play scripts are unusual artefacts, and not designed to be read like prose. For someone who is not theatre literate, nuance and tone can be lost. Presenting a script as embodied and read by actors allows for the totality of the project to speak for itself.

Further, Decent notes, he's never worked with a dramaturg on a verbatim work. He instead prefers to build a "community reference group". These are ideally made up of people "not directly at the centre of the experience, but are still stakeholders in the community". "They are usually the best dramaturgs," he says, "and are the most qualified to offer advice and notes on the piece".

4.4 Community-Engaged Workshopping with Young People

A large portion of our practice focuses on working with youth ensembles in the development of new work. While not specifically working within the framework of verbatim theatre, many of the same principles and theories of practice can be applied, and there is a significant degree of porosity between our ways of working across multiple contexts. It is unusual in many group settings for a set of participants to have a designated "writer", particularly in youth community-engaged work. In our experience, young artists are most passionate about acting and performance. A love of writing, directing, or other theatrical art forms tends to come later. So in a community-engaged youth work charged with creating original content, devising through improvisation, workshopping ideas, and providing opportunities to develop skills in writing, structure, and theatrical conventions becomes an important tool in supporting the participants' theatrical vision.

> **Principles in Practice**
>
> Claire Christian frequently devises new work with young people. She begins by asking participants to submit anonymous, written responses to questions based around a theme. The theme may have been derived from a pre-existing work, from the news, or from other exercises in class. Claire then sorts through the gathered material to come up with new stimulus that will begin students devising scenes and story.
>
> 'I take the content first as a layer of safety,' Claire says. 'Then I will distill that content or hi-light key words and phrases. I will pull out moments that have a dramatic energy, or moments that I can see translating into an image or onto stage. I will usually then compile that into a document, take that back to the group and we will devise from there.'

For a work titled *define adult*, David met with a group of young people, aged 18–22, every week for ten weeks, for three hours a week. The participants had paid for the entry into the program, so David felt it important that each participant be given an equal amount of stage time. Apart from that, the content of the show was entirely up to them. In a series of workshops largely driven by principles of Augusto Boal, David worked to engage the participants in conversations about what they were most enthusiastic about. From this, a list of themes became apparent. The list of themes were then used as stimulus for the improvisation of scenes, as David tasked the participants with manifesting themes in the body and through character. An edited version of their interests (if you could create a show about anything, what would it be?), included:

- Something funny, but also handles serious themes without being overly earnest (the most common request from any youth ensemble)
- "Growing up" and the meaning of "maturity"
- Does age mean anything?
- Relationships: siblings as adults, housemates, "serious" romantic relationships, difficult friendships, online dating
- The value of childhood and play

Examples of how these themes were extracted into scenes and activities are included in the next section. Each scene was recorded. In some cases, when a scene was unanimously applauded as "gold", a participant would transcribe the scene from the recording. After each scene, we explored characters and ideas that had emerged, often than turning this reflection into stimulus for new scenes or new characters.

Thus, a network of scenes, characters, and themes emerged. By weeks five and six, the entire work was overwhelming in its scale. So the improvisations instead became about finding connective tissue between characters and scenes. How could we link this couple in the cafe, for instance, with the other couple in the doctor's office? Through this string of exercises, the group was able to devise enough for two-thirds of a script. The final third, the resolution, required a change in the model we had worked at so far. By now, the group knew certain things needed to happen in a very particular order to resolve the plot. So David wrote the final scenes, in some cases leaving interactions as bullet points only, for the participants to take on and improvise, improve, and edit as they wished.

This system of devising, then, was circular: *Games and improvisation* informed *theme* which then informed *character and scenes* which then informed further *games and improvisation*.

In Sarah's creative development of *Stuck*, three writers each ran a series of workshops with Prospect Theatre for Young People, exploring the theme of being stuck: stuck between ideas, between people, between ideas of who we are and who we want to be. The ensemble had collectively agreed on this theme, and the three writers were then tasked with providing opportunities to interrogate, experiment with, understand, and deconstruct this theme, in as many different directions as possible. Sarah's workshops in this project ranged from provocations around being eternally stuck at the age and with the body the ensemble had now (and exploring the challenges and benefits of this, the lengths people might go to in order to revert back to an ageing process, etc), using soundscapes as stimulus, and writing spoken word poetry in response to difficult conversations. Throughout the workshops the ensemble would often be divided into groups, respond to some initial prompts (often documenting their ideas via brainstorms and notes), devise short moments of performance or write short monologues and then devise/rehearse how these will be presented, and then share the moments of performance with the ensemble. The initial brainstorming, any written materials (monologues or performance ideas), and notes from the reflective discussion at the end of the workshop were all collated and collected. These tangible artefacts from the workshopping process then informed the initial drafting of the play, and when Sarah shared the first version of the script with the ensemble she was able to "point to" which sections of the play had been directly informed by the material they had created in the workshops.

define adult and *Stuck* are both case study examples of how a playwright (or dramaturg, or facilitator, or co-creator – our labels are usually a little more diverse when working with youth ensembles in this way) might approach community-engaged workshops with young people. In each case study we were responding to a specific context and commissioning framework, balancing the needs and expectations of the commissioning organisation with the needs and expectations of the participants in each ensemble.

> **Principles in Practice**
>
> In creating *I've Been Meaning to Ask You*, Dan Evans and Amy Ingram (from The Good Room) worked with a diverse range of young people to build a show based off anonymous, online responses to children's questions. "We became more curators as opposed to creators," he says. "I would curate the answers that we gave back to the young people, often because of safe working practices. We had to redact swear words and things, boring things like that". Beyond this, he notes, the methodology of building a verbatim work didn't alter much. Each piece of data was treated as inherently truthful and worthy of respect, and the young participants were charged with responding to the submissions in their own artistic way.

4.5 Activities and Recommendations

Example Activities from **Define Adult** *and* **Stuck**

Generally, our workshops begin with a check-in process. This might include participants stating their name and pronouns, particularly if it's the first workshop or you haven't seen the group in a little while, perhaps a question relating to the content of the workshop (for *Stuck* Sarah asked participants to share any experiences they had getting a part of their body stuck in something – like a hand in a bangle, or a foot in mud, etc), or any question that gives the participants an opportunity to express themselves and give an insight to who they are (ranging from "what animal do you feel like today?" through to "what makes you most angry in this moment?").

This might be followed by a game or warmup activity, again perhaps something that connects in some way to the activities of the rest of the workshop, or perhaps it is a game or warmup that it is a tradition or ritual of the group to undertake. This would then generally lead into the main activity of the workshop, and we thought it might be useful to include some of the activities we used in the *define adult* and *Stuck* processes mentioned above.

EXAMPLE #1

Small Group Task – Groups of 3

PART A

In groups of 3, consider the following and write down/brainstorm their answers for 10 minutes:

- What would happen if you were stuck with the body you have right now, at the age you are right now, with the skills and knowledge that you have right now, and that it was going to stay that way for the rest of your life?

- What would be the challenges of never changing?
- What would be the positives of never changing?
- What are some of the glorious things about getting older/ageing that you would miss out on because of this?
- What lengths would you go to in order to a) change back to a regular ageing process? or b) make sure you got to keep this gift of never changing? *The group can choose one!*

PART B

Pick one of the challenges *OR* one of the positives, and create a moment of performance that makes the audience really understand why that thing is so challenging or positive. Make me care about the predicament you are in through creating a character that this is happening to – but show me, don't tell me. No monologues or narration – just a scene that shows what it's like for this person or group of people to live in a body that never changes.

- 10 minutes to create the scene, then perform them to each other.

Discussions then Pitch

Divide into three groups, and they each have their own prompts for discussion. They are going to spend 10 mins brainstorming, responding, and creating – and then each group will share their ideas and thoughts with the whole ensemble

What would be the "cure" to this predicament? What would people have to do, or eat or drink, or say, where would they have to travel to, or what might they have to achieve, in order to start ageing and growing again? Brainstorm your responses – think about how finding the cure would be like a quest for people – what is this quest and how might it be adventurous, dangerous, curious, obscure, thrilling?

Why would this be happening to people in the world right now? Would it be targeting anyone in particular, and why would that be? Is this something that people are doing to each other, or is it a quirk of nature? What reasons could you imagine for this to be happening? Brainstorm your responses – think about how the reason for this phenomenon might be discovered by the people it is happening to – how do they find out that this is the reason, and how do they feel about that reason?

In what world/time/era would something like this happen? Would it happen in a world like our own, or in a futuristic land? Is it a fantastical place, or a hyper-real place? Is it a place where other odd occurrences are taking place as well, or is this completely unique and out of the blue? Brainstorm your ideas – think about how you would paint us a picture of the world/place where something like this might happen?

EXAMPLE #2

Using soundscapes as stimulus

- Divide into groups of 4–5.
- Each group will be allocated a different soundscape (one is owls/birds in a forest, one is an afternoon at the beach, one is a crackling campfire).
- Each group needs to decide what the location is for their soundscape.
- Groups will be given the following prompt:
  - A group of 3 teenagers are all in this location
  - They know each other well, but they don't always agree
  - Someone arrives with a message for them
  - They all have a difficult conversation
  - Some of the group choose to stay, some choose to leave
- Using this prompt, the group will discuss:
  - where this story is taking place
  - what the message is which is being delivered
  - and how the group of teenagers feel about the fact that now some people are staying and some people are going.
- Discuss as a group.
- Once they have a sense of their version of events, the group will create a series of 5 freeze frames that tell that story. This task encourages us to think of a story in terms of beats and to be succinct and clear about character, location, emotion. As a suggestion, the 5 freeze frames might tell us:
  - 1 – show us who and where you are
  - 2 – give us a sense of the group and their relationships
  - 3 – show the messenger arriving
  - 4 – show the response to the message
  - 5 – show the decision to leave or stay
- Each group will perform their sequence of 5 freeze frames to the ensemble, with the soundscape playing.

Extension – Using freeze frames as stimulus

- In each group they will allocate amongst themselves one freeze frame each. Their task is to write an inner monologue from the perspective of their character in that freeze frame. What are they thinking and feeling right now? What would be going through their mind if they were this character at this moment in the story?
- Write for 8 mins.
- Share their monologues with each other in the group, and perhaps see if there are any edits/additions they'd like to make.

108 *Transcription, Exploration, and Community-Engaged Workshopping*

- Then, each group will perform their five freeze frames again, but this time during each freeze frame, the person who wrote a monologue for that moment will step outside of the frame and read/perform their monologue (then the group shifts into the second freeze frame and the next person shares their monologue, and so on).
- Respond to each groups story, and discuss what threads, themes, characters, etc resonated with them, which stories they'd like to know more about, etc

EXAMPLE #3

Difficult Conversations

PART ONE

- Divide the ensemble into three groups
- 10 mins – Each group will be asked to brainstorm a number of scenarios where difficult conversations need to be had, but there will be a different prompt for each group (difficult conversations around lying, cheating or stealing). They will brainstorm who is having the conversation and what the difficult conversation is about in relation to that prompt, coming up with as many different scenarios based around that prompt as they can.

PART TWO

- After they have thought of as many different scenarios as possible, pick one for the group to work on for the next activity.
- 5 min– Discuss: Expand on the idea of who this group of people are, and why one of them lied, cheated, or stole. Do they regret it, how do they deal with that? Have they been caught out? Is the lying, cheating or stealing something that a completely different group of people did to the characters they have created, or something they did to each other? Expand their thinking about the situation and what is happening in this moment.

PART THREE

- The groups are going to tell us the story of this group of people and their difficult conversation, through the form of poetry and spoken word (this might be daunting for some and a good challenge for others, so we'll just see how it goes).
- 15 min–20 min – Each group will be given a sheet of words that rhyme (a different rhyme for each group), which they can use as prompts/assistance in the development of their poem/ballad/spoken word performance that tells the story. Their poem should be as detailed as possible, telling us everything we need to know about this group of people and the conversation they're having.

Transcription, Exploration, and Community-Engaged Workshopping 109

PART FOUR

- Once the groups have written their story, we'll all come together to do a vocal warmup, working through some humming and siren exercises, some breathing exercises, and articulation exercises – something to just bring us back together as a group and do some vocal prep.
- Then, the groups will have 10 mins to decide how they are going to perform this story – they might have someone reading the full thing while the others "act it out", they might share the reading, they might sing, it is up to them how they want to stage this story.
- Perform!

EXAMPLE #4

This exercise works with a group that favours improvisation.

Gather a list of themes that the cohort is interested in. Ask the room to split up into small groups or pairs, with each group aligning themselves with a theme or idea they are most interested in.

The participants are tasked with creating a very short commercial – between thirty seconds to a minute in length – that is somehow associated with the theme. Students may be as subversive or as serious as they wish.

Ask participants to present their commercials. Ask the group to extract a single character from each commercial. In total, you will now have a group of characters, each having some kind of relationship to a theme of interest.

As a group, discuss a circumstance in which two or more of these characters could meet one another. Are they related? Do they share a workplace? Are they dating? Did they go to school together?

Participants can now improvise scenes (or imagine and note on some paper or a whiteboard) how these characters interact. Once these scenes are presented, reflect back on the original list of themes that participants devised. Are those themes still represented? Have they become more nuanced? Are there new themes to add?

This circular improvisatory approach can assist in slowly building a network of characters that may then be used to build the narrative.

EXAMPLE #5

This example works best with a highly kinaesthetic group that is comfortable with dance and physical theatre.

Begin with a list of themes or interests.

Put on some music, and gather participants in a circle. One at a time, students are asked to physically embody a theme. Abstract movement is welcome. There is no right or wrong. How does your body move in response to this idea? One by one, participants present their movement, and all other participants copy the movement. Once all participants have presented, repeat with the next theme or idea.

At completion, ask students to recall two or three movements from each theme. Thus, the group builds a library of movements that represent the desired ideas.

Put on music again. Now students experiment with the idea of *copying*. A participant may enter the space and use one of the movements from the assembled library. Participants may volunteer to join their colleague in the space, repeating the exact movement, however *how* they copy is entirely up to them. They may change the axis of the movement – lying or sitting down or facing another direction. They must also be deliberate in their choice of proximity. Close or far away? Thus, a picture of a certain theme is developed.

Now participants experiment with the idea of *riffing*. The copy exercise is repeated, except this time participants are permitted to let the movement evolve or change dependent on their impulse. Other participants may join and copy the riff.

Slowly relax constraints and goals until extended improvisatory movement takes place, using the library of movements as a base. Can participants organically transition from one movement to another? What story is being told through the improvisatory movement? Do characters appear?

Experiment with placing movements directly against a monologue from a verbatim source, or another piece of text relevant to the piece you are devising.

Notes and Recommendations on Transcription Software

Transcription software has recently enjoyed an acceleration in accessibility and advanced technology. Up to five years ago, advanced speech recognition software was the sole property of a few highly-priced products, marketed heavily toward the legal and medical industries. Now, almost every smartphone comes with a very reasonable voice recorder and free transcription software. We are cautious about writing this section because technology so quickly becomes obsolete. Of course, you should do your own research about the latest products. However, there are a few pointers.

Firstly, most word processors, including the perennial *Microsoft Word*, and the free and team-friendly *Google Docs*, come with voice recognition. These are designed to work with one user speaking directly into a mic, often dictating their own punctuation. Setting up a laptop to capture your interview isn't exactly discrete, so we don't recommend it. However, in a pinch, it is possible to play a recorded interview back to your word processor to at least get a starting idea of a transcription.

The most advanced and widely used speech recognition software is generally cited as the *Dragon* suite. However, like the examples mentioned above, *Dragon* is not designed with interviews or group discussions in mind. Professional versions of the software also come with a hefty price tag. At the time of writing, the mobile version of *Dragon* is also very minimal.

There's a large variety of apps on mobile devices available. In the hopes of not becoming too obsolete too quickly, we are recommending two here. The first is *Google Recorder*. This very simple app records using your phone's microphones and transcribes in real time. The transcriptions, in our experience, operate at about a 70% success rate in a quiet environment. They still require significant editing, but it's certainly quicker than transcribing by yourself. We've recommended this app partly because it's published by Google, so the technology is likely to be consistently updated. At the time of writing, it's completely free.

The second mobile app we recommend is relatively new but holds a lot of promise for interviewers. *Otter Ai* is designed to recognise multiple voices. In its transcription, *Otter Ai* will deliver a document that separates voices it detects, which you can then name. Again, the technology is constantly improving, but *Otter*'s initial results are certainly impressive. There's a range of pricing options that start with a free version. We used *Otter* to organise our interviews for this book and were pleased with the results.

Importantly, using third-party software opens up ethical questions about ownership of data. Most reputable software applications come with a terms and conditions of use document that is almost impossible to read in its entirety. But if you're using software extensively for the collection of particularly sensitive material, it's important to make sure you understand how the publishing company is storing the data you collect.

It's also important to consider what you lose in relying on transcription software. Both Sarah and David find a lot of value in the labor-heavy task of transcribing interviews themselves, as it forces a level of intimacy that cannot be achieved through any other means.

Note

1 See https://www.roslynoades.com/the-nightline (accessed December 2022).

Works Cited

Abbs, Peter. "The Pattern of Art-Making." *The Symbolic Order: A Contemporary Reader on the* Arts *Debate*, edited by Peter Abbs, Taylor & Francis Ltd, 1989, pp. 193–206.

Anderson, Michael and Linden Wilkinson. "A Resurgence of Verbatim Theatre: Authenticity Empathy and Transformation." *Australasian Drama Studies* 50, 2007, pp. 153–169.

Bottoms, S. "Putting the Document into Documentary." *The Drama Review* 50(3), 2006, pp. 56–68.

Brown, Rich. "Moisés Kaufman: The Copulation of Form and Content." *Theatre Topics* 15, 2005, pp. 51–67.

Jeffers, Alison. "Refugee Perspectives: The Practice and Ethics of Verbatim Theatre and Refugee Stories." *Platform* 1(1), 2006, pp. 1–17.

Luckhurst, Mary. "Verbatim Theatre, Media Relations and Ethics." *A Concise Companion to Contemporary British and Irish Drama*, edited by Nadine Holdsworth and Mary Luckhurst, Blackwell Publishing, 2008, pp. 200–222.

Turner, Cathy. "Hare in Collaboration: Writing Dialogues." *The Cambridge Companion to David Hare*, edited by Richard Boon, Cambridge University Press, 2007, pp. 109–122.

Wake, Caroline. "To Witness Mimesis: The Politics, Ethics, and Aesthetics of Testimonial Theatre in Through the wire." *Modern Drama* 56(1), 2013, pp. 102–125

Wilkinson, Linden. "'A Day in December'." *Performing Research: Tensions, Triumphs and Trade-offs of Ethnodrama*, edited by Judith Ackroyd and John O'Toole, Trentham Books, 2010, pp. 123–144.

5 Playwriting
Translating Stories into Performance

When writing a play, regardless of style or form, you are deciding how to communicate something to your audience in order to have a particular effect on them. You may be seeking to engage your audience emotionally, politically, cognitively, or most likely a combination of all three. Whether you are writing a verbatim play that strictly uses word-for-word stories from interviews, or something entirely fictional, you have the opportunity to structure the story: to decide what will be communicated when and through which dramatic language. We've sub-titled this chapter "translating stories into performance" because playwriting in a community-engaged process can differ from other forms of playwriting in critical ways. It often means taking stories that have been shared with you in one mode (perhaps through an interview, a conversation, or a newspaper article) and then translating that story into a performance mode using dramatic languages. These include the characters, their relationships with each other, and the narrative of the play, but also the movement on stage and the timing of the dramatic action, the use of space and time in the world of the play, the conventions of specific styles, the mood of the play constructed through dialogue, sound, and design. Translation in a community-engaged playwriting process means taking the idea from the original story and communicating the essence of that idea through performance, using all of the dramatic languages available to you.

Once a playwright has gone through a process of data gathering, transcription, and story immersion, they are usually itching to begin the playwriting process. In this book, we present some processes for doing this in discrete ways and as distinct from one another, but of course, they can overlap significantly. You may have started scribbling down an idea for a scene when you first began immersing yourself in the community before you even began interviewing anyone. The process of transcription and story immersion allows you to sift through those notes and begin writing. This chapter provides information on some of the common conventions of verbatim theatre, and how these approaches to structuring a story can be of assistance when first drafting a new work. We then explore more specific tools of the trade, each with examples and exercises, to assist in helping you shape a new work.

DOI: 10.4324/9781003155706-6

5.1 "Traditional" Verbatim Theatre Conventions

You likely already possess an idea of what "traditional" verbatim theatre conventions look like. It is critical to remember that verbatim theatre as a named form is barely a generation old, with Derek Paget first coining the term in 1987. "Traditional" in this context is nothing of the sort, and it is more true to say that the form is constantly evolving. Verbatim theatre is informed by a variety of political and community theatre forms from late modernism, including Agitprop, Epic Theatre, and the Living Newspaper, as explored in chapter one.

In working with schools and teachers who have verbatim theatre in the curriculum, David and Sarah are most frequently asked about the act of translating stories onto the stage. A comfortable list of conventions is most useful here, and we provide some below. However, it is important to understand that there are no "rules" for how you structure stories in your plays (outside of the ethical commitments you have made in your process): you are free to use the basic elements of drama (tension, character, time, space, and so on), in whatever way you need to so that the play becomes whatever it needs to be. Some of the most innovative and interesting verbatim theatre productions of recent years have included musical theatre (*London Road*, 2011), circus (*We Live Here*, 2019), or dance (enough that Jess McCormack wrote an entire book on the subject, *Choreography, and Verbatim Theatre*). As a playwright, you have permission to use any form that you find suitable to create the dramatic meaning that you're looking for.

The most commonly cited convention and one often referred to as the form's hallmark is "direct address" (Duggan 152; Jeffers 3; Paget 2008, 137; Stuart Fisher 116). Further conventions include the incorporation of monologues, restaging the interview (Watt 193), narration, flashbacks (Chou and Bleiker 565), and "scarce movement and functional design" (Botham 315). All of these speak to a larger diegetic theatricality and assume that you will have actors playing multiple roles. Below are brief explorations of these conventions, each with a helpful dramaturgical question as you write your first draft.

Principles in Practice

Many playwrights we spoke to were quick to point out the importance of finding opportunities for humour in verbatim work. In its most stereotypical form, verbatim playwriting can be overly serious. Campion Decent sees this humour and some kind of "theatrical gesture" as vital. "Things can get quite heavy and bleak, and I'm always looking for opportunities to find a counterpoint. In one scene we've got the Coroner's Court and all these grieving relatives. The next minute there's Bette Midler sashaying onto the stage saying the Prime Minister is a fuckwit".

Decent's playful approach is empowering. Playwrights can be respectful to interviewees without having to be entirely humourless.

Direct Address

Direct address is the most recognisable of the verbatim theatre conventions, frequently utilised to present verbatim material as directly to the audience as possible. Actors in character may address the audience directly, either in monologues or as a group. In many cases, playwrights are often re-staging interviews, endowing the audience with the role once taken by the playwright themselves. The dramaturgical value in this convention is in making the audience complicit to the action and an integral player in the play itself. Thus, the play may "facilitate the audience's access to information, and encourage trust" by looking them straight in the eye and asking them to "hear rather than overhear" (Izod, Kilborn, and Hibberd 202). As a means of building a connection between audience and character (and by proxy, the issue or narrative overall), there is nothing more direct. If this convention is used outside of verbatim theatre, it can be seen as especially performative or expository. Shakespeare's characters offer soliloquies to an audience, for example, as a means of exploring a theme, or by giving critical information on the plot. In other words, this breaking of the fourth wall renders the action "unrealistic" but more theatrical. In verbatim theatre, it paradoxically makes the work more viscerally real, as an audience is brought closer to the interview subject themselves.

> **Principles in Practice**
>
> Of course, it is possible to make a show that is an entirely direct address. In *The Seven Stages of Grieving*, playwrights Wesley Enoch and Deborah Mailman conceived of a one-woman show that combined verbatim theatre, autobiography, stand-up comedy, oral history, and First Nations performance traditions. The singular actor onstage addresses the audience for the show's seventy-minute running time, traversing history and themes in a rapid succession of styles. The direct address employed throughout meant an audience was made permanently complicit in a conversation, charging them as colonists, voyeurs, allies, and more. The power of this kind of interaction, when done properly, can't be underestimated.
>
> > In Sydney in 2014, Enoch recalled – with obvious pride – an old Aboriginal aunty, unknown to the cast, who broke from the Brisbane audience as the curtain began to close on the finale of the second season, and slowly made her way down the aisle. Up on the stage, she tottered across towards Deborah Mailman [the actress] while the audience held its breath. Then, the elder put her arms around the actor and held her, sobbing, for a long minute. Someone had at last borne witness to her life.
> >
> > (Lucashenko)

Diegetic Theatricality

Diegesis, applied to all art forms, simply means a storytelling technique in which details about the world of the work are provided explicitly through the narrative. In verbatim theatre, this most often occurs through the act of narration, where the actor provides the audience with direct address, but in the voice of the playwright, not the voice of the characters. For many plays, including *The Laramie Project* (2000), podcasts (such as the first season of *Serial*), or documentaries (such as *My Octopus Teacher*), this creates a meta-narrative, where the playwright or author themselves becomes a character that goes on a transformative journey through the act of interviewing and meeting characters. As with direct address more broadly, the audience is made complicit in the playwright's journey, mirroring the interview and research process that they themselves have submitted to.

More broadly it's important to understand the essence of diegetic theatricality, beyond just the mere inclusion of a narrator (which is not necessarily present in every verbatim play). Diegesis sits in opposition to mimesis. Mimetic theatricality would ask a script and actors to imitate action, rather than to narrate it. These two different forms of theatricality have been debated for thousands of years, beginning with Aristotle (who preferred mimetic storytelling) and Plato (who preferred diegesis). These two approaches clashed particularly across the modern era, with the realists (such as Stanislavski and Chekhov) advocating for a theatre of mimesis, and the later generation experimenting with a variety of diegetic forms including Bertolt Brecht.

For the playwright, this should come as a reassurance. After months of researching and interviewing, an attempt to stage *everything* that you have sourced can be exhausting and overwhelming. At its heart, verbatim theatre is not trying to imitate in minute detail every aspect of a story or event. Diegetic theatricality allows the play to present just one version of events – the playwright's (hopefully well-informed) version. When the subjectivity of the work is made explicit through the form, it again provokes the audience to participate in moulding *their* own version of events. Verbatim theatre's political roots are exposed here. It is a form that asks an audience to participate and become active. The work essentially *confesses* its process through its presentation.

Actors Playing Multiple Roles

Verbatim plays often feature a long list of characters. For most major projects, where many interviewees are given at least some time on stage, this can mean the introduction of dozens of characters. This can be helpful in a classroom setting, as verbatim plays offer an easy way for a large student population to get involved in a work. In most other settings, however, a small ensemble means most actors are asked to play multiple roles. This may not be a high priority in the initial drafts of your play, but doubling, much like the other conventions, can help solidify and articulate your overall dramatic meaning. In a cast of four to six, for example, most directors would expect the writer to at least provide some notion of age and gender for each role. Race and ethnicity might also be very important. Once you are aware of these boundaries, opportunities for new dramatic meaning may emerge. If all of your cast doubles in multiple roles, for example, bar one character, then an audience will start to impose meaning on that actor (they may be seen as the "protagonist"). If you deliberately swap the genders or ages of your interview participants with your actors, then you are creating new meaning or commentary. More broadly, you might identify certain archetypes and cast each actor in roles that match that archetype: the devil's advocate, the nurturing mother, the idealist, etc. In so doing, an audience will view certain interviewees/characters in a very specific way. Of course, the theatrical possibilities are endless, including using multiple actors to play a single interviewee. Along with creative possibilities are ethical considerations. In some circumstances, you may need to return to your interviewee to ask their permission to be represented by an actor who is significantly different from them. This is particularly true for interviewees from marginalised and underrepresented communities, who have so often been misrepresented or erased entirely in media.

5.2 Making the Literal Theatrical

In this section, we'll talk through some approaches to working with your material and give examples from segments of our own scripts so that you can see the writing "in action". This section is designed to prompt your dramaturgical experimentation within the writing process. Unlike the previous sections, much of the discussion here can be translated across forms and is not solely connected to writing verbatim theatre. We encourage you to consider how you might translate some of your literal material through dramatic languages and into a more theatrical form. Whether you are starting with interview transcripts, reflective observations from your community immersion or discussions generated through workshopping, you can translate the literal to the theatrical through your playwriting. Of course, it's worth noting here that such a process is only ever ethical when done in full consensual consultation with the community with which you are engaging.

Staging the Interview

Let us first begin with the most "obvious" choice, in that sometimes you may just want to re-stage an interview or discussion verbatim. This can be extremely powerful. Staging the interview (or in the case of Tribunal Theatre, staging the court proceedings) should always be an active and purposeful choice. For example, in *twelve2twentyfive* Sarah was commissioned to write a play about the experiences young people have when accessing support for their mental health. The target audience for the work were medical professionals attending a regional health conference, who were there to learn more about their own role in youth mental health support just as much as what the experience is like for young people. This particular framing of the performance meant that staging the interview could serve as an informative and educational framework through which the audience of medical professionals could engage with the characters being staged. Here is an example in the play where a moment from the interview is included directly:

PSYCH 1:   How did Dad react when you told him you had to go and see a psychologist or counselling?
REBEKAH: Um, he thought that it was gonna fix everything.
PSYCH 1:   The old "wave the magic wand".
REBEKAH: Mmm, he thought medication and talking to someone would fix it in the six weeks that I had it and then I'd be fine. He still thinks that, he thinks that – I should be pretty much better, like it's all in my head like, I shouldn't be still acting the way that I'm acting. That I should be cured by now.
PSYCH 1:   And what, all be fixed and/
REBEKAH: Yep
PSYCH 1:   Do you think that when you got that response from Dad, that that sort of coloured how you thought you might be treated when you went lookin' for help?
REBEKAH: Yeah. Well, just the way, when he says, that I should be better, and telling me that it's, like, I've got to help myself, like, of course I know I've got to help myself but, it's not gonna be fixed like that, it's only been six months. It still happens.

Conversely, David has rarely used the technique of "staging the interview", but it is a frequent feature of his first drafts. When encountering a powerful piece of interview, but a little unsure of how to translate it into performance, simply re-staging the interview in the first draft as a placeholder can be a sound temporary option. In the very first drafts of his play *April's Fool*, David himself was a character. Completely embracing the diegetic theatricality (see above), "David" the playwright introduced the work and appeared occasionally in the text. *April's Fool* centres around the death of a young person due to illicit drug use. David didn't know the victim or his family prior to being commissioned to write the work but spent months interviewing his community. It was an incredibly powerful experience for David, and in the early stages of writing it was difficult to disentangle himself from the work.

Each draft went through a creative development, and the backbone of *April's Fool* emerged. The play was strongest when it centred on the direct family's experience of the victim's passing. Anything else felt like a distraction or an unnecessary layer. By draft three, David found himself cutting more and more of his own lines until, at last, he had all but disappeared. Some segments of "re-staging the interview" remain in the finished script, minus the role of an interviewer, as they're not needed. Take this moment from the character of "Steven":

STEVEN: You ever had ecstasy?
DAVID: No.
STEVEN: You ever had any drugs?

Brief pause.

DAVID: Well. Not hard stuff.

This moment became:

STEVEN: You ever had ecstasy?

Brief pause.

                You ever had any drugs?

Brief pause.

Removing the interviewer then allows the character of Steven to directly address the audience, forcing the audience to answer the question for themselves. They become complicit in the conversation.

There are no rules, only a set of tools that will be applied differently to each project. Given that the audience for *twleve2twentyfive* was medical professionals, re-staging the interview very explicitly helped its dramaturgical purpose. For *April's Fool*, the audience were teenagers, so re-staging the interview was helpful for some segments of the text, but only in ways that further challenged and implicated the audience.

Monologues

Turning moments of interview conversation into a monologue can be an accessible starting point when first learning to work with verbatim material. Below is an excerpt directly from one of the interviews Sarah undertook for *bald heads & blue stars* where she has transcribed everything said by both participants. In this moment Sarah and the interviewee are looking through a photo album and have paused to talk about the interviewee's wedding day. Note: when Sarah asks about "patches" here, she's talking about the interviewee's hair.

SP: *[Looking at the photo]* Did you have patches here on your wedding day?
      – well yeah, the thing was on my wedding day I'd grown my hair long to wear it up, and when I went to the hairdressers, because I got married over in England, so it wasn't my normal hairdresser

SP: oh
— um she said, "you can't wear your hair up because you", I had a patch that actually went into my hairline [*demonstrates how the patch was coming up from the back of the neck*], which was odd, first time, my patches were always in the middle of my head, above my ears, around the back [*gesturing*]

SP: yeah
— or low, but they never actually went into my hairline

SP: ok
— and so it was like, almost like, it wasn't triangular, but it was almost like a triangular wedge

SP: yes
— in at the side of my neck, so I couldn't wear my hair up, I had this big piece of hair missing, and that's why I went for this hair style which was kind of up on top with a bun.

When read as part of the interview conversation this moment isn't particularly compelling. However, what is being shared here is that the person being interviewed had meticulously planned how they were going to style their hair, and on the very day of the wedding discovered that she had lost hair in a spot which would be visible. With editing, this story can be written into a short monologue that heightens the theatrical qualities of the story.

> I got married in England.
> I'd grown my hair long to wear it up. I'd never had patches that went into the hairline. Always in the middle of my head, above my ears, around the back. But never into my hairline. So I'd grown it long and was going to wear it up. All planned out and organised.
> Day of my wedding I went to the hairdresser and she said "You can't wear it up because you've got ..." It was like a triangular wedge in at the side of my neck. A big piece of hair missing.

This type of monologue construction is powerful in the hands of an actor and director who understands subtext. Allowing your draft to be read multiple times by different actors, aloud, will give you a sense of how much information or editing you need to give. If you're working with professional actors, often less is more. Interviewees, if relaxed, will likely give you a lot more information than you actually need. Interviewees are different people to characters. Interviewees will likely repeat information, but characters rarely do. Interviewees will likely talk beyond the punchline of a joke, or the emotional beat of a story, but a character won't. Sarah chose "A big piece of hair missing" as the final line for the monologue because it gives the greatest emotional punch to the scene. But of course, the original interviewee talked well beyond that point.

Fundamentally, monologues are dramatic instruments, so require tension and a narrative. They are not the same thing as "re-staging the interview" (see above), as a monologue requires editing in order to be made dramatic.

Principles in Practice

Talking to Brick Walls is a verbatim theatre piece written by Claire Christian in partnership with Ari Palani and the Empire Youth Arts Ensemble. The piece centres on the communication breakdown between adolescents and their parents. There were many monologues throughout the play, but in one of the most memorable moments, the monologues were unseen by the audience. Claire describes the scene:

> We got our young participants to write our children letters. Then we filmed their parents reading their letters live. No one got to read those letters except the parents. So our audience didn't know what the kids had said, but simply watch their parents react to that on a video screen. While that was happening we had members of our ensemble get parents out of the audience and dance with theme. Visually, as an audience member, it's a beautiful moment.

Even though no words are being said in this scene, it still is, of course, community-engaged verbatim theatre.

Show Don't Tell? Show AND Tell?

While verbatim-based works can use a lot of past tense re-telling, these moments can be made more theatrically dynamic by writing in a performance of the moment. Caroline Wake distinguishes between "diegetic realism" which is a staging of the interview context, and "mimetic realism", which is moments of re-enactment designed to mimetically represent the actual experience (*To Witness Mimesis* 106). To extend on this, character-narrated realism uses moments of narration and direct address juxtaposed with moments of mimetic realism. This allows the playwright to have the connection with the audience that direct address and narration provides, while also capitalising on the power of theatre which allows the audience to suspend their disbelief and imagine that what they are watching is really happening in a time or place different to where they physically are. Moments of character-narrated realism give you the best of both worlds.

Here is an example of an early draft of *Blister* where Rosie is injured while walking the Camino:

ROSIE: I was silently and self-righteously judging the people who had instant blisters from their brand new shoes. Amateurs.
Then I kicked my toe on a bedframe and knocked off half the nail. So, stupidly, I pulled the rest of it off.
N1: That was clever.
N2: Didn't think that one through did you.

Rosie is limping.

ROSIE: Ow. Ow. Ow.
I hobbled into the first town and sat down in a café to take off my boot. It was a bloody mess. And I'm not just being Australian when I say that – the top of my sock was soaked in blood. I was cleaning my foot with tissues then trying to find a way to wrap it so I could put the boot back on. Two French guys came over but no one spoke English, and I was trying to explain.
"My toe nail. The nail on my toe has come off. I pulled it off when it wasn't ready and now it's so swollen I can't put my shoe on. Um, swollen?"
"Blister?"
FM1: Ahhh! Blister
FM2: Si si, blister, awwww
ROSIE: Some things are beyond translation.

In the revised excerpt below you can see how much of the description of the injury has been removed, and the action placed in the stage directions instead of being described.

ROSIE: All these pilgrims with their instant blisters from their new shoes. Ha. Amateurs.

Rosie runs into the bedframe.
Ow. Fuck. Ow. Ow.
Rosie limps to the table. She pulls off her sock tenderly, and she realises that she has knocked off half the nail. She gathers herself and pulls off the rest of the nail. It hurts.
    Two French guys enter and see Rosie's foot.

FM1: ça va? [trans. Are you ok?]

She tries to explain, but they struggle to understand.

ROSIE: It's my toe nail.
I kicked my toe and half the nail was knocked off, so I pulled off the rest. I pulled it off when it wasn't ready and now it's so swollen I can't put my shoe on.
Um, swollen?
Blister?
FM1: Ahhh! Blister
FM2: Si si, blister, awwww

ROSIE: Some things are beyond translation.

Character-narrated realism can be flexibly applied. In the excerpt above the direct address is minimal and the mimetic re-enactment of kicking the toe takes up the majority of the moment. In contrast, character-narrated realism can also focus primarily on monologues being spoken in direct address with brief moments of dialogue or interactions with other characters re-enacted around them, as in the following example from *bald heads & blue stars:*

> 3 (45): *(to the audience)* I've got a six year old and she said to me/ I mean I don't ever criticise her, I always say "oh look your hair is beautiful, and you've got the prettiest freckles" and she said to me the other day,
> 6yr old: You've got very wobbly legs mummy.
> 3 (45): And I guess it was just an observation and she said
> 6yr old: And your tummy's a bit fat too
> 3 (45): And I was like, *(to her daughter)* "well we don't use the word fat in this house, and I know my tummy's a bit wobbly but that's because I've had three babies".
> *(to the audience)* And I just thought, where does she get that from? I mean you hear other stupid women who say ridiculous things about themselves in front of their children, and the children are attune to go "oh we have to criticise each other, that's what our job is" you know?

Narrating a scene that you're also presenting must be an active choice. It's worth experimenting while drafting to see if you need to justify the use of both the narration and the presentation.

In *April's Fool*, a character named Bob describes a scream from the character of Helena. David originally wrote in that the actor was to scream in that moment. Then he tried Bob not saying anything, but just letting Helena scream. Finally, he settled on the narration with a scream. For him, the audience imagining the scream in their minds was enough. This was in contrast to an earlier scene in the play, where the same character of Bob hugs another character in a meaningful embrace. Again, David tried every possible iteration. Narration without a hug, a hug without narration, and then both. Because of how the scene ended up blocked in the original production, David settled on both. David found that seeing the hug was emotionally impactful, and including narration allowed the audience into this moment – to be a part of it – instead of being passive observers. They got the hug too.

In *St. Mary's In Exile*, David played extensively with narration and presentation. The majority of the play were scenes written by David, re-staging an event that he'd learned about through extensive research and interviews. The play periodically cut back to a central narrator figure, a character named Peter, whose dialogue was largely taken from interviews. The narrator was able to underline, foreshadow, reflect, and pause on moments that were either about to be seen, or had just been seen, giving the action another dimension.

Amalgamated Characters

Two ways that you can combine a broad multitude of experiences in a refined way is through amalgamated characters and collective choruses. You might choose to create a fictional character that is informed by a multitude of people you have met or interviewed. These amalgamated characters are technically fictional, but they are informed and imbued with the authenticity of each of those individual people that have been woven together to create this one character.

In *Eternity* there is a character called Jaz, a young girl trying to come to terms with her brother's terminal cancer diagnosis, managing the responsibility of working in a family business and feeling pressured by her girlfriend to come out to her Mum. The characters in *Eternity* were created through workshops and letter writing with undergraduate theatre students, and the character of Jaz has been informed by a variety of stories and experiences shared across this process of creative development by multiple students. These experiences and fears were combined in one character so that we could explore the tension between the needs of an individual versus the perceived needs of a family.

IVY: No Jaz. Please, let me say this. I get that right now doesn't feel like the "right time", but I don't know if there's ever really a right time. But that means that there's never really a wrong time either. There's just what we've got and what we know, right now.
And I know how I feel about you.
JAZ: Is this, some sort of ultimatum or something?
IVY: No! God no, never. I just think that, surely, if anyone is going to help you to do this, it's going to be me right?
And I'm not talking about the whole world, I'm talking about your mum.
JAZ: Mum is my whole world. But right now, Andy is her whole world.

There is an ethical line here that can be difficult to navigate and is reliant upon informed consent from your interview participants and a great deal of care from the playwright. Be careful in how you present your future work to interviewees. A promise to ensure "every voice is represented" may be noble in spirit, but interviewees can interpret this literally and feel their voice has been missing (or worse, deliberately struck from the record) if you've amalgamated it with several others.

More tricky territory occurs when you amalgamate several voices into one actor's body. A particularly heinous example would be to amalgamate several First Nations people's voices into a white character. Or to take several women interviewees and place those stories in a male body. Unless the dramaturgy of your play allows for recognition and acknowledgement of the process by which it's been made thus making a comment on the amalgamation itself, then a playwright needs to be very deliberate in how these matters are worked through in the drafting process and through communication with the community whose stories are being told.

For *The Time Is Now*, David worked with two other co-creators and ten young people. This community-engaged work required the creation of a script and a professional production in a matter of weeks. In order to accelerate the process, a typical morning session was spent with the co-creators informally interviewing and recording the participants on themes. David would then take these transcripts over lunch and edit them into a scene to be rehearsed that afternoon. To make line-learning more convenient, the young participants spoke in a certain order throughout the entire show – thus, they always knew when their next line was, as they would always speak after the same person. David, in trying to edit the verbatim script into a workable scene, would mix up the verbatim responses. So in the afternoon, participants would pick up a draft script of their scene, only to find that the lines they were saying on stage weren't necessarily the lines they said in their interviews. Sometimes this was fine, but others occasionally objected. The reasons for their objections were sound and dramaturgically complex. The script became a negotiation, but it also meant the young people were becoming articulate in the show's dramaturgy in real-time, allowing themselves to think through every moment and their intention for each line. In the end, they were all unique and yet all an amalgamation of each other, a complex refracturing of their personal identities and their identity as a community.

Such complex discussions and revelations are all part of community-engaged practice, as participants build critical reflexivity skills. Of course, the same can be true for an audience in simply viewing the work, as they witness their own community amalgamated and mixed up on stage. It results in the "exercise of the mental ability ... to consider themselves in relation to their (social) contexts and vice versa" (Archer in Akram and Hogan 607). The next tool, collective choruses, also provides opportunities for this reflexivity to be exercised.

Collective Choruses

A collective chorus who often speak in what Stuart Young describes as fragmentary language (Young 81), can be informed by the verbatim from multiple interviews, such as this excerpt from *bald heads & blue stars* which allowed Sarah to convey just how different the alopecia experience is for each individual:

1: I had this big piece of hair missing, like a triangular wedge
5: At that stage there was like 3, 3 twenty cent piece bits missing
3: It was actually the hairdresser, um, yeah she goes "If I cut your hair too short you'll see the bald spot". I'm like, um, bald spot?

4: That's when I started to worry
1: Patches from like 7 or 8
4: My husband said "Oh looks like a bald spot on the top of your head"
3: It's the weirdest thing
4: You've just got no bloody idea what's going on
5: And it just kept coming
1: I'd run my fingers through my hair and they'd just be covered
5: With hair
4: My hair
1: I just kept thinking it's gonna stop, it is gonna stop, it's always stopped
3: Dribs and drabs
5: Handfuls
3: A bit more here, then here
4: Excruciatingly slow
1: It happened so fast
3: One minute I had hair and then I had
All: Alopecia

Or the chorus might be a way to navigate between scenes and characters. In *Eternity* Sarah wrote lines of verse for the "spirits", a collective chorus made up of as many people as the production allows, and this chorus guides the audience from one moment of the play to the next, creating thematic links between scenes and offering verbal illustrations to contextualise each new time and place in the play:

SPIRITS: It's getting colder,
everyone a little older,
and it's messy and it's complicated,
but in this moment under the stars
they know who they are.
In each other's arms
what could do them harm?
Love is love
is love is
love is love.
The world keeps on spinning
breathing
moving.
A shared bedroom
three blocks across town
cushions and pillows scattered around.
Clothes of all sizes askew on the floor,
old tattered posters blue tacked to old doors.
Stickers of stars that glow in the night,
Lily to the left and Idalia to the right.

This is particularly useful for large casts such as may be used in schools or universities. In practice, we find it best to leave the script pretty much as above. That is, don't bother assigning lines to individual cast members in a chorus scene until you're working on the floor with actors.

Structurally speaking, the use of collective choruses can often be used as punctuation points to a larger narrative. While narrative scenes may allow us to zoom in on just one interview or one set of relationships, chorus scenes can let the audience zoom out to a wider context or larger set of opinions. This may be as simple as a chorus scene built on a mix of news reportage, in effect becoming a montage of media. Or, it may be more abstract discussions on a play's theme.

In works written by David and produced by Queensland Music Festival, the "chorus" took on its more musical meanings as the productions were pieces of musical theatre. As was featured in many of Bertolt Brecht's early works (*The Threepenny Opera, Round Heads, and Pointed Heads*), a song can serve as an opportunity to expand a script's limits from one narrative to larger themes. In the Queensland Music Festival shows, working as a lyricist (or sometimes selecting pre-existing popular music), David was tasked with interviewing hundreds of people living across regional Queensland. Finding phrases and clips from interviews and conversations that could be moulded and morphed into lyrics was challenging, but served the dramatic purpose of these community-engaged projects.

For example, in 2017's *The Power Within*, David worked with Music Director Steve Russell to write a finale song that would summarise eighteen months' worth of conversations with residents of the Isaac Shire council region in Central Queensland. The shire was defined by its enormous mining industry, meaning conversations with locals often revolved around economic prosperity. Isaac Shire includes some of the youngest colonial towns in all of Queensland, built in response to the mining industry. Moranbah is the capital of the Isaac Shire, but there are very few "generational" locals. The population is transient in the medium term, coming to Moranbah for three to five years to build up enough savings to buy a home on the Queensland coast or in metropolitan areas. Working in the coal mines in particular was dangerous, but the work was worth it, according to the locals, in order to secure a future for their children. This narrative thread occurred in almost *every single* conversation David had with the residents of Moranbah, numbering at well over two dozen. For the finale song, David and Steve also knew, because of the logistics of rehearsal, that the verses needed to be split between the assembled men, women's, and children's choir. And so they settled on these lyrics to go to the male choir, in the second verse.

In hard times
When the odds are stacked up high
When your family's doing rough
You break your back to build a home for them
Sometimes all you can provide is love

This was the tonal bottom of the song, its darkest moment. The third verse would go to the children's choir, rising with a hopeful key change at the very end:

There'll be times
When the dawn breaks out anew
And you'll feel your spirit rise
You look back at the days that are behind you
You've done more than just survive

And so the arc of the song, of a collective chorus, summarised (both musically and lyrically) the journey that had been encountered organically in interviewing dozens of Moranbah locals.

Principles in Practice

Alana Valentine's *Dead Man Brake*, which depicts the circumstances around a horrific train crash, included a series of songs inspired by what Valentine refers to as "generic verbatim": commonly expressed sentiments and phrases that she came across as part of the playwriting process. Valentine explains:

> A feature of the play was the poems I wrote that Daryl Wallis turned into songs to make a kind of verbatim musical, or, as we started to call it, a requiem drama. The songs attempted to capture not the individual speaker, but a sense of the community – to shape broad phrases, ideas and feelings that I perceived from the interviews. For instance, many people I spoke to shared a survivor's guilt but did not express it in a way, dare I say it, that was succinct enough to make it into the play. So I shaped their response into poems and the sentiment became part of the song lyrics instead. When I was asked at a forum where the lyrics came from, I described them as 'generic verbatim'.
>
> (Valentine, 63)

In 2015, David worked with Queensland Music Festival in the more urban centre of Logan, on Yugambeh land. David and the creative team worked with the local Yugambeh Museum Language and Research Centre to talk about Logan's past, present, and future. Logan's population was incredibly ethnically diverse. Like many working-class immigrant towns across the world, Logan suffered from a largely inaccurate perception that it was unsafe or racially divided. A united musical chorus held potentially profound power. In working with local choir masters, in particular, Cath Mundy and Jay Turner, David, and director Sean Mee collaborated with the Yugambeh

Museum Language and Research Centre to construct a new Australian national anthem: first presented in Yugambeh language (translated from English), and then sung in English but translated from the Yugambeh translation. This complex linguistic route created new lyrics that the community could sing together:

(Karalboo panyahra ngali)
All of us be glad
(Ngali baling nga kandayjam)
We are young and free
(Boogoorahm jagun wahng-gu naranyen-ngur)
Very good country and happiness through work
(Toomgan galgulmahla jagun ngalingah)
Our land is surrounded by sea
(Karalboo malgerri jageegan panmahla jagun ngalingah)
Beautiful gifts cover our country
(Gaureima ngalingah nambahla yagruma)
Our story always says
(Wandah Jageegan Djagun)
Rise up, beautiful country.
(Yerabai ngali naranyen ngur)
With happiness let us sing.
(Wandah Jageegan Djagun)
Rise up, beautiful country.
(Wandah Jageegan Djagun)
Rise up, beautiful country.
                                             (Mundy and Turner)

Lyrically and musically, the song transforms the national anthem into a new, contemporary meaning, meaning the gathered chorus becomes an explicit symbol of unification.

Principles in Practice

Importantly, scenes in a verbatim theatre play needn't tell a "narrative" in the traditional sense or have clearly defined characters. Here, the use of a chorus can be useful, especially when showcasing a wide range of short responses as is commonly found in data gathered from surveys. Claire Christian utilised this technique in *Talking to Brick Walls*, a show built around the communication gap between teenagers and their parents. Claire worked with the ensemble to build several scenes based around one-word responses or simple phrases. Claire identified the staccato rhythm of these scenes having their own "drive" that propels the work forward.

> For example, in response to the question, "what is a smell, a song or a moment that defines your adolescence?", Claire gathered simple responses from both parents and teenagers, allowing for comedy and tragedy in the direct juxtaposition of these elements: *Peace Train* by Cat Stevens, the smell of Lynx Africa (a deodorant), the moment when parents tell their child they're getting a divorce.

Juxtaposition and "Conspectus"

One of the best things about a community-engaged project is that you can put very different stories and very different opinions and perspectives side by side, to show the diversity of lived experiences even within the same community. In fact, this can be one of the central aims of community-engaged work and applied theatre more generally. Neelands, cited in Saxton and Prendergast (2009) discusses the distinction between *consensus* and *conspectus* within communities:

> The former involves a homogeneity of perspectives, the latter a rainbow of differing opinions, all of which are to be recognized and included within a dramatic process ... These "artful collisions" and dissonances of identity and location allow for a theatre that challenges accepted beliefs and histories and works toward new versions of community actions and social change (135–6).

This conspectus of opinions might serve to show the range of experiences, but can also provide moments of humour and irony when putting two very different opinions side by side. This is demonstrated in the following excerpt from *bald heads & blue stars:*

> 3 (45): I want to try and lobby the health funds to get cosmetic tattooing as part of Medicare, you know, cos its $600 to get it done, its bloody expensive, to have a face. As soon as you get those eyebrows on you feel your face, you've got your identity back you know, I'm me again.
>
> 4 (25): Originally when I first got "em done they were the cosmetic tattoo that are like 400 bucks and they only last like 3 years and then you gotta touch it up again. It took em like a friggin" hour an eyebrow cos I'm sitting there and they're trying to do all these hair strokes all this crap. So then when they faded I actually went to my tattooist and said "hey can you just, whip a line across, make em a bit darker" and he's like "yeah no worries", you know, ten minutes nnnnnnn, cos most like proper tattooists won't do your face, won't do cosmetics cos apparently it's a different needle and all that sort

of stuff so that's why they can charge so much for lashes and eyebrows and that cos it's a different sort of procedure. I just said to him, "dude, you've tattooed people's faces, just do that on my eyebrows and make em darker", "ok no worries lie down", fifty bucks. You know?

1 (45): Someone said "oh you can get them tattooed on" and I said you've got to be joking, how terrible would that be? And don't they look disgusting?

More confrontationally, community-engaged works allow space for conflict to emerge. In fact, they must in part attempt to wrestle with some community tensions and difficulties. How and when to do this is up to the playwright's sensitivity. In the Queensland Music Festival works, David was challenged by the repeated pattern of oppressed LGBTIQ+ voices he found in regional Queensland. But the parameters of the projects didn't allow space to stage comprehensive discussions on same-sex rights in these politically conservative communities, *especially* when David and his co-creators would effectively leave town on closing night, potentially abandoning vulnerable LGBTIQ+ people to reckon with their new explicit identities within the community. Instead, finding ways to welcome and celebrate LGBTIQ+ people within the production, as cast members or crew, and offering acceptance and encouragement, created opportunities for them to find belonging (Burton and McDonald 2021).

Conversely, finding ways to integrate the First Nations narrative within each town's community identity felt paramount and timely. In interviews and discussions across the communities of Mount Isa (for *The Mount Isa Blast* 2019) and Logan (for *Under This Sky* 2015) the topic of multiculturalism occurred again and again. For David, in examining transcripts and immersing himself in these communities, the integration of First Nations narrative felt tense and delicate, but he also felt the community wanted a pathway to healing. For *The Logan Project,* this ended up meaning the integration of the Australian National Anthem sung in the local Yugambeh language, and then translated from Yugambeh back into English. Thus, "Advance Australia Fair" became "Rise up Beautiful Country". In *The Mount Isa Blast*, the main character of Megan, a First Nations local singer, went on a journey from feeling isolated and fed up with her community to feeling integrated and accepted, especially after meeting the local Kalkadoon people, hearing their stories, and meeting their totem, an emu (a large puppet built by a local artist). At the climax of the play, Megan kneels to the emu and the emu utters its only line: "You are welcome here". Such moments, crafted over many drafts and many community discussions, are designed to hold space for conspectus. Both shows also featured white colonial narratives of local history. One wasn't represented as superior to the other, but each added new dimensions to the other, and the stage was big enough to hold them both.

132 *Playwriting*

> **Principles in Practice**
>
> Playwright Tom Wright worked with director Wesley Enoch on *Black Diggers* in 2014. The play attempted to tell the story of over a thousand Indigenous men who fought in the First World War – a fact largely forgotten by history. The enormity of the task meant a "broad acceptance of truth" by Enoch, who drew upon the South African post-apartheid Truth and Reconciliation Commission to find a four-part definition of truth:
>
>> Personal truth – the thing you believe to be true; Social truth – what a group believe to be true through discussion and debate; Forensic truth – the truth that can be proven through science and records; Public truth – the value of telling the truth for the greater good.
>>
>> (Wright, 5)
>
> This framework allowed Wright and Enoch to wrestle with "conspectus" in the work. This was further ameliorated by the absence of real names from the production, says Wright, "in case of an innocent factual mistake, and out of respect for the difficult tension within communities and families between fact and myth" (6). In assembling the play, then, Wright and Enoch allowed for a broader definition of "truth" that aided their larger aim of telling a story long forgotten.

Theatricality and Imagination

Along with the dramatic and theatrical languages at our disposal, artists also have the opportunity to play with metaphor, symbolism, abstract concepts, and imagination. As Rossiter et al. (2008) remind us, "the act of theatricalizing data allows for a whole new form of interpretation and analysis, one that uses theatre's fantastic, imaginative possibilities" (136). These imaginative possibilities can sometimes render the emotion of an experience in more tangible ways than a mimetic re-enactment can, as "what was invisible becomes visible" (Feldhendler 94) through theatre.

I Should've Drunk More Champagne was created by The Good Room's Dan Evans and Amy Ingram, who received over 100 submissions from anonymous contributors responding to the theme of regret. Evans describes their process of working through these submissions, and their initial impulse to respond in a highly theatrical and devised way:

> Some of the submissions were just a name. Some of them were a sentence, some of them were six pages long. We printed them all out and began to muddle our way through a process that involved reading them all, and then

asking "what feels like the lightest one?" And "what feels like the heaviest one?" So "I should have worn more lipstick" that feels quite light and then finding the anti chamber, the darkest, darkest of dark. And I remember that I do recall that submission and it was so horrific, it was so horrifyingly bleak. I think we only read it once and we were like "that's the heaviest".

So then we had this continuum that we kind of placed those submissions on, and we started to look at themes, thematics, recurring words, images that started to come out of it. There were a few submissions that mentioned like oranges, and the color orange came up a lot, this idea of space or the universe kept coming up in a lot of people's submissions.

Then we set about responding to those submissions in a devised way. "Amy go away and respond to submission 76, like create a theatrical image that responds to it". Don't read it, respond to it, either create a mini installation, or put yourself into that installation. But it can't be text based. And it can't be a performative moment, it has to capture the energy, it actually has to capture the feeling of what is inside that submission. So take me to the marrow of the feeling of that submission.

We would do a roulette of those over about a week's time. Just kind of throwing up images, seeing things that we liked. And it was random and bizarre. And then all those things, those little snapshots, those verbatim vignettes we were kind of making, got logged on index cards and out of that we would begin to shape the show.

Principles in Practice

In Suzie Miller's *Driving into Walls* (2013), dance and physicality is used as theatrical gesture to animate material drawn from over 500 interviews with young people in West Australia. Reviewer Robin Pascoe describes the production with Barking Gecko in 2012: "a glass box, five young physical performers, five chairs, pulsating music, and lighting … through a blend of verbatim stories, statistics, and physical theatre, the play captures the rhythms and vernacular of young people". She describes how the cast "throw themselves with energy and fearlessness at, through and around the Perspex box that sits centre stage. Their sweaty physicality effectively captures Danielle Micich's choreography, blending street and contemporary dance" (2012).

5.3 Structuring Your Script

Questions of structure come late for some and early for others. In verbatim or community-engaged work that focuses on a singular historical event, the structure can be quickly resolved by recounting the narrative in a chronological function. At its most complex, however, a verbatim or community-engaged work may need a structure that is able to dramaturgically straddle multiple themes, genres or even forms of performance. For Sarah and David and most playwrights, a simple system of index cards becomes incredibly useful in the drafting process. As you make your way through your research, give each moment, scene or storybeat an index card and arrange these on a wall so you can begin to see the overall shape of your work. Beyond this simple tool, however, it can be useful to have a basic knowledge of narrative structures that are available to you. We will address "The Hero's Journey", but this is a "traditional" playwright structure (more accurately described as "Western" and "patriarchal") that you may want to impose upon a work. For most verbatim playwrights, however, they let the *stories* inform them of the structure to be implemented.

Story-Led Script Structures

In our research, we found that most playwrights resist imposing a dramaturgical structure on the stories and data they gather. Rather, they let the *stories* lead the structure of the script. This may be a very natural evolution from how you organised the gathered stories and information in the first place. It may be by chronology (a linear plot structure), theme (an episodic plot structure) or tone (a non-linear or post-dramatic approach). Importantly, there are no "rules", and particularly in the twenty-first century all dramaturgical shapes and collisions are valid. For community-engaged work, the only rule is that of ethical community engagement. Your choice of structure will have a dynamic relationship with your ethical framework, as it will implicitly prioritise some voices over others, or potentially erase some contributions entirely. By letting the stories tell us what structure would suit it best, we are hopefully placing the community's desires for representation above our own "vision" for the work.

You might structure your play as a list, a guidebook, a map, a video game, a "choose your own adventure" novel, or an instruction manual. The structure of the play might be informed by the location and action. In the 2021 production of *That Boy* at Adelaide Fringe (written and performed by Martha Lott and directed by Yasmin Gurreeboo), the play opened with a child's messy bedroom. Books and toys scattered across the room, clothes piled high on the bed, on the floor, and draped over the dirty clothes hamper. Lego spread out all over the carpet centre stage. The single character enters the room looking for a toy and across the duration of the play alternates searching for the toy with tidying the room, returning books to shelves, toys to boxes, and clothes to drawers. At the play's conclusion, the room is tidy and the toy is found. The play was structured around this action of searching and tidying, and the rhythms that connect to these actions informed the rhythms of the dialogue (and vice versa).

Even a relatively "simple" structure, such as linear time, can be more complex than one might think at first. Dean Bryant's work *Gaybies* takes interviews from dozens of children with queer parents and presents them in a series of monologues that roughly translates to the growth of a child: through primary school into adolescence, the discovery of their own sexuality, to having children themselves. But the play also circles back upon itself, returning to characters across the course of their lives, juxtaposing stories alongside one another so that disparate voices may work in harmony along themes of belonging or loss. This is further complicated by the inclusion of music, which Bryant leaves open for individual directors to choose. In so doing, the potential for new dramatic meaning explodes exponentially. In the case of *Gaybies* then, the approximate chronology of a developing child provides a structural foundation that allows for countless opportunities for expansion and play.

You might like to experiment with a cyclical structure, arranging your stories and characters in such a way that they circle around a particular theme, or perhaps spiral in and out of themes, rather than progressing in a linear structure. Many verbatim plays, like *Gaybies*, allow for the existence of a linear and cyclical structure simultaneously. In *bald heads & blue stars* Sarah has a linear structure with the dramatic action of the central character Violet (we follow her across her life from age 5 to age 30), and has juxtaposed this with a cyclical structure to include multiple stories and vignettes from the women interviewed for this play. We have a scene with Violet in high school, and then the play circles out, sharing stories from the other 15 women interviewed in the project which all connect in some way to a high school experience, before returning back to Violet at the next juncture in her journey. David's play *April's Fool* operates in a similar manner, with a young man's week-long coma in a hospital providing a linear "spine" to the work. Scenes based around theme spin out from this spine and interact with each other, before always returning to the "home base" of the central plot.

Tom Wright describes puzzling through research data the size of several phone books when writing *Black Diggers* (a play about the experience of First Nations soldiers in World War One). In working with dramaturge Louise Gough and director Wesley Enoch, they arrived at a dramaturgical structure that allowed for sixty scenes broken into five parts (much like five "acts" of a Shakespeare play, or the five movements of Freytag's pyramid):

> Pre-nation – a reflection on the wars and experience of Indigenous people before nationhood; Enlistment – the process of Indigenous men signing up; The Theatre of War – the stories from the front as reported in journals, letters, official records and oral history; The Return – the effects of returning and the expectations of both the men who returned and those they were returning to; Legacy – what has been left behind for us (Wright 5).

Such a structure implies a linear chronology and allowed for Wright to sort through his enormous research. Again, however, this linear structure also allowed for a fragmented dramaturgy. "It's like the shellshock experience of those in war", reflects Enoch, "fragments of story mixed with emotional responses" (Wright 6). Wright continues: "It deliberately tries to be a patchwork quilt of the past, presenting a variety of short sharp scenes, as if the theatre itself is suffering from shellshock". This marriage of theme and structure is the essence of good dramaturgy: where form meets function.

In *I Should've Drunk More Champagne*, Dan Evans collaborated with Amy Ingram in creating a production centred around regret. The pair received over a hundred anonymous submissions online. By chance, many of the submissions used metaphors or repeated images around space (many mused on ideas of choices they would've made "in an alternate universe"). One submission talked about a comet landing by a lake. "Weirdly enough", says Evans, "that comet became the dramaturgical structure. We related it to regret as an event that just *plows* into your life and then there's debris everywhere". Evans took that structure to its most literal manifestation. The first half of *I Should've Drunk More Champagne* "feels very much like a verbatim spoken word show", reflects Evans, "and we fool the audience into thinking that's what the show's going to be. Then we blow it up. Basically, the rest of the remaining forty minutes of the show are these fragments floating out into space".

Evans reflection on dramaturgy echoes other post-dramatic forms that intertwine image, theme, and symbol together into a script structure into "heterarchical dramaturgies". In this field of knowledge, plays take on the shapes of organic, living structures such as archipelagos or even geological systems like stratification (the layering that is found in rocks) (Trencsényi, 2021). These make sense when considering community-engaged work, where playwrights are effectively organising their research around complex and dynamic social systems. In its ideal form, the structure of a piece of verbatim theatre should mirror the structure of the community who shared it.

The Well Made Play and Hero's Journey

The "Well Made Play" is an invention of modernism, developed around 1825 by playwright Eugene Scribe and Gustav Freytag (who created Freytrag's pyramid), informed by the Aristotelian view of drama from Ancient Greece. This recognisable form evolved over time into mainstream narrative structures that buttress most Hollywood films. The most popular of these is the "Hero's Journey", written about extensively by Joseph Campbell in his famed book *The Hero With a Thousand Faces*. Many screenwriters have elaborated on Campbell's initial outline, writing books that are considered "bibles" for today's screenwriter: Robert McKee's *Story* and Blake Snyder's *Save the Cat*. Most recently, Dan Harmon's spin on the hero's journey, the "story circle" has gained industry traction. All of these forms usually centre on a protagonist who is going on a journey or quest to reach their destiny, but they must overcome many trials, an encounter with an antagonist, and the darkest parts of themselves.

These forms can be seductive to the contemporary Western playwright, if for no other reason than we are immersed in it constantly from watching cinema and television. While the theorists above are worth reading and considering for any playwright serious about their craft, this conservative view of structure begins to buckle when we look at verbatim theatre, and especially community-engaged work in particular. The well-made play preferences a singular story where we focus on a protagonist. By necessity, this means eliminating other stories or voices or pushing them to the background. Here we run the risk of erasing one of verbatim theatre's greatest assets in its unique ability to showcase a range of "truths" (we discussed this previously as the notion of "conspectus"). It's also important to note that this story structure historically precedes the forming of early verbatim theatre by almost a century, so verbatim theatre was never really designed to fit into a linear narrative. In fact, some of the earliest practitioners who experimented with community-engaged forms (at times flirting with verbatim styles) would have been in staunch philosophical opposition to thinkers like Scribe and Freytag. More broadly, the Aristoltean view of drama is one that preferences *conflict* as the driving source of narrative. This can be inherently problematic for community-engaged works. At the time of writing, there is a significant movement in contemporary dramaturgical research to move more meaningfully away from Aristotle's rules for drama (Bilodeau 2016).

This is not to dismiss these structures as irrelevant to the form entirely. Importantly, these are the structures that your audience is most likely to be the most familiar with and find comforting. A useful way of thinking about these structures, particularly if the draft you are building is made cohesive by theme alone (as opposed to consistent characters or a plot), is to consider the audience as the hero on their own quest. Mapping out your scenes to guide the audience through an experience on their journey can be helpful. If we were to apply Harmon's story circle, we might think of the audience's journey through the work in four "quarters". Importantly, these quarters may not be equal in length (typically the second and third quarter will be the longest), but they are rather four distinct parts of the work.

- Firstly, a "normal" world is established. The audience understands certain rules about the world that they are viewing. There is a call to adventure, which at first we may refuse. This is a possible foreshadowing of a darker tone to come. Then, something occurs that dramatically shifts us, and propels us forward
- Secondly, we are thrust into a new world. We meet new ideas or characters that are challenging to us. The road ahead becomes uncertain until we arrive at the mid-point of the work, where we might come into contact with the object of our quest, or we may arrive at our darkest moment. We may "meet the goddess", who reveals a central truth that changes us
- Thirdly, we must wrestle with the largest demons to get what we truly want. In order to do this, however, we need to pay a price or make a sacrifice. Doing this allows us to return home
- Finally, we return home, with a new understanding of who we are and our relationship to the work. We are changed

If nothing else, this structure may help you organise your piece tonally. While we've started here with a structure that is likely most familiar to you, the structural possibilities are endless. It depends on what you are wanting to achieve with your play structure, what experience you'd like to aim to give your audience, or the effect on the audience that you're aiming for. We say "aim" here because as much as the playwright can position and guide an audience through the choices they make in writing, those choices will also be interpreted by the creative team producing the play, and also interpreted by the audience. If you've ever seen a play (or a movie, or tv episode) and thought "I think they were trying to make us feel (insert any feeling here), but I just couldn't stop feeling like (insert contrasting feeling here)", then you'll know what we mean – audiences have a mind of their own, and will read meaning into a story in ways that you never could have imagined (or intended!).

Principles in Practice

In an article by Kate Hunter on performance makers use of sound, Roslyn Oades reflects on how her politics and values inform the way she structures her headphone verbatim stories:

> There's a real politics in it for me as well. I feel like I want to create opportunities for people to hear their world differently and hear their world deeper. I feel like whenever I'm making a work, I'm trying to create an opportunity for people to listen closer, or listen differently to those around them, and to play with shifting power structures through sound as well. I've done a lot of mismatching of sound [between] what you hear and what you see. And I find that has a lot of potential for sharpening, or focusing on things that I'm interested in. That's what I'm mostly drawn to – that imaginative space of sound.
>
> (Oades in Hunter 343)

5.4 Playwriting Activities

Dramaturgical Questions

Direct Address

- How might you use direct address to provoke questions and emotions in an audience that you yourself felt when interviewing subjects?
- How might you use/subvert the use of direct address to position your audience sometimes as interviewer, sometimes as friend, sometimes as oppressor, etc?

Diegetic Theatricality

- What you are attempting to provoke in an audience, and how might that be achieved through the use of narration or other diegetic theatrical means?
- Will you as the writer be a character in the play, or is there a different meta-narrative arc that may be used to anchor the work?

Playing Multiple roles

- How might you use cast doubling to assist in the creation of new dramatic meaning as the playwright?
- How might you use vocal captioning, projection, physical performance (or some other mechanism) to introduce the different roles for the actor (and is this even necessary)?

Exercises in Stage Directions

If you've never experimented with stage directions before, it is worth devoting some time to exploring the possibilities. This can be done in any setting, but is most useful in a moderately large group when you are drafting a script. Take a scene and picture it in your head as best as you can. Write down *every single stage direction* as it appears to you, including set, blocking, and patterns of speech. Now delete *everything*. If possible, you can even delete dialogue attribution if you wish (so the dialogue is simply floating, and not attributed to a particular character).

Give these two wildly different versions of the script to two different groups. Ask them to prepare a short presentation of the script. If possible, don't tell the group what you're experimenting with.

There are multiple learnings here, but as a writer crafting a script, it is often the similarities between the two scenes that will reveal to you *what the scene is truly about*. It will also likely reveal to you the stage directions you do need – and if you're like most writers, there will be substantially fewer stage directions needed than you thought.

The Audience as Your Hero

When considering the structure of your piece, think about your intended audience as your "hero" about to embark on a quest. Are you able to plot their journey onto the hero journey structure? Being able to do so isn't a sign of success or failure, but going through this exercise may illuminate new possibilities for you in composing your script. The steps of Joseph Campbell's Hero's Journey can be found below, but are summarised further in countless places online.

1. The call to adventure
2. Refusal of the call
3. Supernatural Aid

4 Crossing the threshold
5 Belly of the Whale
6 Road of Trials
7 Meeting With the Goddess
8 Woman as Temptress
9 Atonement With the father
10 Apotheosis
11 Ultimate Boon
12 Refusal of Return
13 Magic Flight
14 Rescue from Without
15 Crossing the Return Threshold
16 Master of Two Worlds
17 Freedom to live

Your Community Map

Compose a list of your interviewees. Using a wall and some index cards, create a "map" of the community, assembling these interviewees in relationship to each other. What power structures are in place? Do some interviewees posses relationships that may be unknown to them, such as through theme or even repeated images?

Now consider some natural systems, listed below. Can your community of interviewees be mapped onto any of these systems?

- A forest, including the roots of trees and rotting undergrowth, new and older trees, insects, and birds that occupy the canopy
- A coral reef, with fish of all shapes and sizes, and colourful plant life
- A mountain with a summit, but also home to a rich network of interconnecting caves that house crystals, dead-ends, or man-made shafts
- A continent with a diverse range of interacting weather systems, and perhaps civilizations with their own politics, history, and diplomatic relations

Works Cited

Akram, S., and A. Hogan. "On Reflexivity and the Conduct of the Self in Everyday Life: reflections on Bourdieu and Archer." *The British Journal of Sociology* 66 (4), 2015, pp. 605–635.

Bilodeau, Chantal. "Why I'm Breaking Up with Aristotle." *Howl Round Theatre Commons*, 2016. https://howlround.com/why-im-breaking-aristotle

Botham, Paola. "From Deconstruction to Reconstruction: A Habermasian Framework For Contemporary Political Theatre." *Contemporary Theatre Review* 18.3, 2008, pp. 307–317.

Burton, David and Janet McDonald. "Performance 'Training' in the Dirt: Facilitating Belonging in a Regional Community Theatre Musical Theatre Event." *Theatre, Dance and Performance Training* 12(3), 2021, pp. 425–439.

Campbell, Joseph. *The Hero with a Thousand Faces*. New World Library, 1949.
Chou, Mark and Roland Bleiker. "Dramatizing War: George Packer and the Democratic Potential of Verbatim Theatre." *New Political Science* 32.4, 2010, pp. 561–574.
Duggan, Patrick. "Others, Spectatorship, and the Ethics of Verbatim Performance." *New Theatre Quarterly*, 29.2, 2013, pp. 146–158.
Feldhendler, Daniel. "Augusto Boal and Jacob L. Moreno, Theatre and Therapy." *Playing Boal: Theatre, Therapy, Activism*, edited by Jan Cohen-Cruz and Mady Schutzman, Routledge, London, 1994. pp. 87–109.
Hunter, Kate. "A Sound Conversation: Performance-Makers and Sound Practices with Roslyn Oades, Madeleine Flynn and Tamara Saulwick." *Australasian Drama Studies* 79, 2021, pp. 337–385.
Izod, J., R. Kilbron, and M. Hibberd. *From Grierson to the docusSoap: Breaking the boundaries*. University of Lutton Press, 2000.
Lucasheko, Melissa. On *'The Seven Stage of Grieving'*, by Wesley Enoch and Deborah Mailman. Griffith Review. Available at: https://www.griffithreview.com/seven-stages-grieving-wesley-enoch-deborah-mailman/
McCormack, Jess. *Choreography and Verbatim Theatre*, Dancing Worlds. Palgrave Pivot, 2018.
McKee, Robert. *Story: Substance, Structure, Style and the Principles of screenwriting*. Methuen Publishing Ltd., 1999.
Mundy, Cath and Jay Turner. QMF 2015 - '(RISE UP! Beautiful Country)', Under This Sky, 2016. https://www.youtube.com/watch?v=xyLxJkNxhBY
Paget, Derek. "New Documentarism on Stage: Documentary Theatre in New Times." *Zeitschrift fur Anglistik und Amerikanistik* 56.2, 2008, pp. 129–141.
Pascoe, Robin. "Theatre Review: Driving into Walls." *The West Australian*, 28th February 2012. Available at: https://thewest.com.au/entertainment/arts-reviews/theatre-review-driving-into-walls-ng-ya-328501
Rossiter, Kate, et al. "Staging Data: Theatre as a tool for analysis and knowledge transfer in health research." *Social Science and Medicine* 66, 2008, pp. 130–146.
Saxton, M., and M. Prendergast. *Applied Theatre*. Intellect Ltd, 2009.
Snyder, Blake. *Save the Cat! The Last Book on Screenwriting You'll Ever Need*. Michael Wiese Productions, 2005.
Trencsenyi Katalin. "Heterarchical Dramaturgies." *Critical Stages* 24 , 2021.
Valentine, Alana. *Bowerbird: The Art of Making Theatre Drawn from Life*. Currency Press, Sydney, 2018.
Wake, Caroline. "To Witness Mimesis: The Politics, Ethics, and Aesthetics of Testimonial Theatre in Through the wire." *Modern Drama* 56.1, 2013, pp. 102–125.
Watt, David. "Local Knowledges, Memories, and Community: From Oral History to Performance." *Political Performances, Theory and Practice*, edited by Susan Haedicke, Editions Rodopi, 2009, pp. 189–212.
Wright, Tom. *Black Diggers*. Playlab Publications, 2014.
Young, Stuart. "Playing with Documentary Theatre: Aalst and Taking Care of Baby." *New Theatre Quarterly* 25, 2009, pp. 72–87.

6 Verbatim and Community-Engaged Work in Rehearsal and Beyond

6.1 Introduction

During the rehearsal component of production, the playwright is positioned in a unique manner, and this is particularly true for verbatim playwrights. They are the "experts" on the events and source material and have spoken to the real people whose stories are being shared through the performance work. Often, the actors, director, and technical creatives haven't had the same level of interaction with the subjects of the show. This position is made further complex if the writer is also producing, directing, or acting in the work. In these situations, the playwright plays many functions and is required to nimbly pass between a variety of roles. A further complexity occurs if the community of participants are also involved in the performance or production process, perhaps performing versions of themselves or in some other way are related to the community at the heart of the script and performance.

While this may all seem unique for verbatim and community-engaged theatre practice, in reality, rehearsal rooms are frequently sites of complex relationship dynamics. Every production is unique in this regard. Relative giants of the Western canon such as Caryl Churchill and Tony Kushner have both developed some of their most famous works in dense collaboration with actors and directors (Aston 2009, Butler and Kois 2018). Shakespeare himself, writing in the time before the invention of the "director", was also an actor in his company. The idea of a playwright with an all-encompassing vision to be obeyed by all other creatives is, in most cases, a modernist myth. Even in the case of verbatim theatre, where playwrights are generally regarded as the expert who's embedded in the research and has the benefit of relationality through the community immersion process, will need to make room for the director, actors, and technical creatives to have their own artistic impulse and impression of the script.

In this chapter, we explore some of the intricacies that arise when rehearsing a verbatim theatre work, both inside and outside of a community-engaged context. We begin by exploring some of the nuances of working the script with actors, taking time to make an important distinction between actors who have had no previous knowledge of your verbatim research, and

Verbatim and Community-Engaged Work in Rehearsal and Beyond 143

those who have. We then discuss areas that may require the playwright's attention on opening night and beyond, including a discussion on elements of technical design, interactions with the audience, and critical reviewers.

6.2 Early Days – Working the Script

In community-engaged practice, it is rare for a script to be "complete" before it enters rehearsal. Some scenes may only be in their primordial form, while others are clear and specific. In other practices, especially commercial theatre, there is often a clear line between a script's "development" stage and when it is "rehearsal ready", but even this is more uncertain than it may appear. In the first part of a rehearsal for any performance, a script is most likely to change to some degree. A playwright may write an entire new draft (or several) in the first days of rehearsal. This is not unusual, although the changes should hopefully not be too seismic. In a commercial or professional context, a playwright generally aims to have the script relatively locked down by the third week of rehearsal, to allow for the actors and the director to have time to build the work. The playwright may reappear in "tech week" before a show's opening to make any final amendments. If a playwright is lucky enough to have previews for their show, they will be allowed further time to collaborate with actors and the director to edit the work in dialogue with audience responses, although this opportunity is rare in Australia outside of large-scale companies.

Community-engaged work with non-actors can be far less structured. Full-time rehearsals are often impractical, and so part-time rehearsals may take place over many months before a show's opening night, giving the writer ample time to make changes. Previews are often impossible in a community-engaged context, so the playwright will be left largely unprepared for how an audience will respond to the work. It is often the case that the audience for a community-engaged work is largely made up of members of that broader community (or people connected to the community), so there is some element of the "known" which can exist in the relationship between the playwright and the audience in a community-engaged project that isn't the same as an audience in a solely professional or commercial context. Still, a playwright is charged with guarding narrative cohesion for the audience and may find it necessary to make changes right up until opening night.

With all of the peculiarities of individual rehearsal rooms, it is difficult to make all-inclusive statements about the playwright's role in these circumstances. While a playwright's role may be altered by many factors, there is an essential singular component that has the most influence over their behaviour, and thus this section is split into two:

- The first part describes a rehearsal room where the acting company and the community whose stories are being shared through performance are different from one another. This may be the case for a professional

production where actors and director are completely separate from the community with whom the playwright has interviewed or interacted with
- The second part describes a rehearsal room where the acting company and the community are the same, as may be in a youth work, or a focussed community-engaged work. Actors on stage may be people whom you've interviewed, or may otherwise have a personal stake or relationship to the community of study

The Acting Company and the Participating Community Are Different

A playwright may exist in isolation, or in collaboration with a small team, for months or even years before a producing company mounts a full production. With this commitment, an entirely new team of professionals come into the work's orbit. In essence, the acting and creative company in this scenario become a *new* community that the playwright must engage with. This new community is adjacent and largely parallel to the original community of study that was the source of the writer's data. Some of these new creatives may have prior knowledge or experience with the community of study, while others may have very little. Regardless, the playwright has special knowledge that may be useful to a director, acting company, and technical design team. In contemporary theatre practice, how intrinsically collaborative a rehearsal room becomes is largely dependent on the director's leadership style. Discussion may be largely open, and the playwright may be in the rehearsal room on a daily basis to assist in the development of the production. In other scenarios, roles may be more strict, and a playwright will need to be sensitive to a director's vision and an actor's right to interpret a character, potentially leaving the creative team alone for days or weeks at a time during rehearsal. For the playwright to navigate these roles, while also remaining an expert on the community of study, can be a delicate process. Not to mention, of course, that in most large-scale works of this kind, the playwright isn't strictly paid for their time in rehearsal. Usually, they are paid a commissioning fee and some royalties at the box office. So anytime they spend in rehearsal can be "volunteer". If this is a point of contention, it's worth discussing at the time the theatre company and the playwright are drawing up their initial agreement.

There is some nascent language in the field around the role of the playwright in a rehearsal room. It is vital to understand that there is real economic capital at play here for many playwrights. In commercial theatre-making, the stakes can be high for all creatives, who are banking on the success of production for the sustainability of their careers. The entrepreneurial part of a playwright's role is frequently marginalised in scholarly discussion, but it is a crucial ingredient as it hints at the power dynamics that can be in play inside a rehearsal room (Ainsworth 2008). An emerging playwright, for example, is unlikely to contradict a more experienced director, even if the director has not engaged in the hours of research that the playwright has undertaken. It can be helpful in these circumstances to locate the playwright in a network of "communities of practice" (Wenger 9), a term derived from sociology research, used to describe a community that is united by a particular set of pre-conditions. A playwright may be navigating up to three communities of practice at once inside a rehearsal room: their relationship to the original community of storytellers (or source data to use the lexicon of research), their relationship to the other creatives in the room, and their relationship to their employer who has commissioned the work. There is no set template in how playwrights can achieve the agility required to navigate all three communities at once. Decisions can only be made in a moment-to-moment basis. It is also worth saying that there are significant differences in playwriting cultures internationally. In some countries, it is fashionable to emphasise the role of the playwright, even above the director's vision for a production. In others, it is far more common to mirror the experience of screenwriting, where director's wishes are given precedence over playwrights, or at least for these two parties to compromise. In Australia, most theatrical new work is largely dependent on the playwright and director forming a happy and productive partnership.

There is no single "right" approach in these situations, although (as will be explored further in the next chapter), the playwright possesses unique ethical responsibilities in these situations that are worth careful attention. The playwright has access to all of the "on-the-record" data, but also those gathered "off-the-record", with nuanced understandings of sensitive relationships and narratives. It is certainly incumbent upon the playwright to speak up if they feel the director's vision will be defamatory or unfair to a subject of study (hopefully as early as possible, which is why the playwright's presence early in the rehearsal process can be valuable). But where else to draw the line is up to an individual's ethics. In community-engaged practice, the playwright would go beyond "defamatory" or "unfair", and likely also take umbridge if a director's interpretation was at risk of being offensive or dismissive. For more deliberately provocative or political theatre, however, a work being offensive to a particular group of people may be vital to the dramaturgy of the work (quoting and damning certain politicians, for example).

In traditional theatre productions, the playwright can often be limited in halting a production once rights to the work have been handed over. Cases of an extreme falling out between the playwright and the director are rarely discussed openly. One such example is from 2013, when Australian playwright Lachlan Philpott publicly distanced himself from Perth Theatre Company's production of his work *Alienation*. In the production's rehearsal, the script had been altered enough that Phillpott asked to be removed in the credits as the "author". Philpott also left a note on the seats for audience members, stating: "I would like to acknowledge the people who bravely shared their stories and the actors and creative artists who contributed to this work in good faith ... However, the outcome of this production does not reflect my original scripted or communicated intentions as the playwright". The removal of his name as the author was not done "as a result of the type of differences in artistic vision and interpretation that are part of the usual and constructive interplay between artists", an additional statement issued by the Australian Writer's Guild stated (Watts 2013). The play, which revolved around the experiences of real people who claimed to have alien abductee experiences, ultimately remains under Philpott's copyright. Philpott's reputation was also largely undamaged, as he continues a career as one of Australia's most celebrated playwrights. We provide the example of *Alienation* here only as a means of citing that extreme disagreements do occur, perhaps more often in verbatim-centred works than in others, as the visceral connection to "real" people makes for difficult ground to navigate.

As another example, when writing *April's Fool*, David was in his first years as an emerging playwright. The director of the original production, Lewis Jones, was also the person who had commissioned the work and had several decades of experience. Jones enabled a mostly collaborative rehearsal room, and for the first week, David was very present to answer questions from actors and Jones on different characters. It became clear in the ensuing weeks, however, that the cast and director were becoming united in their vision of a particular character as a "bad guy". David saw the story as essentially absent of villains, particularly because he had spent a lot of time with each interview subject. The character in question was very complex, but a critical part of the play's narrative. In the final production, the character was introduced with a snarl from the cast and was positioned on a corner of the stage, in isolation. The lighting state for this character's monologue was the darkest for the show. David was sympathetic to Jones' point of view and could understand the allure of creating a villain to make a compelling narrative for an audience. At a different point in his career, David may have objected, but in the circumstances for this first production, he didn't feel he was able. Ethical concerns about the character being treated unfairly were comforted by the fact that their name and several identifiable details about the character were changed. An average audience member wouldn't make the link to the real-life "villain". As a playwright, David navigated ethical obligations to the original source material (changing the name of the interviewee), his own interest in protecting his relationship with his employer Jones (by not objecting to Jones' interpretation), and the actors and directors' intrinsic right to have their own interpretation of the script.

The nature of Sarah's verbatim playwriting practice means that there have often been characters that are (to varying degrees) based on Sarah herself. In *Blister* the central character of Rosie is based primarily on Sarah's experience walking the Camino, however, there was a professional director and cast for the 2019 production. The *Blister* team had a week of creative development prior to the start of rehearsal, and this was an invaluable opportunity for Sarah (as producer/playwright on this production) to refine and tighten the script, and for the cast and director to ask Sarah questions about the experience of walking the Camino. During this week Sarah was challenged to rework some moments in the play so that instead of being past tense descriptions of experience they could be performed as present tense "in the moment" action in the world of the play. The director and cast also asked excellent questions which prompted Sarah to delve a little deeper into her own experience and lay bare some of the vulnerabilities she experienced on the Camino and consider how these might be echoed in the text. These prompts and moments of reworking are great examples of how a cast and director might develop the script with the playwright, bringing their own experience and knowledge of performance into the development process. In these moments of conversation, brainstorming, and development Sarah was holding space for multiple communities of practice. She was navigating her own intentions and goals for the structure, form, and content of the play, being open to feedback and interpretation by the cast and director, keeping her knowledge and relationship with the pilgrims whose stories were included in the play in the mix of decision making, and figuring out whether some of the suggested changes would be taken on board in the script itself, or whether they might be interpretative choices that would be made in this production, but not written into the text itself.

In most instances, the changes which emerged across the creative development process were written into the text, except for the occasional stage direction which had been removed during the creative development and which Sarah later decided to add back in. Echoing David's reflection on *April's Fool,* there were two characters in *Blister* who ended up being interpreted in a highly comedic manner, providing comic relief through their caricatured interpretation. While definitely written to add levity, Sarah was at times concerned that the interpretation meant that some of the full complexity of these characters was lost and that the people who had informed these characters might react negatively to their portrayal. Theatrically it was hilarious to watch the actors push these characters to the limits of comedy during rehearsal, and they provided a much-needed juxtaposition to some of the heavier content across the play. Yet what was "good" for the play, might not be what is "good" for the community being represented. By being in the room for rehearsals Sarah was able to express some of these concerns, and the cast and director worked these into their experimentation, finding ways to soften the edges of the caricatures at key moments in the story, inviting the audience to engage with these characters in a more multidimensional way. It was a relief to Sarah when the people who had informed aspects of these characters saw the show and loved it – but in reflection, the fact that she was still concerned or unsure how the portrayal might land for those members of the community, means that more work could have been done to check in with them about their representation during the rehearsal process.

Principles in Practice

The premiere production of *The Campaign* in 2018 (written by Campion Decent and directed by Matt Scholten) is a great example of a production where some of the acting company are also members of the participating community (the people interviewed), and some of the acting company were not. Matt reflects on the experience of having Robert Jarman in the cast, who was also one of the original campaigners who had been arrested in 1988:

> Robert's interview was quite funny, because he was very much like, 'I don't remember, I don't remember, I don't remember'. And then in the process of playing himself and other characters in the play – and he was playing a lot of the people you might consider to be, you know, less than supportive shall we say, of the activists – Robert was having a lot of memories in that first week. I was very concerned, and I'm always concerned about this with people, of triggering them or making them go through a traumatic experience, and so I'm very clear that it's important that we try and protect people when they're going through these kinds of things. But Robert, being the resilient creature that he is, was affected, but also he had these memories of things that came up that first week. So on the floor, rehearsing the show, he would stop me and say, 'oh, I need a moment'. And of course, I'd say, 'Yeah, of course, you know, just do what you need, you know, go outside, and whatever you want to do'. And he took me outside one moment and said, 'um, there are things I remember and I haven't told you or Campion about but I really want to, you know if they're useful to you then they should go in the play'. So a couple of moments like that did end up being in the play, including the scene where he's in jail, playing himself.
>
> Because Robert is an actor, he's a great communicator, but it was such an emotional thing for him that I remember him not being too – I do remember a moment after the initial interview Campion and I both saying 'well, he didn't really talk about what we thought he'd talk about'. And so we were like 'do we need to press him or do we need to just let it be?' and my instinct was to let it be. So it was just so fascinating that in that first week, Robert was being an actor, being himself contributing this to the story even then, so those things went into the play as well. And certainly the moment when he is alone in jail ... it's interesting to see with a verbatim piece, to see that actor who is playing himself is also able to, through the process of rehearsing, remember stuff and was open enough to contribute that to us as a team.

In this premiere production, Robert was the only cast member who was both a part of the interviewed community and a member of the performing ensemble. For the four other actors, the experience of sharing the script with the interviewed community was a different experience. Matt recalls:

On our first day of rehearsal, we had as many people who were available come in who were also living in Tasmania, they all came in on that first day. So we had literally, I think about 20 people and they listened. That was like a double edged sword in a way, because it's like, 'Well, I hope you like what we've done'. Because, you know, everyone's gonna be there. And these people, this is their life. This is their actual real life. Well, it's our version of their real life. Firstly, it's their version of their history. And our interpretation or our edit of their story. Everyone's memory is affected by many, many things. We were like, 'Oh my God, what are we? What if they hate it?' ... and on the day we hadn't actually told the actors this because we thought it's enough for Campion and I to know this, we don't want to scare them, we thought we'd save them the fear. On the day of the reading, I had to read all the stage directions, because Campion just wanted to sit back and listen to it. So everyone's assembled, and then Rodney chose to sit next to me. Fantastic. And so we begin and then I realized the first stage direction in the play, speaks of Rodney dancing and being a DAG, or being a bad dancer. I'm realizing this, as I'm saying it out loud, sitting next to the person who the stage direction is about, who was looking at me. So that was fun.

[After the reading] the real people were holding corners talking, and in some cases debating whether events actually happened or not. So it was kind of fascinating to me. People sometimes interpret verbatim as being the truth. But I think the truth is such a nebulous concept. And certainly when it comes to people's memory, and this is like 30 years ago, memory. So these people in most cases are in their late 50s, early 60s, some are even in their 70s. And that also affects your memory, and also the fact that so many of these recollections that we got through the interviews, were so personal, like people were so prepared to share really deeply personal stuff with us. There was a lot of crying involved in the interviews ... and that's going to do two things. It's going to really heighten the work and make it really kind of unique, but also it means that when you are in an emotional state, it's possible that you might either be forgetting some stuff or embellishing some stuff or whatever happens when you remember things. So yeah, I remember that first day really clearly for lots of reasons.

The Acting Company and the Participating Community are the Same

In situations where the acting company and the participating community are identical, the playwright's role is significantly altered from that of a "traditional" theatre-making model. These are more likely to be community-engaged works, where the act of presenting new work has a multitude of intentions beyond simply executing a theatrical production. Social values underpin community-engaged models, and so a playwright's job description is often entirely different in these circumstances. They are not simply entrusted with the task of "writing" a script, but are frequently also charged with mentoring non-actors in performance and text analysis, collaborating with non-writers on scenes or monologues, and curating and adapting a script that sets all participants up for success, while still being an accessible and necessary document for a stage management team. "Facilitator" (or "Lead Artist" in many Australian-based grant applications) is the broader term that has been adopted colloquially by the Australian working industry for this kind of community-engaged arts practitioner.

The idea of a "facilitator" invites an open and collaborative approach to playwriting. The playwright can not see themselves here as the arbiter over an artistic artefact, but rather the curator of an experience. In working with non-actors especially, a script becomes futile if it only sets up the performer to essentially fail at the task that has been given to them. A scene that relies on complex comedic timing, for example, may frustrate a performer and leave an audience silent. As written on the page, the scene may be intrinsically genius, but if it doesn't empower the performer or connect with an audience, then what's the point? A smarter approach is to listen to the performer's natural sense of comedy and storytelling, and devise and create a scene that allows them to display that natural sense of humour on stage. This is a particularly clear process in community-engaged projects informed by verbatim theatre methodologies. If a script has been co-written by the same people who end up performing it, then they can never really "get their lines wrong", as it is their own words and a version of themselves, that they are ultimately portraying. Thus, written scripts become necessary instruments for stage management and technical teams, but may ultimately be only a guide for your performers, depending on the parameters or style of performance you're undertaking. Balancing this quality of open-ness while protecting dramaturgical integrity and clarity is the work of the playwright/facilitator, who always has the ultimate purpose of the production in mind. Ultimately, we find it's a process of simple compromise and collaboration. An instruction to a performer may be: "as long as you're talking about that theme, you can discuss it how you want for about thirty seconds, but make sure you end on that line so our technical team knows your moment is complete".

David has found this degree of open-ness to be invaluable when working with First Nations non-actors in particular, in the context of the Queensland Music Festival Signature Community Events. These large-scale events often featured moments of First Nations history as told by elders or young people. As a white man, David committed to lengthy relationship and trust-building, and wrote scripts based on verbatim conversations he'd had with the relevant First Nations participants involved. Humility and vulnerability have been crucial tools for David's artistic practice in this regard. To start an interview or rehearsal process by saying, "I'm unsure about this, but I want to work with you to make this amazing" has a profound effect on building relationships of trust that deliver high-quality results. After initial conversations, participants were able to change the script as much as they wanted, but for all of these performers, after an initial few edits, they preferred to settle on set "text" that they could learn. Only on the closing night of some of these performances did performers get especially daring, and take the opportunity to riff a little on the script that had been provided for them. Importantly, because they were witness to David's transparent artistic process, and to their place in the show overall, these riffs weren't contrary to the integrity of the final artefact of the show itself. By this late stage in the process, the community were empowered in their sense of ownership of the show, and their contributions were in line with a cohesive vision of the final artefact.

In some circumstances, a playwright may find it useful to structure a script working backward from what they know will be logistically possible to achieve in rehearsal. With a cast of non-actors, part-time rehearsals are common. Sudden withdrawals by cast members who are otherwise volunteering their time can be unavoidable. This was the case in the *Lockdown* project, where one of the actors had to withdraw from the project ten days before the opening night at Adelaide Fringe. People should always come before the project, and this participant's withdrawal was supported by Sarah and the cast. In this instance, Sarah was able to reach out to another young performer who had met the ensemble while creating the educational resource for the production, and she was able to step in and rehearse the role. Having the opportunity to ask someone who was not completely unknown to the rest of the cast assisted in making this transition smoother than it otherwise would have been, and meant that the ensemble already had the beginnings of a relationship with their new cast member. While in this scenario it was luck rather than forward planning, scripts can be written with contingencies built-in so that the work can withstand the bumpiness of a community-engaged process. An episodic dramatic structure, for example, is more resilient to change than an intricate and inter-connected narrative. It is easier to organise rehearsals for self-contained "episodes" than attempting to request an entire cast for every single rehearsal. In youth work, rehearsals often collide with class time. Creating scripts that feature a collage of duologues, monologues or small groups means that all students can rehearse parallel to one another. This means time is used efficiently, and students aren't left bored, waiting for their chance to rehearse their scene or moment. In community-engaged work, it is essential for playwrights to consider how a work will be rehearsed for these very reasons. Early planning can create a smoother rehearsal process for all participants.

Most of David's community-engaged work has followed a specific verbatim theatre model. David interviews participants, edits the responses, and presents them back to the participant for them to "perform", with permission for them to edit as they wish. In almost all cases, the participant is grateful for the reliability of a script, and will only seek to tweak some phrases or keywords. It has always been important to let the participant know how their words fit into the larger story the work is telling. If available, diagrams of set drawings and familiarity with the venue itself can help a non-actor imagine what the experience will look and feel like.

Principles in Practice

In working with non-actors in community performances, playwright Alana Valentine calls for an observance of performers' "assets" or strengths. The playwright is then tasked with creating a role that essentially capitalises on that strength.

> Writing for community performers or youth theatre performers is different to writing for trained actors. As the writer you can build work which supports amateur performers and uses their assets to their best effect – assets such as sincerity, authenticity and enthusiasm. In the case of *Watermark,* the play about Katherine's flood, I structured a long poem to embody the flood waters and provide a central narration for the work (Valentine, 120).

This poem was informed by the community participants and drew on their vocal strengths as performers, without requiring that they have the same ability for characterisation and embodiment as professionally trained actors.

Principles in Practice

In some of Roslyn Oades work these lines are blurred, with both professional artists and community-based participants contributing to the performance outcome. "Part love-letter to the ocean, part site-specific audio documentary, *Sea Stories* is a listening experience designed to accompany sunrise over the ocean" (roslynoades.com/sea-stories, accessed 2022). Commissioned by Festival 2018 as part of the Gold Coast Commonwealth Games Arts and Culture Program, audiences were invited to a sunrise audience experience at 5:30 am, to take a seat in a beachfront deckchair, nestle in with a wireless headphone system, and be aurally immersed in this site-specific storytelling event sharing five first-person stories from ocean-lovers about their experiences of the sea. The audio-documentary comprises written and performed elements, alongside voice recordings from community participants.

6.3 To Opening Night and Beyond

In the final stretch to opening night, activity accelerates for all members of a production company. It's easy to assume that this is a time when playwrights may have very little to effectively do. In many cases, especially in community-engaged settings, the playwright's workload becomes more nuanced and complex. The following is split into three sections, each with very specific discussions. The first is specific to a verbatim theatre context where the community of participants are different to the company of actors performing the work. Curating the experience of that community viewing the work is essential. Secondly, it is worth briefly exploring the ramifications of technical design for the playwright. Finally, we focus on how a playwright may think about interacting with the audience of the work, and the impact that viewing theatre based on lived experiences can have on audiences (particularly when they share those lived experiences yet weren't involved in the development of the play).

When Two Worlds Collide: the Play and the Real Meet

In situations where the subject of study and acting company are different, it is important to carefully consider how the subject of study will first encounter the production. In most cases, this consideration falls to the playwright, as they are the most acquainted with the community of storytellers. A playwright may advise a director on the best course of action. Sometimes, the consideration is quite simple. For small, targeted productions that are particularly community-based, such as in a school or church context, for example, the subjects of study may also be the targeted audience for the work. As such, they are invited with other community members to a final "showing", and see the final work at the latest possible moment. Deviating from this model might occur when the production is especially large, or the material is especially sensitive.

When writing *April's Fool*, David was interacting with a community in deep grief. Of particular concern were the parents of young Kristian Terauds, whose tragic death was the focus of the work. David intuitively felt it was important to develop the work without their direct input, allowing several drafts to evolve without reaching out to Kristian's parents. However, David was very aware that it would be inappropriate, and likely traumatic, for Kristian's parents to first encounter the work among an audience of many hundreds on opening night. David worked with director Lewis Jones to schedule a special performance in the middle of the rehearsal period. The timing of this was critical. If Kristian's parents sought changes to the work, it was important that they requested these changes early enough in the rehearsal process that those requests could be duly considered. Too early, however, and the actors would still be getting a grasp on the material. As such, the performance occurred approximately two-thirds of the way through the rehearsal process. The cast were just beginning to "run" the show without stopping. While the set, lighting, and sound design had been imagined, none of these elements were present in the room. In a special, surreal, and emotional rehearsal, the actors performed the work for Kristian's parents. It's difficult to describe what occurred. Of course, all parties were incredibly emotional. Both the actors and Kristian's parents said it was "cathartic" and extremely helpful. For the performers, the stakes of the play were at full tilt: they viscerally experienced the "real-ness" of the subject matter (something which verbatim theatre is particularly positioned to truly deliver upon). The parents were able to understand David's intentions in writing the work much better than if they had seen it only written down. They had very little to offer as "suggested changes", but the conversation that followed naturally with everyone after the performance was helpful to all parties, including director Lewis Jones.

Many years later, David penned *St Mary's In Exile*, a play which focussed on a community of church-goers and a very public scandal. Here, David feels he made an error. In an effort to be transparent, David offered a reading to all interview participants for the play's very first draft. While everyone was polite, the nature of the material meant that opinions on what the play "should" stage were vast and overwhelming. The reading didn't help anyone, least of all David. Importantly for *St. Mary's In Exile* and *April's Fool*, the works were informed by verbatim theatre, but they were not *community-engaged*. They were pieces of theatre commissioned by theatre companies for the sake of producing commercial works for as broad an audience as possible. David's loyalty ultimately lay with the producing company, not the community of study, although the tension between these two parties sometimes made for difficult but necessary decisions based in an ethical code of practice. Still, two figures in *St. Mary's In Exile* were invited to a late rehearsal in the same manner as Kristian's parents were for *April's Fool*. These were two priests at the heart of the scandal, Peter and Terry, who had been particularly vulnerable in interviews with David. David felt it only fair to give them a more cohesive preview of the production. Prior to them seeing the rehearsal, they had read several drafts of the script, but it wasn't until they saw actors performing that they understood all of the nuances of the play. Playwrights can often forget the intrinsic odd-ness of play scripts to those who aren't used to reading them. Seeing a rehearsal reassured them and made them feel more prepared for what they were to witness on opening night.

In summary, it's important to consider special previews of performances in circumstances where there is particularly sensitive material at play. The timing of this is essential. Unless the subject of study is particularly theatre-literate, sharing written scripts isn't advisable (although in some instances, this still may be better than nothing. For example, in *bald heads & blue stars* the community of women interviewed were geographically dispersed, so attending a rehearsal or preview performance wasn't practical. In this case, Sarah had sent the script to the community of women long before rehearsals began, along with an explanation of the script formatting, detailing why some of the text is written in italics, etc). Seeing a rehearsal with actors communicates more of the vision for the final work, and can be incredibly helpful for the actors, director, and community to take part.

> **Principles in Practice**
>
> Alana Valentine reflects on a public reading of *Watermark* on the 10th anniversary of the Katherine flood:
>
> I will never forget the moment, almost towards the end of the play, commemorating the people who had died as a result of the flood waters. Using the transcript from the Territory parliament, it named the people and detailed the circumstances. At the time, the parliamentarian reading this had asked his fellow politicians to stand for a minute's silence. I included this as an authentic part of the record. We had asked a few people associated with the cast to stand at this moment, to see if it might encourage others in the audience to do the same. We needn't have bothered. Almost before the invitation to stand was issued, the entire house got to its feet and stood, silent, respectful, grateful to be able to respond to the pain and heartbreak outlined. It was a precious moment that anyone who works in community theatre will know well – that moment when the work of art becomes a conduit for spontaneous community feeling (Valentine, 121).

Technical and Design: the Community Expands

In the weeks before opening, the community of the production expands further to welcome more expertise. The playwright in a traditional setting may be absent from this process, but in most community-engaged work they are usually present. Regardless, a playwright has more of an effect on the technical design than they might realise (and the direction) in the simple use of stage directions throughout the script. A certain amount of pedanticism is welcome and necessary in how a playwright considers stage directions. This is by no way to assume that playwrights can *dictate* the choices of directors, lighting, sound, and set designers, but they can certainly inform them.

For example, a simple decision that all playwrights must make is how they move from scene to scene, or moment to moment. Clearly defined scenes, with scene headings, create a certain level of expectation among the rest of the creative company. It suggests the work will be punctuated, either by blackouts or significant beats of sound design, to transition from one space to another. Take the following as an example:

STUART: And that's when I realised we'd never be the same again.
            END SCENE.
            SCENE FOUR
            MALCOLM is on stage.
MALCOLM: We were working out of the warehouse that day, and it was raining.

This simple act has more of an effect than one might realise. A competent stage manager, on instinct, will likely devise a rehearsal schedule based on scene numbers. As such, for the first section of rehearsals, scene "three" and scene "four" may be rehearsed separately, and imagined as separate entities in the minds of the designers, director, and cast. Stuart's final line may come with some music, a significant lighting change (a blackout even), and then we may get sounds of a warehouse, sounds of rain, and a very different lighting state for the start of scene four. Malcolm presumably enters once Stuart has finished his line and at some point in the transition. A particularly literal set designer may decide they need something that indicates a warehouse space. Of course, this is absolutely fine as long as such ideas are intentional on the part of the playwright. If a playwright eliminates scene headings (or some of them), we end up with a very different result. For example:

STUART: And that's when I realised we'd never be the same again.
            Change.
            MALCOLM is onstage.
MALCOLM: We were working out of the warehouse that day, and it was raining.

Now it is up to the director and the company as to how to interpret "change". "Malcolm is onstage" is also very generous to the team, as it is entirely their choice as to when Malcolm would enter. His entrance isn't described, only the moment in which an audience would begin focussing on him. These moments are more likely to be rehearsed right next to each other, which means the director will think about the transition with actors in mind, instead of relying on technical design. The sound of rain may fade in earlier, or later. A set designer is less likely to take a literal approach, particularly if spaces change frequently. If we eliminate "MALCOLM is onstage", then we also allow for the possibility, depending on the context of the rest of the work, that Stuart *can become* Malcolm (or of course, you can state this literally in the stage directions).

There are no "correct" answers here. In Australian professional practice, most playwrights leave stage directions very open to interpretation by the director and cast, using them sparingly. As verbatim theatre methodologies have evolved out of the community and political theatre contexts playwrights of verbatim works tend to emphasise design that is utilitarian and symbolic. A brief note from the playwright at the start of the script can be incredibly informative. Take this example from the beginning of *The Laramie Project* by Moises Kaufman:

> The set is a performance space. There are a few tables and chairs. Costumes and props are always visible. The basic costumes are the ones worn by the company of actors. Costumes to portray the people of Laramie should be simple: a shirt, a pair of glasses, a hat. The desire is to suggest, not re-create. Along the same lines, this should be an actor-driven event. Costume

changes, set changes, and anything else that happens on the stage should be done by the company of actors. (4)

The above description could be applied to hundreds of other verbatim theatre performances. Kauffman's distinction to *suggest* rather than *re-create* is essential. While film and television may attempt to re-create history, verbatim theatre has different aims. As discussed elsewhere in the book, verbatim theatre, particularly in a community-engaged context, has complex aims that desires to engage its audience in a dialogue. Understood with this purpose in mind, technical design takes on an important role.

Principles in Practice

Claire Christian frequently works as a director for youth-devised, community-engaged works. In these settings, it is typical for a technical team to only be available in the last few days (or hours) before opening night. Claire places importance on the role of the director in these moments to be clear and precise in their vision. It is ultimately the director, who may or may not be the playwright, who must make the various elements of technical design come together.

Claire also talked about working with youth ensembles who had previously had no theatrical experience. In some instances, trying to explain to them the full technical vision in Claire's head was impossible: "So I often say, I need you to trust me. Because they can't see what's in my head yet. Everyone needs to trust we're all making choices that ultimately serve the work. Then you get into a tech and they go, "holy shit! This is amazing!"

Audiences and Reviewers

Some playwrights love to interact with audiences, while others dread it. Regardless of your personal preference, in a community-engaged work in particular, you're more likely to continue an ongoing dialogue with the community. If you've done your job well, the piece will be deliberately provocative and evocative, for better or worse. Verbatim works invite an intensity of emotion from an audience. If you and the production succeed in engaging them, there is likely to be a deep resonance. How the playwright prepares themselves for this, and how they can navigate an ongoing conversation with an audience, will be the focus of this brief section. Before doing so, it's worthwhile pausing briefly to discuss the role of reviewers or the professional press.

In the context of professional productions, reviewers, bloggers, and professional journalists are generally expected to attend. There is little that can be done by the playwright to control this process. One can only hope the reviewers are aware of verbatim theatre as a form and will possess enough sensitivity to critique the production, rather than the personal content of interviews. With this in mind, it may be sensible to talk to any interviewees about their potential appearance in the press, especially if they're not used to public life. In general, the smartest advice is the same that is offered to professional actors and artists: just don't read reviews! But of course, it's a personal choice.

In a community-engaged context, the role of a reviewer or blogger is more complicated. This is especially true in hybrid models, where professional companies may work with non-actors. For an ill-informed journalist, the outcome may *look* as though it should be judged to a professional standard. In reality, the product of community-engaged work is not the best judgment of the relative "success" of a project. Rather, the product is best viewed in the context of an entire making process. As such, it is ideal if a journalist can interview a director or playwright *before* seeing a production. Rather than writing a "review", journalists would be encouraged to write a feature piece on the entire project. This is usually not a domain that the playwright has a lot of control over, but it's an important conversation to have with a marketing and publicity team.

Even a casual theatre-goer will still have an opinion on what they've witnessed, and they may want to share this opinion with you! This is actually a good sign, in that the performance has provoked a strong enough emotional response to warrant a discussion. In David and Sarah's experience, this is rarely a negative experience, but it can be overwhelming. Verbatim theatre often deals with sensitive topics, and the act of sharing stories can give audiences implicit "permission" to share their own stories with you. Verbatim plays are excellent models for how stories can be shared, and after witnessing this modelling, an audience can be compelled to contribute their own story to the mix. We explore this in a little more theoretical detail in the next section.

Principles in Practice

Playwright Campion Decent doesn't fear interaction with audiences. In fact, he loves it.

> If you're going to write these sorts of things,' he says, 'then you have an obligation to hear the audience response. You'd prefer people respond than just walk straight out the door. There's a duty of care around that as well. For several of my shows after the performance we've directed people to mental health resources, and there's been signs up in the foyer to help too.

Audience Impact

All theatre may provide opportunities for social connection, or as Meeks, Shryock, and Vanden suggest from their longitudinal study with audiences, attending theatre can create a sense of belonging and provide social engagement which enhances well-being (122). Sarah has previously explored this connection between belonging and the dramaturgy of verbatim plays, suggesting that the processes of verbatim theatre (conducting interviews and being immersed in a community) mean that the community of storytellers have opportunities to express identity narratives about who they are and how they understand themselves in relation to their lived experience. These identity narratives are then written into both the form and content of the verbatim play, modelling a process of belonging through the play's dramaturgy (Peters 2019).

Making sense of experience, and expressing this "sense making" to our friends and family is also a process of belonging (Meinhof and Galasiński 73). In Sarah's research around participant impact in the *bald heads & blue stars* project, the community of storytellers expressed similar sentiments, with one reflecting that they "experienced a whole range of emotions from sadness, fear, anxiety (esp knowing my family were now more closely aware of what I had been thru – a point that I had always try to protect them from my pain to a greater extent [sic]" (survey response 3). Another expressed feeling proud to have been involved and that the play would "hopefully help people become more aware of the condition ... It has made me optimistic that these experiences can be explained and demonstrated" (survey response 5). Two storytellers reflected that it was the form of theatre that helped enable their personal experiences to be so clearly expressed, that verbatim theatre is "a great medium for discussion" (survey response 3) and that "the translation of our stories was beautifully done, maintaining the raw emotion but ensuring it was eloquent" (survey response 5). One element of this translation was the choice to embody the condition of Alopecia as a character in the play. This personification of the condition allowed the central character (Violet) to have a tangible relationship with Alopecia, and this theatrical abstraction enabled the frustration, anger, and hurt experienced by the women to be expressed in a way that they described as genuine, truthful, and honest, despite not being a "naturalistic" representation. Translating a feeling, place or thing into something tangible and multifaceted like a character is one way that plays can help make sense of experience for the audience members whose stories were being told, and enabled the complexity of who they are to be communicated to others in an authentic way. Sarah's 2017 article in the journal *Social Alternatives* further discusses the impact of participating in the *bald heads & blue stars* project not only for the women with alopecia, but for the cast and creatives involved in that production as well.

Sarah has continued her research into audience impact in subsequent productions. Audiences who attended the 2019 production of *Blister,* and who had at some time walked a Camino themselves were invited to participate in an anonymous post-show survey about their audience experience. Despite not being as engaged in the entire process (from interview through to performance), the survey responses were similar to those collected after *bald heads & blue stars,* with an emphasis on how valuable it was to see the experience of walking the Camino conveyed authentically and with a complexity resonant of their own lived experience. One walker described *Blister* as "an emotional re-enactment of a time that lives within me. The play became a mirror and conduit back to those experiences, as if they were shared also" (survey response 2), and another that it gave them the opportunity to "re-live my own Camino" (survey response 5). *Blister* also uses the convention of personification through the character Mother Camino, and through the embodiment of Rosie's (the central characters) inner voices as characters in their own right. One walker reflected that this enabled a particularly accurate depiction of the Camino experience where they were, "[q]uestioning yourself about whether you had the capability to complete the task" (survey response 3). This walker further reflected that the play "made the intangible become seen. I have never been able to explain the wrestling with yourself while simultaneously [being] physically challenged".

Martin Welton describes meaning-making by audiences as being a process of feeling, that audiences understand theatre through feeling it emotionally, cognitively, and through touch (Welton 2012, 5). He describes this as "a perceptivity founded on the movements of attention" (6). When watching a live performance the audience is physically present in their bodies and in order to perceive or understand the performance they move in order to get a feel for the show. Welton explains that when "watching or performing theatre, we undertake practices of perception which are founded in certain kinds of movement – of visual or aural attention for example – and in doing so 'get a feel for how it goes'"(3). An audience's embodied experience of the play (which in the case of verbatim theatre, is also *about* embodied experiences) provides the conditions for understanding a play through this felt process. The walkers' reflection that the performance made the intangible become seen and served as an emotional re-enactment could be understood as how they felt the performance. The story of the play is perceived "feelingly", and for the research subjects in both *Blister* and *bald heads & blue stars,* this felt perception is also a reminder or echo of an experience they have lived through personally and felt before. This may contribute to the walkers' sense that their experiences have been explained in a more tangible way than they'd previously achieved, and contribute to understanding how verbatim theatre impacts those who are an audience to their own story (or even to stories similar to our own).

Verbatim theatre and community-engaged practice provides the opportunity to use multiple dramatic languages to convey very real relationships, emotions, and experiences in abstract ways, comprehensively representing them emotionally, cognitively, and aesthetically. This opportunity to have experiences evoked, validated, and understood by others, through the depth and complexity of representation afforded by verbatim theatre, creates the conditions for audiences to participate in a process of belonging. This can occur whether the storyteller is involved from the outset of a verbatim project (such as *bald heads & blue stars*) or shares the same lived experience as that being portrayed (such as *Blister*). This research reminds us how precious the arts are to our sense of self, and that the opportunity we have as artists to express, explore, challenge, critique and be curious about the world can be understood simultaneously as possibility and responsibility. What we do as artists can have far-reaching impacts on the audiences to our work and remind us to continue walking this balance with an ethic of care and understanding.

Principles in Practice

Australian playwright and lawyer Suzie Miller explains that "Because you are in the same room and breathing the same air as the actors as they play out characters, [it] gets under your skin and makes you think differently about things" (Miller qtd in Coade, 51). In response to her play *Cross Sections* (2005), which explores the experiences of homeless clients she has worked with in Kings Cross, Miller reflects that "When the play was put on, it was interesting how many people came up to me and said 'I walked back through the Cross and saw the people on the streets, and had a sense that they could be my sister ... I suddenly saw them as people'" (Miller, qtd in Coade, 51). This impact on the audience's degree of understanding and compassion was a significant contributor in Miller's decision to continue to pursue playwriting.

6.4 The Legacy of Your Work

It is incredibly common to accelerate towards opening night, through a season, and into closing, without really pausing for breath. Before you know it, after months or years of work, the project is over. You've been through a process where you've deliberately immersed yourself in a community and likely formed very tight bonds. Without the impetus of an upcoming performance outcome, what is left to bind you together?

In community-engaged contacts, particularly those with non-actors, the feelings of connection and social health can be incredibly powerful for the participants. This may trigger conversations about the future. Could we stage this again? Could we do it all again? Could we "go professional" and take this show on the road? While enthusiasm of this sort is fantastic (and a sign that you've done a great job!), they should be approached with an open mind. Theatre, by its necessity, is temporary. It is impossible to replicate specific productions and their feeling as if they were products on a conveyor belt. Theatre works, particularly of this sort, are most akin to complex social organisms that are dynamic and adaptable. If the community wants to move forward with another creative project, it is up to the individual playwright how much they would seek to be involved in that new outcome.

> **Principles in Practice**
>
> Matt Scholten reflects on the experience of stepping away from *The Campaign* after it premiered in 2018:
>
> > It's a remarkable thing to have done. Everything about it, the fact that the people whose lived experience we based the story on were happy – and they also were happy for us to sometimes make fun of them or to show the less than attractive side of them as well, the competitive side of them, show their humanity and all the colours of what that means as well. I'm really proud of it. And I'm glad it went on and had other seasons as well. I was asked to direct the other shows in Melbourne and Sydney and I respectfully said 'No', because I thought to myself, 'how am I going to beat this? Am I going to get to dance out into Salamanca place? No'. I had the two other directors very kindly ask for my advice. And I didn't give much advice, because I thought 'you just take it and run with it. Because it's for you now'.

In Australia, for successful verbatim mainstage works, there are two central channels for longevity. The first is touring, which was the case for Dan Evans' and The Good Room's work *I Want To Know What Love Is*, which completed a seven-year run in 2022. The second is through publishing, which is common in works that are suited for a youth and education audience in particular. As schools pick up the scripts and perform their own versions, the playwright is usually very removed. In some instances, the playwright may be invited by the school to give workshops or to watch the final show. Importantly, for better or worse, the playwright has no control over these moments! By publishing the work, either on paper or on stage, the playwright forfeits control of what happens after (for the most part, unless productions deliberately alter the text in ways that are defamatory or break copyright laws).

Five years after closing the original production of *Talking to Brick Walls*, one of the playwrights, Claire Christian, found a clip published online of a school production. She sent the clip to the group chat of the original participants. Claire's work often involves work with youth, and her social media inbox is filled with group chats from projects over the years that occasionally light up with discussion. In this way, the legacy of the work is much more than a script or a show. A community that is bound together by a unique experience, that is able to come together in a matter of seconds, to gather in each other's company.

Verbatim and Community-Engaged Work in Rehearsal and Beyond 163

6.5 Frequently Asked Questions and Post-Show Activities

I really disagree with a choice that an actor or director is making in interpreting the script. What can I do?

It can be especially frustrating for a playwright to hand over control of a script, but it is an essential part of theatre. Theatre is, by its nature, a collaborative art form, and a director and actors must be allowed to bring their artistry and expertise to the table. However, a playwright must also be allowed to bring theirs. As playwrights, we feel naturally attached to our scripts. It is first ideal to attempt to imagine the decision made by directors and actors as not antagonistic to your aims, merely different. By all means, voice your different opinion on the matter, but do so as a suggestion, not a demand. As with any conflict resolution, see if the parties are open to a compromise, and do your best to explain your reasoning behind the concern.

If it is a matter of ethics, or if the playwright feels that decisions by the director and actors openly mock or disparage the interviewees, then the matter should become relatively simple. A brief explanation of the concern should open up a discussion for compromise.

If you're finding your relationship to the director or actors especially antagonistic, take some time away from the rehearsal room. Perhaps organise a meeting external to the rehearsal room, with a stage manager or trusted third party present, to help talk through the main concerns.

An interviewee is really upset with how they were presented in the show. What do I do?

If the season is ongoing, there may be the opportunity to change their portrayal. Call a meeting with the director, stage manager, and producer to discuss. If their complaint has merit, then it certainly behooves the team to try and find a solution as quickly as possible. Their complaint may also come from shock, embarrassment or fear and come from a very instinctive reaction. Take time to talk things over with them. Explain the process of rehearsal and decision-making that led to that portrayal. Hopefully, all parties should leave feeling better after this conversation. If not, attempt to find a solution. If you feel overwhelmed or unable to handle the situation, make sure to ask your producer to step in and begin a conversation with them.

In years of doing this practice and many many hours of study, these cases are extremely rare. While some participants may be uncomfortable with how they are being portrayed, most of the time they understand (because they have been told repeatedly and kept up to date) that it is an artistic process. Being made anonymous in the play can greatly help alleviate most fears.

Post-Show Activity: Capturing Audience Impact

We can often be so obsessed with opening night that we forget about carrying on a conversation with our audience. In community-engaged work, opening night may be an emotional climax, but it is certainly not the completion of the project. Here are a few brief ideas on capturing audience (and participant) impact.

- A brief online survey that can be filled out on a phone via a QR Code that is given to audiences immediately after seeing the show
- A workshop series that takes place any time after the performance, using the script as a starting point to provoke discussion and reflection, or ask audiences to re-stage the work
- Publishing an e-mail address in the program of the work, or making one very visible, and inviting audiences to email with impressions
- Filming the show and publishing a digital copy, organising a screening night for participants and audiences a year later. Use this as an opportunity for all to reflect and discuss the show. What has changed? What hasn't? Is there enough fuel here for a sequel of some kind? Even if we can't stage it, what would we imagine it to be?

Works Cited

Ainsworth, R. *The Entrepreneurial Playwright: A Relational Approach to Marketing Plays in the Regions.* Queensland University of Technology, 2008.
Aston, E. "On Collaboration." *The Cambridge Companion to Caryl Churchill.* Cambridge University Press, 2009, pp. 144–158.
Butler, I. and D. Kois. *The World Only Spins Forward: The Ascent of Angels in America.* Bloomsbury, 2018.
Case Study Data. *Bald Heads & Blue Stars.* Survey responses, 2015
Case Study Data. *Blister.* Survey responses, 2019
Coade, Melissa. "Class Act." *Law Society Journal* 56, 2019, pp. 50–51.
Kaufman, Moises. *The Laramie Project.* Random House, 2001.
Meeks, S., S. Shryock, and R. Vandenbroucke. "Theatre Audience Members' Positive Affect, Belonging, Social Interaction, and Flow Related to 2-Year Well-being." *Innovation in Aging* 2.1, 2018, pp. 122–123. https://doi-org.ezproxy.flinders.edu.au/10.1093/geroni/igy023.450
Meinhof, Ulrike and Dariusz Galasiński. *The Language of Belonging.* Palgrave MacMillan, 2005
Peters, Sarah. *Bald Heads & Blue Stars.* Australian Plays Transform, 2017
Peters, Sarah. "The Impact of Participating in a Verbatim Theatre Process." *Social Alternatives* 36.2, 2017, pp. 32–39.
Peters, Sarah. "Verbatim Theatre and a Dramaturgy of Belonging." *Australasian Drama Studies*, 74, 2019, pp. 39–63.
Valentine, Alana. *Bowerbird: The Art of Making Theatre Drawn from Life.* Currency Press, Sydney, 2018.
Watts, Richard. "Playwright Speaks Out over 'Derogatory Treatment.'" *ArtsHub*, 11 July 2013. Available at: https://www.artshub.com.au/news/news/playwright-speaks-out-over-derogatory-treatment-195979-2308196/
Welton, Martin. *Feeling Theatre.* Palgrave MacMillan, 2012.
Wenger, E. "Communities of Practice and Social Learning Systems: The Career of a Concept." *Social Learning Systems and Communities of Practice*, edited by C. Blackmore, Springer Verlag and the Open University, 2010, pp. 9–18

7 Ethical Practice
Private Lives, Public Stages, and Making Space for Stories

This chapter explores some of the ethical considerations involved when telling stories through performance. A lot of what we discuss here is relevant for any storyteller, performer or theatre maker, however, there is a specific focus on the practices and strategies that we feel are particularly important when using verbatim methodologies or engaging with a community in your storytelling practice. We'll unpack what ethics means in the context of storytelling and how other artists have described their ethics of practice. Woven across every chapter of this book are examples of our ethics in action, and through this final chapter, we wanted to gather some of them together and discuss them explicitly, with a particular emphasis on community immersion, relationship building, and informed consent – as these are practices which occur across the lifespan of a project. We finish the chapter by posing a range of critical questions that you can use to consider your own approach to ethical practice.

7.1 Ethics and an Ethics of Practice

The Oxford dictionary defines ethics as "moral principles that govern a person's behaviour or the conducting of an activity". Ethics are the principles that guide a person's behaviour. Some principles are embedded into our system of laws and actively policed, and some aren't (for example, we can understand that something doesn't have to be "against the law" for us to consider it to be "wrong"). Our personal principles are often informed by our context and our intersectional identities. Our experiences and "different cultures and traditions have generated different approaches and theories to inform the moral life, offering rules and guidance as to what it means to do the right thing and to live well" (Gallagher 17). Tania Cañas discusses how ethics is relational and rather than being one size fits all, it moves "from moment to moment, context to context and project to project" (42). Relational ethics is holistic, looking at "socio-positionality, privilege and power" (42) and Cañas advocates that "a creative project is an opportunity to interrogate, interrupt, disrupt and reconsider existing norms and modes of thinking" (43). In this way, while the field of ethics has much to offer the arts, so too can the arts offer insights and new knowledges to the field of ethics. This can relate to theatre-making in many varied and complex ways. You could consider the ethics of characters and their choices, the ethics of representation, the ethics of telling particular stories, the ethics of asking people in the arts to work for less than minimum wage – the list is endless.

For the purposes of this chapter, we are focusing on the ethics of using verbatim theatre methodologies in community-engaged practice. Put simply, what are the principles that guide your behaviour as an artist in your creative work and the way you work with communities? As James Thompson explains, community-engaged projects often take place "within regions that are marginal to the mainstream" (125). It is always vital to consider the ethics of your creative practice, particularly so when working with communities who may already be marginalised, vulnerable, and underrepresented.

Many artists name and define their own ethics of practice as a way of sharing their approach and thinking with others. Jan Cohen-Cruz outlines a theory of practice called "engaged performance", and we have used her work as a model when defining our own. Cohen-Cruz describes the engaged performance as a dialogue between the social call of a community and the cultural response of an artist, where the overall process "must benefit the people whose lives inform the project, not just promote the artist" (2). Derek Paget emphasises that engaged theatre marks a shift between "generalised political commitment ... to the specificity inherent in theatre of the single issue" (175). This specificity in verbatim theatre is defined by the community of storytellers who participate in the project, combined with the playwright's intent for the play. Cohen-Cruz describes the engaged performance as having "social justice aspirations" (8), "without being dull and pragmatic" (13). The goals of engaged performance are "aesthetic and something else" (11), and we engage with this assertion that you can have multiple aspirations for a work "without compromising either" (12). Cohen-Cruz describes this as reminding actors that they "can walk and whistle at the same time" (12).

A further model is Callaghan's coining of the phrase "aesthetics of marginality" (262). Rather than use the term feminist aesthetics, Callaghan posits that aesthetics of marginality "designates that intractable space between politics and aesthetics and denotes the liminality of the theatrical space itself, the osmotic membrane between text and performance" (262). Callaghan uses the practice of Joan Littlewood and Buzz Goodbody as examples and outlines that Littlewood's aesthetics of marginality included collaboration, a focus on the form as much as the content, emphasis on physical and vocal expression, altering genre conventions, viewing theatre as a catalyst for action and a space to create social and political awareness (268). You can see in these two examples that when artists define their ethics of practice there is always a combination of values/principles and practical strategies. Ethics of practice in a creative context is all about action and creativity, and finding the liminal porosity between a principle and its manifestation in the creative work.

In *Creating Verbatim Theatre From Oral Histories* Clare Summerskill provides "Guidelines for Working Ethically in Verbatim Theatre Processes" (47). Summerskill acknowledges that across the literature on verbatim theatre, there is engagement with the possible tension between ethical practice and artistic licence, and that artists often speak about their work being guided "more by their own individual moral compasses than by an external rules or law" (46). She advocates for artists informing their practice by Oral Histories disciplinary ethics, suggesting the following as a potential framework:

1 Identify the agenda of the playwright and the aims of the production
2 Identify power dynamics between the theatre makers and the narrators
3 Secure informed consent from narrators
4 Endeavour to increase the narrators level of agency during the production process
5 Make ethical decisions about the naming of the narrators in the script
6 Demonstrate sensitivity and respect for narrators in their theatrical representation – particularly those who come from marginalised or vulnerable communities (47)

We include this here as a further example of how artists and academics strive to think about, explain and share their moral principles and ethics of practice. There is porosity between the three examples provided here and the theory of ethical practice that we want to share with you, and we hope that by offering up this collection of approaches there will be something that resonates and usefully speaks to you.

Representing a Community, or a Theme?

Importantly, the ethical framework that is applied to individual works is reliant on the context of those works. In considering your own ethical practice for a project, it is important to first consider your own values and intentions in creating the work, as we discussed at the very beginning of this process in chapter two. An intention to accurately represent a community demands a level of rigour of ethical consideration that is different to a work based on anonymous responses to a theme, for example. In the former, a playwright is tasked with reflecting the essence of a particular community. There will already be existing "official" accounts of this community, and the playwright will construct their work in knowledge of those pre-existing accounts. In the latter, a playwright is able to interpret the gathered data by themselves. They are the only ones with the viewpoint on this particular set of data, and so have more broad permissions to interpret it as they wish. This was true for Dan Evans and The Good Room's work in building productions based on themes of regret, love or forgiveness. It is also true for Claire Christian's work in classrooms and educational settings, using data submitted anonymously in response to a theme. When Campion

Decent was tasked with writing about bushfire survivors, or Sarah Peters wrote about the alopecia community, or David Burton wrote about a specific First Nations community, there was less room for their own individual artistic interpretation.

> **Principles in Practice**
>
> Matt Scholten reflects on his and Campion Decent's intentions for *The Campaign:*
>
> We were determined that we would tell the truth, whatever that means. And the truth, being I guess that we would give the characters that might be considered heroic, we wouldn't consider them heroic, we would consider everybody to be human. And, you know, we're all human. As humans, all we are trying to do is avoid pain and suffering all of our lives. I understand that very deeply. But we were determined that we would make sure that all the voices were heard and the voices that some would probably consider to be negative voices, we still made sure that they were heard because you can't just hero worship someone like Rodney or Nick or Lee-Gwen, or Robert or anyone, you can't just do that, because then it just becomes a self-aggrandizing act. It's not really theatre, there's no conflict. You have to hear from everybody. You have to hear from the people who you have things in common with and who you would normally gravitate toward ... But also you have to hear from the hate, you have to hear the hate, you have to hear the anger and the vilification of these people, because unless you hear those voice you don't understand. You don't understand what they're up against.

7.2 Developing a Theory of Ethical Practice: Engaged Verbatim Theatre Praxis

We have taken up Cohen-Cruz's call that "practices that share a similar impulse" should "claim kinship" (9). We seek to honour this space between principles and practice, and we name and define our ethics of practice as Engaged Verbatim Theatre Praxis.

Engaged Verbatim Theatre Praxis is a decision to practice and create theatre inspired by a community's verbal stories in a way that:

1 Values listening to and sharing personal experiences and community stories so that people are heard, visible, and empowered through connection, relationship, and community

2 Embraces collaboration, dialogue, and experimentation with theatrical languages and conventions throughout the process of development to create innovative, engaging, and theatrically dynamic performance
3 Challenges normative and oppressive politics and policies, broadening our consciousness and transforming our understanding of the human and non-human world

It is crucial to emphasise that this theory of practice, like most verbatim theatre practice, is one of potential. The following statement by Deirdre Heddon most significantly captures the infinite balancing act inherent in a practice grounded in potential:

> I recognise its potential to also do harm or to fail in its politically aspirational or transformational objectives. This is precisely the liminal quality heralded by the word 'potential' – it can always go both ways. Some performances might well 'fail' to communicate, or 'fail' to move us, teach us, inspire us, challenge us. Some might prescribe to essentialist notions of self and identity, thereby further repressing or constraining us. Some might speak 'for', rather than 'as', while others might be appropriated in unexpected ways or might appropriate other's stories in inappropriate ways. Some performances might use the politics of the personal in a less sincere way, recognising that 'the personal' functions as a useful marketing tool in today's culture where the personal is a popular and cheaply manufactured commodity. In acknowledging the potential of autobiographical performance, we need also to acknowledge the dangers. Though I am an advocate, I am not a naïve one. (7)

In chapter one, we referred to a number of theoretical frameworks which we have found useful to develop our thinking around ethical practice: critical theory and critical pedagogy, feminist theatre practice, and ethics of care. In this next section of the chapter, we want to take you on a deep dive into these frameworks – both as an opportunity to get you thinking about how our ways of understanding the world directly inform the way we create art and tell stories, and also as a potential starting point from which you can begin to articulate your own theory of practice.

Critical Theory and Critical Pedagogy

Critical theorists perceive that there are different kinds of knowledge and different ways of knowing (How 116). Crucially, these knowledges are dependent on products of historical, geographical, and social context. It is a theory based on speculation, that we do not "dogmatically accept" perceived given circumstances (3) but rather understand that what constitutes "truth" is dependent on a person or communities experiences, discourses, and context. Therefore, seeking to know and understand the context of others enables a broader understanding of knowledge, reason, and the multiplicities of truth (6). Broadening "the horizon of our understandings" (120) teaches us not only about others but makes our knowledge of self simultaneously more comprehensive. Critical theory promotes engagement with opposing ideas (or conflicting understandings) "in hopes of finding a third position that embraces, but also transcends both" (185). This echoes Hegel's theory of dialectics and is also evident in Anderson and Wilkinson's assertion that verbatim theatre embraces the intellectual and the emotional, creating a synthesis that transcends both in order to "empathetically inform and empower through authentic story" (156). The verbatim theatre process involves communication with a community and on behalf of that community, and it is this aspect of the process that aligns verbatim theatre practice to the critical theory framework. As Agger states "communication provides an ethical base for critical theory" (94) particularly when that communication is a dialogue based on respect. Through respectful communication with others, we are able to broaden our understanding of the multiple ways in which people understand the world, and as community-engaged practices often embrace a broad cross-section of experiences, identities, and perspectives, this process has heightened potential to generate opportunities for that understanding to take place.

Critical pedagogy is one application of critical theory in systems of education and learning. Joan Wink defines the dialogue of critical pedagogy as:

> talk that changes us or our context ... Dialogue is two-way interactive visiting. Dialogue involves periods of lots of noise as people share and lots of silence as people muse. Dialogue is communication that creates and recreates multiple understandings. (41)

This is an intent we hold for the dialogue in our practice as theatre artists and community-engaged practitioners. In the critical theory paradigm, selves are products of their societal context. So therefore it follows that understanding other contexts enables a greater understanding of other individuals. Kanpol describes it as being "entwined", that self and society are "intimately related" (94). Verbatim theatre enables engagement with other societal contexts. First for the artist in the process of community immersion, and secondly for the public audience when the voices of people from those "other places" are dramatically presented in a public way. Just as Kincheloe suggests "a complex critical pedagogy is always searching for new voices that may have been excluded by the dominant culture" (24), Heddon argues that verbatim theatre enables the marginalised voice to "literally take centre stage" (3). Audiences engage with those voices through performance and are given the opportunity to "feel the other's position in life" (Kanpol 94). Burbules and Berk outline that the "primary preoccupation of critical pedagogy is with social injustice and how to transform inequitable, undemocratic or oppressive institutions and social relations" (47). Just as the values of critical pedagogy are evident in

Heddon's assertions around her intents for verbatim theatre, we also acknowledge the discourse of critical pedagogy in our intent. We aim to share kinaesthetically in the stories of others and thereby begin to construct a knowledge of other communities and identities, critically engage with social injustice, and potentially, broaden an audience's understanding of self.

The values of critical pedagogy are also evident in some of our processes of verbatim theatre. Wink outlines a process for critical pedagogy that involves learning, unlearning, and relearning (18). The learning occurs as part of our context, it is what Kristeva described as our chora: "the Greek word for space, place [and] locality" (Ziarek 328). Kristeva argues that our experiences of chora are how our bodies become embedded with cultural constructs: family and social structures. The learning of our chora forms the lens through which we see and understand the world. Wink's "unlearning" refers to the broadening of our horizons, it involves "a shift in philosophy, beliefs and assumptions" (19). A shift instigated through the process of speculation and one that challenges "what currently passe[s] for reason and extend[s] it into something more comprehensive" (How 6). This challenge and extension occurs through engagement with or exposure to difference. Often classified as the "other", interaction with this difference provides opportunities for us to reflect on our own context and understandings. Wink acknowledges that unlearning can be a challenging and traumatic experience that takes the subject on a journey through defiance, confusion, and doubt as they consider the nature and content of their knowledge. However, at the other end of the journey is the opportunity to "see beyond" (Wink 25), or in terms of critical theory, to "transcend" (How 185) what we thought we knew and expand our understanding to something more comprehensive.

Learning, unlearning, and relearning in the field of theatre practice occurs through praxis, a way of working that bridges the gap between theory and practice (Taylor 5). Verbatim theatre is an example of praxis as it bridges the *thinking* to the *doing*. This occurs on a number of levels. On the macro level when groups are interviewed in a verbatim theatre process they are thinking about their experiences. They are remembering, naming, and representing stories, ideas, and discourses through verbal and physical communication. The playwright then bridges the gap to the *doing:* they creatively shape this thinking into a practical act through the artistic process of scripting and writing stories into performance. Verbatim theatre, therefore, combines theory and practice in a macro sense. On a micro level, the continual dialogue between the interviewer and interviewed, and then later actor and director or between collaborators provides opportunities for continual reflection on and improvement of practice (Taylor 107). Each party in the dialogue is given the opportunity to voice concerns, successes, interpretations, and revelations. These voicings then inform, stimulate and provide impulse for improved practice. Dialogue, discussion, and interviewing are practice, and at the same time are theorising. Throughout the interview, the verbatim theatre artist is simultaneously *thinking about* as they listen for the theatrical potential in a

172 *Ethical Practice*

story and *doing* as they play the role of the interviewer and the practice this involves. At all times throughout the interview, playbuilding, and performance process, the playwright and other theatre artists can be enacting praxis, the constant incorporation of critical reflection on active doing.

The transformative power of praxis when viewed on this individual level has been articulated by Peter Abbs through his description of the five phases of art making.

The five phases begin with an impulse. This impulse is akin to an idea, a flash of energy, a "desire for an image" (Abbs 199) that comes from our contextual imaginings. The artist then pursues this impulse through engaging with a particular medium. This medium will have its own rules, "its own inner propensities, its own laws, its own history. It allows and forbids ... the impulse can be lost in the material or ... taken to an expected consummation" (Abbs 200). Abbs describes this phase as the most problematic as it involves taking a personal, contextual, and inner idea and then wrestling with the requirements of a medium in order to express that idea in a public way. It is the binary of form and content that Kaufman and Valentine describe experimenting within their work. The artist begins their reflective practice in this phase as they critically question whether or not their chosen medium is enhancing their initial impulse or limiting it. As the artist enters the third phase, the realization of final form, they begin to "discard, to select, to consider, to evaluate" (Abbs 201). These decisions are made by frequently consulting with the expected audience, either imagined or real: "it is as if a continuous inner dialogue is taking place between the artist and critic, between the creative subject and the sympathetic onlooker" (Abbs 202). Valentine described presenting readings of *Parramatta Girls* throughout her process in order to clearly shape the work and make decisions about its further development after hearing feedback from the storytellers and invited audience.

Abbs describes art as a public category, requiring communication with and recognition by community. This is the presentation or performance phase of art making, however, this is not the end of the process as the audience is "an essential part of the art-making" (Abbs 203). Their responses, combined with the critical reflection of the artist themselves, provides the platform for the next artistic impulse. The whole experience of art-making contributes to an artist's cultural context, so each experience broadens this context and influences the next work. In this model, all impulses can inspire the possibility of a new idea. Critical theory and critical pedagogy are built on the foundation of the possibility of transformation, which is expressed in practice through the concept of praxis.

Feminist Theatre Practice

Elaine Aston, Sue-Ellen Case, and Lizbeth Goodman each provide extensive overviews of the development of feminist theatre practice: its history, political agenda, and innovative expression of content through the form. Goodman asserts that not all women's writing is feminist, "feminist theatre is defined by its politics (feminism) rather than by its form (theatre)" (*Comic Subversions*

243). This is a crucial distinction and one we have considered in our own practice. Feminist theatre has a certain political agenda and those politics also translate into certain ways of working. "A Theatre offers possibility for feminist intervention on a number of levels" (Laughlin and Schuler 18), and it is these interventions that are demonstrative of a theory of practice. The politics of feminism is generally grouped into what Aston describes as "the three dominant feminist positions" (*An Introduction* 8): bourgeois, radical, and materialist (although these positions have been titled differently across the literature). Case outlines that feminist theatre practice situated within a materialist position is "built on mutuality and inter-subjectivity", operating by enactment and engaged dialogue and rooted in everyday life (46). This description echoes Stuart Fisher's depiction of the verbatim theatre process as one built on reciprocity: that the community of storytellers choose to be involved in the project and are engaged throughout the process.

Feminist activist and author bell hooks outlines the feminist movement as occurring "when groups of people come together with an organized strategy to take action" to eliminate any form of oppression, dominance or hierarchy (xi). Ackerly describes this organised strategy as "collective action" (2) and suggests it is a hallmark of feminist theatre practice, with a focus on collectively speaking and sharing in an effort to "make an otherwise insecure environment one in which [...] voices are heard" (3). Specifically, Ackerly asserts that these voices can be everyday people in everyday places (5). This valuing of lived experience and community story links feminist theatre practice to the hopefulness of verbatim theatre outlined by Dolan who suggests verbatim theatre makes unique connections between both individuals and ideas. She states verbatim theatre attempts "to create a 'we'" (*The Laramie Project* 114), a community of people "who might not otherwise have spoken to each other" (113). Our projects exemplify the collective action of everyday people, as the storytellers volunteer to be involved in the project and to voice their individual experiences to benefit and share with the broader community. Verbatim theatre and feminist theatre practice enables a collective space for this sharing, a platform for a multitude of listeners. Verbatim theatre influenced by feminist theatre practice is a "theatre which aims to achieve positive re-evaluation ... and/or to effect social change" (Goodman *Contemporary Feminist Theatres* 37) and thereby enabling performance to "be a transformational act" (Heddon 3).

Heddon and Goodman both include consciousness-raising as being a key outcome of feminist theatre practice, and Joan Scott outlines that this often occurs through the evidence of experience. This experience becomes visible through others seeing, and in the context of feminist theatre practice, through the specific seeing of the audience. Scott finds the use of experience as evidence problematic: that making visible the experiences of others is not enough to raise the consciousness of an audience or community as the experience does not speak for itself (83). Rather, making visible the "inner workings or logics" of the experience, and asking how the experience was constructed (83) then allows for a critique of normative experience and the raising of consciousness. Scott argues that "what counts as experience is neither self-evident nor straightforward: it is always contested, and always, therefore, political" (96). She states that analysis and critical viewing of experience can become the work of the artist or playwright. Rather than allowing words and experiences to speak for themselves, the practitioner's aesthetic mediation or "massaging" (to use Valentine's phrase) of the material enables a critique of those words through artistic juxtaposition, staging, and editing. Making the ideology visible and highlighting the inner workings and contested nature of experience can form part of the artistry of the verbatim theatre practitioner and also parallels the consciousness-raising and social change agenda of feminist theatre practice. Dolan states that:

> feminism at this historical moment seems caught between reifying experience as truth, and proclaiming that although experience does dictate a certain material reality, it is a reality necessarily constructed in relation to social ideology and cannot be the basis of any fixed objective truth.
>
> (*In Defence of the Discourse* 96)

In developing our own theory of ethical practice, critical theory and critical pedagogy have been influenced by a feminist theatre practice, which by its very nature challenges and questions pre-conceptions of reality. The very notion, then, that verbatim theatre is somehow more "real" because of its use of verbatim material is tantalizing. Part of the appeal of the form may be that an audience feels as if they will finally see some "truth", but of course, the playwright knows they will witness a multiplicity of truths. This complex negotiation of truth and dramatic license is bound by an ethics of care.

Principles in Practice

Claire Christian strongly identifies with a feminist theatre practice, and sees it as fundamental to her working ethical framework.

> I don't think you can make great theatre unless the people in the room feel safe. And I think we have an inherent culture, in our sector, where we have top down structures, and have spaces where people do not feel heard and safe at all. So for me as a community arts maker, that's number one. People feel safe. I think it makes better art. If you feel safe, you'll be vulnerable, you'll show up authentically, and you'll take more risks.

Thus, the playwright or facilitator's chief concern is often simply about creating a space that allows for safe and vulnerable exploration or discussion of themes and ideas.

Ethics of Care

A feminist ethics of care is "a way of thinking about politics, social practices and the everyday-life considerations of people in diverse circumstances" (Barnes et al. 233) which actively considers the relationship between values, actions, and systems in order to critique and transform policy and practice. Hankivsky defines an ethic of care as contextualising the human condition, sensitively responding to individual differences, considering the consequences of specific actions and decisions, and "opens new ways for understanding experiences of discrimination, suffering and oppression" (2). In addition, Simola *et al.*, emphasise that an ethic of care means that rather than managing the needs of a group on a hierarchical basis, "a care orientation would focus on identifying creative ways of simultaneously fulfilling competing responsibilities to others" (181). This acknowledgement that often we can be drawn in multiple directions (or have competing responsibilities) and yet can still approach our practice with a mindfulness for others and ourselves, a mindfulness-based in a caring consideration for the project/community/context as a whole, is one of the ways ethics of care informs our Engaged Verbatim Theatre Praxis.

Central to an ethics of care is the imperative to take the time needed for meaningful connection and thoughtful creation. Maggie Berg and Barbara Seeber state that slowing down "is about allowing room for others and otherness" (59) and so the act of taking time, of prioritising connectedness and reflection, of making space across time for the messiness of life, is in their view an ethical choice. In *Slow Ethics and the Art of Care* Ann Gallagher describes slow ethics as an approach that is "slow and sustainable, rather than fast and short-termist" where part of the intent is to "promote flourishing in humans and non-humans" (3). Gallagher outlines the six elements of slow ethics as sensitivity, solidarity, space, sustainability, scholarship, and stories. Along the lines of our earlier reflection that people who propose an ethics of practice often do so through a combination of principles and actions, Gallagher outlines some of the ways that slow ethics might be implemented, that it requires you to "listen carefully and judge slowly", to "pause, balance, breathe, laugh and listen", to endeavour to "be kind to others and to ourselves – considering ourselves and others with a just and loving eye", and to understand that slowness is "not just about pace but about giving other humans, other species, our environment, and artefacts our full attention as far as possible" (12). We hope that our approach to community immersion discussed in chapter two echoes this focused attention, kind consideration, and making room for others and otherness.

Principles in Practice

In some community-engaged practices, a duty of care and ethical protocols are already built into the environment. Such is the case for schools, where teaching artists have a very clear duty of care for participants. Claire Christian often invites anonymous submissions from students as a means to trigger stimulus for themes, characters or scenes. Importantly, however, she reviews all submitted material first.

"As teachers we have a duty of care to the participants to keep them safe", Claire says. "So if there was content that we couldn't navigate or handle in a manner that was consensual and supported, or student felt like they may trigger other students, than that material is not used in the classroom". Considering the intended audience and acting ensemble is critical for this analysis as well. If, in devising, a topic surfaces that Claire feels as though the maturity of the performers, within the time limits, could not address properly, then it is put to one side.

7.3 Authenticity and Ethics

In a community-engaged project, you are often working with people about their lived experiences – stories and experiences that are "actual" or "true" for them. A large portion of the field of literature on verbatim theatre focuses on this concept of what is true or real, particularly in the highly constructed space of theatre and performance. It would be remiss of us not to address this conversation in some capacity – yet we are mindful to assert that this is by no means an exhaustive engagement with these ideas. If this discussion ignites a spark for you, we encourage you to follow up on the readings referenced in this section.

Manipulating the Truth or Creating Fictional Authenticity?

Reverberating across the field is an engagement by scholars with the theme of reality and truth. Professional practice mirrors this debate, where notions of authenticity become confounding in the writing, editing, and rehearsal of verbatim theatre works. The questions that result are fundamental to the form. Just how *verbatim* does a work have to be for it to be verbatim? Can a scene or character be faithful to the *spirit* of an interview while not necessarily replicating it? When does an artists' interpretation of an event become an unfair or unethical imposition? These questions are doubly crucial for community-engaged practice, where artists and communities collide in an artistic space, where truth is negotiable and often messy.

Principles in Practice

Suzie Miller adds a further layer of reflection in this space, which has come from her background as a lawyer. She questions how it is possible to decipher when clients are being honest and telling the truth in their

> accounts of events. Reflecting on the interviews and research she conducted for *Transparency,* Miller shares:
>
> I had nightmares for weeks about some of the details I was told, all told quite matter-of-factly, by these young men in prison. I was shaken when later I realized some stories I was told, and had fully believed, were entirely fabricated. Others I felt had not told me the story to their best advantage, and when I read their files and case reports I was afraid that they had missed a few opportunities for defence ... What part do we all play in covering up truths and lies? Is there ever any objective truth when we construct narrative about our own memories to make them more savoury to ourselves?
>
> (81–83)
>
> In a similar vein, Valentine reminds us that "when you are using verbatim material you cannot forget first rule of dramatic characterisation on stage – don't believe what a character says, look at their actions. In theatre, just like in life, what people say isn't always what they do (or don't do)". (64).

Cantrell describes this central theme from the scholarly field as "questions of authenticity" and is one of many scholars who interrogates the relationship between the testimony documented from storytellers and the resulting performance (*Acting in Documentary Theatre* 4). There are two main perspectives. Firstly, in verbatim theatre (and other forms of documentary performance), there is material collected from lived experiences and events that maintains its status as "real" when incorporated into a production. It infers a quality of "truth" on this material. This data exists alongside material specifically developed for the performance. This first perspective approaches the playwright's role as one of shaping, editing, and weaving the "real" and created material into a script that tells, to varying degrees, "true" stories. This perspective emphasises a hybridised reading of a performative text: some material is "verbatim", while other material is "created". However, the second perspective suggests that all material in verbatim theatre *is* essentially created material, and collaboration and engagement with communities and lived experiences creates authenticity in the performance of that material. This perspective posits that replicating the "truth" onstage is impossible, but stories can achieve a quality of "authenticity" through performance.

The first perspective, which implies a quality of unshakable truth in dialogue derived from interviews, opens up discussions about reflexivity. In the act of script creation, to what extent should real/true material be explicitly differentiated from created material? Is such a differentiation for the audience's benefit to prevent manipulation in their reception of the story? Is such a thing even possible? A playwright or director may make this difference

178 *Ethical Practice*

obvious by sign-posting "real" moments in many ways. This may be through a clear staging delineation or by the establishment of a meta-dramatic framework, allowing actors to speak directly to the audience ("This next bit you're about to see is from an interview …").

The second perspective eliminates this debate, positioning all material as fictional and removing all notions of universal or essential truth. It enables discussions on the value of fictionalising experience to more effectively convey an authentic representation of that experience and the artistic practice of verbatim theatre. It's worth looking at both of these perspectives to introduce ourselves to some of the ethics that underlie verbatim theatre methodologies and community-engaged practice. Thus, this section explores both of the perspectives mentioned above, and their practical applications for artists.

"Real" Material in Performance

Proponents of the first perspective advocate that the "real" material in a performance should be marked as such to enable the audience to better differentiate between the facts and the created material in a play (Luckhurst; Duggan). Luckhurst suggests that the "lack of clear sources in some verbatim plays is an ethical issue" (214). She praises Alecky Blythe's headphone verbatim practice, where the actors listen to recorded verbatim stories through headphones while performing, clearly foregrounding the source of the play's verbatim material. Luckhurst also applauds the work of Tanika Gupta in *Gladiator Games* (2006), which notes specifically the source for dialogue on the script itself and states that anything unmarked is a dramatization. Luckhurst applauds this as an "interesting model of notation for verbatim plays which incorporate invented material" (214), implying similarly to Duggan that the verbatim material is un-invented or "real".

Luckhurst does acknowledge that verbatim theatre "like other documentary forms, is always stretched on the rack between a pursuit of "facts" – a loaded word in its own right – and an engagement with artistic representation" (203). This has led to a debate over reflexivity in verbatim theatre and has become "one of the more contentious issues" within the field (Megson 531). Particularly "the extent to which processes of theatrical mediation should be acknowledged reflexively within the verbatim performance itself" (531). Bottoms argues that to prevent a disingenuous presentation of truth, theatrical self-referentiality is "precisely what is required of documentary plays if they are to acknowledge their dual and thus ambiguous status as both 'document' and 'play'" (57). Bottoms uses Moisés Kaufman as an exemplar of reflexivity, describing Kaufman's *Gross Indecency* (1997) as an example of a work that constantly reminds the audience where and when a verbatim text originated through the vocal captioning of the actors. Bottoms advocates that "such performances need to foreground their own processes of representation" (61) and expresses a desire for this reflexivity in performance as a reminder to the audience that "this story is being mediated: that what is being presented is not simple truth" (62). He argues that while many verbatim theatre performances (in London specifically) are "worryingly un-reflexive" (67) in *Gross Indecency* Kaufman encourages his audience to think, not only about the content but about how all information is shaped and delivered for a specific purpose.

We can see some exemplars of this approach in some of our own case studies. In *April's Fool*, for example, *all* dialogue is sourced from verbatim sources, except where an actor is interrupting that dialogue to caption it, or to narrate the story more generally:

ARI: I knew it was a music festival so I knew Kristjan and his friends would be drinking, possibly taking drugs.
ACTOR: Ari, Kris' little brother, now 15.
ARI: But um, yeah I didn't know it what music festival it was, but it was a big one.

Thus, the script constantly interrupts the theatrical machinery of actors, lighting, and sound to remind the audience that the dialogue is "real".

But such mechanisms for sign-posting "truth" to an audience are open to critique. The most prominent artistic critique may be that this approach to conserving "truth" can eschew the theatrical imagination. It's in this quest to preserve and identify accuracy that verbatim theatre may get a bad wrap. Those un-initiated in the possibilities of the form might only think of it as actors standing still and reciting lines with minimal design or production intrusion. This view is reflected in Barnett's "The Poverty of Verbatim Theatre", where he argues that the "wonderful riches of imaginative theatre production are rejected, or perhaps simply ignored, in the name of reproducing 'the truth'" (19). There is a prevailing assumption here that all artists universally approach verbatim theatre as a vehicle for truth or with rhetoric of "meticulousness" (Frieze 153). However, Young does acknowledge that some playwrights "often informed by feminist and queer theory ... endeavour to interrogate and subvert strategies of documentation ... thereby destabilising notions of truth and reality" (73).

In contrast to the reflexivity advocated by Bottoms, Botham contends that the verbatim theatre process inherently promotes an "intersubjective version of the truth" (*From Deconstruction to Reconstruction* 307). She argues that while "a greater degree of reflexivity might improve verbatim drama's ethical/political aspirations" (316) one of the form's strengths is its inclusion of both information (through verbatim material) and deliberation (through the artistic voice of the playwright), without "relinquishing its artistic character" (317). It is precisely verbatim theatre's potential lack of deconstruction that positions it as a form that promotes inter-subjectivity by emphasising the diverse experiences of a community or event. The very process of verbatim theatre engages with various expressions of experience and identity, therefore reflexively questioning the notion of "truth". In community-engaged practice in particular, verbatim theatre methodologies can be used to place multiple "truths" onstage, de-stabilising how a community sees itself and opening up opportunities for learning and greater engagement. For many artists, this is the entire point of the form.

Authenticity in Performance

Amanda Stuart-Fisher is at the forefront of the second perspective within the academic field. Her alignment of verbatim theatre with testimonial theatre instead of the documentary is a critical differentiation that frames her engagement with the theme of "truth". Stuart-Fisher argues that the intention to tell a community's story (as opposed to using elements of their story as research for a separate narrative) "engages the writer in an ethical contract with those offering up their life experiences". For Stuart-Fisher, these subjects "should have some agency within the process" (*That's Who I'd be* 197). Rather than making claims to truth, Stuart-Fisher suggests verbatim theatre conducted in this way shares "subjective encounter[s] with an event or a situation" (197) to authentically tell stories of "personal perspectives and life experiences" (197). Rather than equating authenticity with "standard conceptions of truth", we should instead "consider a more existentially nuanced articulation of truth grasped as 'authenticity'" (*Trauma, Authenticity* 112). A dramaturgy that "is less concerned with factual truth and instead embraces the poetic and the metaphoric" (115) as well as collaboration with and commitment to a community, enables a greater authenticity in the performance. There are clear examples of embracing the poetic and the metaphoric across the case studies discussed in this text, such as in *St Mary's in Exile, Blister, Eternity,* and the QMF Community Signature works.

This position is echoed by Waters, a British playwright who argues that the "genuflection to journalism" (140) evident in much British verbatim theatre is merely an observation that does little to investigate or explore events and experiences. Waters critiques what he perceives to be a general approach by artists to allow stories to speak for themselves as this "merely reveals the surface of actuality and rarely penetrates into the secret recesses of experience" (139). Waters and Stuart-Fisher suggest poetic and metaphoric shaping of verbatim material can provide closer authenticity to lived experience than a word-for-word dramaturgy. This poetic or metaphorical shaping of material *is* a reflexive intervention that emphasises "the process of writing ... [and] highlights the issue of the relationship between representation and reality" (Young 75). Young suggests that failing to theatricalise verbatim material manipulates audiences into receiving the work as fact and may result in outcomes that "collude with the mechanisms of injustice which they seek to expose" (86).

We agree that the question of "truth" should not form the ground of verbatim theatre's critique. However, it is an ethical and dramaturgical consideration that is at the core of much community-engaged practice and verbatim theatre-making. In an Australian context, verbatim theatre is consistently discussed within a framework of authenticity. Valentine shifts the notion away from authentically representing reality and suggests authenticity relates to the language of a community in performance, to the rhythm and patterns of speech specific to an individual or community. This idea is something which, again, many of the case studies in this book exemplify.

Similarly, Paget's 2008 discussion of verbatim theatre suggests that it focuses on "the sinewy language that often emerges from testimony" (132). Anderson and Wilkinson explain that people's voices and their vernacular link to place, and texts resulting from these voices "inspire relatedness and identity" (157). This relatedness is what Anderson and Wilkinson and fellow Australian academic David Watt propose lend verbatim theatre credibility and authenticity, not the prescriptive recounting of transcribed word-for-word or signposting of sources.

Australian playwright Damien Millar, author of *The Modern International Dead* (2008), explains the authenticity of his work in terms of actuality: "all of these events happened. But it is a play and should not be mistaken for a work of history or objective journalism" (i). Campion Decent describes this creative process as a synthesis between conceiving ideas, collecting material, and collating stories (6). These playwrights acknowledge that their works build on recognisable material, whether that be the language, lexicon, event or experience, however, they work from the position that they are artists, and the work they create is theatrically fictionalised. The playwrights mentioned here are well-established Australian artists, who have each arrived, somewhat accidentally, at a consensus on verbatim theatre's problematic relationship with the truth, or to be more precise, how the *playwright* relates to their data. These playwrights interpret, emphasise, and connect the community that is the subject of their work. To do this without veering into exploitation, is where reflecting on our principles and ethics of practice, and holding ourselves to the highest standards of integrity, courage and care, is vital.

7.4 Consent, Permission, Celebration, and Care – EVTP in Action

Engaged Verbatim Theatre Praxis is the set of principles which guide our behaviour and ways of working. We have sought to make connections to this ethics of practice in each chapter, highlighting how these principles inform the decision to act in a particular way during a particular juncture in a project. However, there are some practices that are ongoing and take place across the duration of a community-engaged project, such as community immersion, continued communication and relationship building. These are the practices we want to focus on in this section of the chapter.

Community Immersion and Being Invited to Continue

Community immersion is a practice that acknowledges the importance of time, presence, and care, and gives you the space to build meaningful

Ethical Practice

relationships. We gave examples of some of the different approaches we've taken to community immersion in chapter two, as well as a guide for practice:

Community Immersion

1 Contact peak bodies, media outlets and support services connected to the community
2 Engage in activities that serve the goals of the community
3 Have conversations with the community
4 Provide creative service to the community
5 Maintain connection with the community
6 Ensure accessibility to the project outcomes

In this section, we want to take the opportunity to reiterate the ethical principles underpinning community immersion and further discuss how a community might be invited to participate in a project and, conversely, an artist might be invited to continue their collaboration with a community. In *The Relationship is the Project* Jade Lilie describes community-engaged practice as "a deep collaboration between practitioners and communities to develop outcomes specific to that relationship, time and place" (9). In Lillie's introduction to the book, she outlines a series of considerations that artists should make when choosing to work in a community-engaged way. First up, invitation. She states "you don't have to wait for an invitation to start talking about a project, but it is very important that you are invited to continue" (11). In some projects, this invitation process might occur between the artist and an organisation. This was the case with Sarah's *Time* project, where she met with the managers of a residential care facility and the project only continued after they invited Sarah to return and to facilitate a series of storytelling workshops with the residents. In other projects this invitation occurs on the individual level, and while some members of a community might not wish to continue with a project, others will.

Research and design are the next two steps in Lillie's approach. What other projects have taken place in this context before and what can you learn from them? When designing the project you might choose to co-design it with the community or design it yourself and take it to the community for input. "Both ways are appropriate at different times – it really depends on the context" (11). Be flexible and prepared for change in the delivery of the project, and while the final outcome might not be known from the outset, make sure the project has the time it needs and is something "that everyone can be proud of" (12). Finally, celebrate the project and factor in time for reflection with all of the stakeholders, making sure to "leave the door open for the next conversation" (13).

Meaningfully Informed Consent

It is a crucial aspect of our ethical practice that people are informed (meaningfully – cognitively and emotionally) about the project, and that communities are invited to participate but in no way pressured or forced to do so. Australian playwright Alana Valentine describes it as being "strategically responsible even to people who think they will be fine" (59). She explains that this is where having a chain of connection between your participants can be useful, as it means that each person you're interviewing or involving in the project knows of someone else who they can talk about their participation with. While we have a responsibility to the creative work nothing is more important than the physical and psychological safety of the communities you work with and the play is not more important than the wellbeing of another person (Valentine 60).

Promoting a project (using the mediums relevant to your community) and inviting participants to get in touch with you is an excellent way to ensure that individuals are exercising their own agency in being involved. You can then provide as much information as possible about the intent and focus of the project so that participants understand what is being asked of them, how their stories and words might be used in the resulting creative work, and what they can expect of you as the leader of the project. If they still choose to participate they are doing so in an informed way, and have the opportunity to voluntarily give their consent.

In Sarah's *Verbatim Theatre and Healthy Ageing* project a promotional blurb about the project was shared in a variety of aged care service newsletters and on social media platforms. This blurb was a brief synopsis of the project and invited people to get in touch with a member of the project team for further information. Below is an example of what this further information might include, demonstrating the breadth and depth of information that could be communicated to your participants:

Description of the study

This project uses interviews, workshops and surveys to research the experience of receiving and providing aged care support services. These experiences will inform the writing and performance of a play and other modes of digital storytelling that share the experience of transitioning into aged care.

Purpose of the study

This project seeks to research the lived experience of ageing and transitioning into aged care from the perspective of people accessing aged care support services, the carers and families of those transitioning into aged care, and staff members who provide aged care services. It will then present this research through a work of theatre and other digital storytelling mediums with participants invited to engage with the creative development of this work, and share their response to viewing the creative work.

Participant involvement and potential risks

If you agree to participate in the project you will be invited to participate in any of the following ways:

Attend an interview with a playwright that will be audio recorded. The interview will take about one hour. Participation is entirely voluntary, you may bring someone along to the interview to support you if you choose, and you may stop the interview and opt out at any time. The project team will transcribe the interview and send the transcript to you for review and approval.

Attend a storytelling workshop with other participants that will be video recorded. The workshop will take about 1.5 hours. Participation is entirely voluntary, and you may withdraw from the workshop at any time.

Attend a focus group after seeing a playreading based on the experiences shared in the research and providing feedback that will be video recorded. The focus group will take about one hour. Participation is entirely voluntary, and you may opt out of the focus group at any time.

Fill out an online survey after seeing the playreading or performance to reflect on the experience of seeing this creative work and the impact this has for participants. The survey will take about 15 minutes. Participation is entirely voluntary, and you may opt out at any time.

For any of David's work that includes deliberate interviews that may be transcribed or recorded, David issues a "letter of consent" before the interview begins. This letter is usually written by David but then shown and approved to the commissioning theatre company. David provides two copies of the letter to all interview participants. Both he and the participants sign in front of each other. David also takes time to explain the contents of the letter. This all occurs before any recording has taken place. Below is an example of a typical letter of consent. David used this letter when researching *St. Mary's In Exile* in 2015.

Dear participant,

My name is David Burton, and I am conducting research for a theatrical production that has been commissioned by the Queensland Theatre Company. I am collecting stories and anecdotes from a wide variety of people in connection with the St. Mary's South Brisbane and St. Mary's In Exile community. The data gathered from this research will result in a public theatre performance, using direct quotes from interviews.

I request your approval to digitally record interviews with you at a pre-arranged time and place, and then to transcribe these interviews and use direct quotations in a public theatre performance. The recording of the interview will be in my possession as a digital file, and destroyed in December of 2017.

Your participation in this activity will be voluntary. If you wish for your name not to be referred to or used in any way, you may ask for all of your comments to be given anonymously. If you choose not to participate or withdraw from this process up until the commencement of a rehearsal process, there will be no penalty and it will not affect your treatment in this process.

Although there may be no direct benefit to you, the possible benefit of your participation will help to advance the awareness of an important Brisbane story.

If you have concerns about your role in the study before or after the interview, you are free to call or contact me.

In the event of a dispute, or if you feel you have been placed at risk and do not feel you can speak to me, you may request to speak to Queensland Theatre Company's Programming team, who are happy to talk through any concerns.

Sincerely

Comparing this letter of consent to Sarah's examples above, we can see many common elements. Describing the nature of the project, the nature of the participation, and any risks or benefits to the participant is necessary. Specific terms are at the playwright's discretion. For *St. Mary's In Exile*, David deliberately left the choice of anonymity in the participants' hands. David also gave participants the option to withdraw their data. Even if you don't give participants these options explicitly in a letter of consent, it's important to consider your responses if a participant requests anonymity or for data to be withdrawn after the interview has been recorded. In all instances, it is best to take the request seriously. If possible, we advise to engage the participant in a conversation for their reasons and fears. Almost all of the time, an easy compromise can be reached.

Importantly, consent is not something that participants only have one opportunity to provide. We suggest that a rigorously ethical approach means seeking informed consent prior to the initial participation, and then following up after the interview with either a transcript of the conversation, or a draft of the play or performance, and confirming that you have the permission of the storyteller to use their material in the creative work. This iterative consent process can form part of the continued communication with the community of storytellers. This continued communication ensures there is an open dialogue between the theatre artist and the community.

This practice includes supporting that community and helping to raise awareness about the complex and sometimes contradictory stories that emerge from within it. As Valentine advocates, the role of the artist is not necessarily to proselytise for the community, the creative outcome might be complex and confronting, but "if you are authentic, strategic and genuine, you may become a broker between the wider public and the specific community as they sit together in the audience" (67). This will manifest uniquely depending on the community and the project. For *bald heads & blue stars* it meant sending a draft of the script to each storyteller and providing an opportunity for feedback, questions, and discussion in either a direct or anonymous format. For *Time* it meant talking through the goals and intentions of the play with each of the three contributing participant groups, and acknowledging, together, that their experiences were sometimes contradictory.

This aspect of the model is an opportunity to keep the community actively involved in the process and enrich the script through expert feedback about the content of the work. It gives dynamic agency to the concept of informed consent and keeps the community involved for the duration of the project.

Meaningful Consent and Communication

1 Discuss the project with the community
2 Invite participation, or wait to be invited yourself
3 Give multiple opportunities for consent
4 Continue communication across the project
5 Structure in opportunities for co-creation
6 Make space and time for the community and the project

Documentation and Celebration

Like every other practice discussed in this book, the documentation and celebration of a project are also informed by your values and ethics as an artist. In Fisher and Shelton's *Face to Face, Making Dance and Theatre in Community* they refer to this component of the project as "the rituals of closure" (116). What a glorious phrase! Rituals are a means to acknowledge, to legitimise, to honour. Marking the conclusion of a project through a ritual of closure acknowledges the work that has taken place. Fisher and Shelton list celebrating, gift giving, "handing back the keys", and writing references (or stating your availability to write references in the future) as being among this ritual of closure. Paschal Berry suggests that not taking the time to "sit with communities to dream up a realistic timeline and exit strategy" is one of the biggest failures of community-engaged practice, and that part of our role as artists is to know when we are no longer needed (151). Acknowledging the end of a project and celebrating what has taken place also provides a juncture for change, the opportunity to reflect, and in some cases handing a project or idea over to someone else.

Documentation processes such as taking photos across the life of a project can also enable meaningful gift-giving at the end of a project, as a token of remembrance. Depending on the nature of the project, you might choose to document timelines, workshop plans, photos of the group working on the project (with permission), photos of the place/location of the project or outcome, a filmed recording of the live outcome, photos of the work in progress (paintings, sculpture, drawings, etc), emails, project drafts or messages from people connected to the project.

The following questions might be a useful starting point for you to consider documentation in your project:

- What will be documented in this project?

- How will you document this project?
- Why are you documenting these aspects of the project (what is the goal of documenting these particular components, and what do you want to remember in the future)?
- Who will do the documentation in this project?
- What permission is needed, and from who, for you to document this project?
- How will you share project documentation with the community stakeholders?

Document the project in a way which makes sense for that particular project. In *bald heads & blue stars* Sarah kept an archive of every newspaper article which mentioned the project, because raising public awareness about Alopecia was one of the goals of the work. In *Stuck,* it was useful to document all of the contributions from participants by collecting their written brainstorms and creative responses during the workshops. When Sarah first shared the draft of this play with the ensemble she was able to refer back to all of the creative work that the group had developed and point to where and how it had been included in the final outcome. The ensemble could see the direct link from their collaborative work in the process to the realisation of a character or a theme in the play. In the Queensland Music Festival Signature Community events, the company went to some expense to professionally film the productions. Given the unique nature of these productions, the 2015 production *Under This Sky* was the subject of a feature-length television documentary by SBS titled *The Logan Project*. These acts of archival served many purposes. They were used as important souvenirs to participants, many of whom were very young. They also served as important publicity artefacts that QMF then used to leverage future artistic partnerships with bodies across the state.

Documenting a project is also often a requirement for funding bodies and vital to the acquittal process. Often our work is made possible through grants and government funding, and part of this process involves providing an artistic, financial or statistical report back to the funding body, as a means of demonstrating what you did in the project, how you spent the funds allocated, and what the outcomes of the project were. An acquittal might ask you to give a detailed report on how the final project unfolded (compared to what you had initially set out to do), who were the artists and communities involved, how was the project successful, and what, if any, challenges were faced. Funding bodies might assess "success" on a variety of metrics, including how the project enhanced an individual artist's practice or skills, the impact that the project had for a community, the "bums on seats" or number of people who attended the final outcome, and the benefit of the project for the participants, the community, and the arts and culture sector more broadly. If you have documented the project well, you will have plenty of material and "evidence" to include in this acquittal, such as anecdotes from audiences and participants, photos of the process and outcome, or perhaps a

188 *Ethical Practice*

short video or "sizzle reel" of the performance outcome. We encourage you to think about how you might emphasise stories and creativity in your documentation and acquittal processes and to develop your own criteria for success as the primary way that you will reflect on and evaluate your project.

Celebrating the project is vital! People have given their time, energy, focus, heart, creativity, and story to the work, and this should be acknowledged and celebrated. As Valentine says, working closely with a community is relational. "It is premised on the idea that love, ideas, art, humour, and life itself is about the relationship between people and the energy created when any community of people – small or large – get together to make meaning out of character in action" (215). So celebrate the people, the art, and the experience of creating something together. Celebration is a ritual of closure, an acknowledgement of the work, and a sign of respect. The end of a project doesn't mean abandoning the community with whom you've developed meaningful relationships, but it does allow you to shift into finding what Berry refers to as sustainable ways of retaining connections (155).

7.5 Questions, Templates, Activities

Creating a Letter of Consent

No matter how large or small your project, pressuring yourself to articulate your values and methods in a letter of consent can be illuminating. You may find that there are parts of the project that you (or your students) haven't considered. You may want to run through some worst-case scenarios for your participants and imagine how all parties might be protected. In writing the letter of consent, any nervous energy you may have around interviewing people may dissipate, as you're able to articulate your purpose and protect yourself and others. It can also help in giving your questions a tighter focus, allowing your conversations to stay more on track.

We suggest using the letter of consent example used earlier in the chapter under 7.3: Consent, permission, celebration. From there, begin writing your own letter of consent, considering the following questions:

- What, in simplest terms, is your project about?
- Why is it important that you talk to your chosen participants about this topic?
- How will the data be recorded? Where will that data be stored? When will you delete the data and how?
- What is the possible risk to you, the playwright? What is the possible risk to the participant?
- Can the participant be anonymous? If so, *how* anonymous? Can you share their job title? A description of how they look or talk?
- Is it important to the topic, to the participant, or to you, that in the final casting of the work you remain loyal to participant's gender and racial

identity? Do you need to warn participants of any potential variance in casting?
- What happens if none of the interview data you gather from a particular participant ends up in the show? How can you make them feel they have still made a valuable contribution?
- If someone has an issue with you and doesn't feel they can come to you, where can you direct them?
- Can someone withdraw their data after the interview? If so, how late in the process can they decide to do so? Is the script negotiable right up until closing night? Or before then?

Role-Playing Unethical Behaviour

For first-time interviewers or young and emerging practitioners, role-playing interviews *before* they occur can be a worthwhile practice. In so doing, it's easy to dramatise and satirise unethical (or just rude) interview behaviour. This may mean the topic can turn into a joke. There's nothing inherently wrong with experimenting with this in a classroom, but keep in mind that it's often the more nuanced and subtle communications that can make participants feel uncomfortable or unheard. This exercise is designed to highlight some of that *outside* of the interview process, but inside the later stages of editing, casting, and staging work.

Below are some sample monologues. All of them are entirely manufactured, but are presented so as to replicate data one might gather from raw interviews. Below the monologues are suggestions for experiments and provocations. Leave plenty of time for discussion and reflection, always focussing on the ethics behind each decision.

Monologue 1 – An anecdote from a young male athlete

Yeah. So um. I can't even tell you what happened. Um. So it was the final. Everyone was there, obviously. And if I got this I'd go to the state championships which was a big deal. My parents were there. My sister and her mates. Um, she had this one friend who, like was watching and it's not a big deal but we'd been texting and that. And they were all, like especially her, they were all "Go for it! You've got this!" Anyway, I felt fine all morning and they were all there and then just, just as we were watching the race before I felt a bit weird. Just, I don't know, like, yeah, weird I guess. That's the best word. And then we were lining up and the pistol went and it was like I didn't … yeah, it's so stupid but it's like I didn't hear it. I just stood there. And I looked up and it was my sister and her mate and they were looking at me like I was this idiot and I just hear them scream, like "run". And I ran. And I came dead last. And afterward I like, couldn't talk hey. We didn't talk about it. I just felt … .um, panic I guess. Like I hear on TV they talk about panic attacks and this felt like that … .yeah.

Monologue 2 – An anecdote from a young mother describing the birth of her first child

There's tremendous pressure to get it right. From everywhere. And I just wanted to do the right thing and I'd been reading all of these books and my Mum – yeah, she was intense about it. I wanted a home birth but my husband was worried about that. It's a good thing we didn't because – well we never got the chance. 35 weeks out and the GP takes my blood pressure and I knew immediately it wasn't right. The GP keeps telling me to relax, and I'm like – I can't relax you're freaking me out. And that makes my blood pressure come up more. And everybody starts acting like the baby's going to explode out of my stomach like on *Alien* – you know that film? The like … .rahhhh! Anyway, we rush to the hospital and everyone's shouting at me to relax and I'm like I CAN'T BLOODY RELAX. And I burst into tears and then I feel stupid and my husband – when I cry he freaks out – so he's useless now. Um, so … yeah, it was not great. Pre-eclampsia and an epidural and obviously a bit early. So I was pretty scared a lot of the time and really um, yeah took me a long time to recover.

- Experiment with *editing* both monologues. Can you edit either monologue to be funnier? Or more dramatic? In so doing, do you feel you've crossed a line and messed with the intention of the speaker?
- Experiment with *casting* both monologues. What happens if you cast the actors in cross-gender roles? Can the actors perform caricatures of the interviewees? Can the actors perform the interview to get as many laughs as possible? Can the actors perform the interview to give both interviewees a sense of rising panic? Can they perform it so that the interviewees appear unhinged or disturbed? At what point do you feel you're being unethical or unfair?
- Experiment with the *staging* of both monologues. Experiment with lighting, sound, blocking, and choral work. In making artistic decisions of this kind, how do you affirm and subvert the interviewee's perceived intention when telling the story? And when is this ethical and unethical?

Reflective Questions on Ethics

These questions have been derived from pre-existing literature around ethics and verbatim theatre methodologies in community-engaged performance. Use these as a way of provoking discussion at any point during your artistic process, or as a way to guide discussion in your journal.

- What biases and intentions do you bring to the project? (Cañas 47)
- What power and privilege do you bring to the space?
- Should you be the person telling this story or doing this work? ("People have asked me how non-Indigenous writers can help tell Indigenous stories and the short answer is 'Wait to be asked'"(Valentine 189))
- How are you ensuring safe spaces of solidarity, particularly for vulnerable groups? A space is not safe just because you say it is.

- The personal is the political – how political (or politically aware, reflective, forthright, challenged) are you prepared to be?
- Do not presume that experiencing oppression or discrimination in one form means that you are able to understand it in other forms. Who are you, what are your intersectional identities, and what gaps/blind spots/assumptions does this mean you might have?
- How will you ask people what they need in order to participate? Caroline Bowditch explains that "The Social Model of Disability is a philosophy, or way of thinking, that recognises that people are disabled by barriers created by society, not by their condition or impairment" (53). What assumptions might you have made about access and inclusion and how might you explicitly consider these? What access and inclusion barriers exist in your project?
- Who is not in the metaphorical "room" of the project? Why? Should they be?

Works Cited

Abbs, Peter. "The Pattern of Art-Making." *The Symbolic Order: A Contemporary Reader on the Arts Debate*, edited by Peter Abbs, Taylor & Francis Ltd, 1989. pp. 193–206.

Ackerly, Brooke. *Political Theory and Feminist Sociakl Criticism*. University of Cambridge, 2000.

Agger, Ben. *Critical Social Theories, An Introduction*. Westview Press, 1998.

Anderson, Michael and Linden Wilkinson. "A Resurgence of Verbatim Theatre: Authenticity, Empathy and Transformation." *Australasian Drama Studies*, 50, 2007, pp. 153–169.

Aston, Elaine. *An Introduction to Feminism and Theatre*. Routledge, 1995.

Aston, Elaine. *Feminist Theatre Practice: A Handbook*. Routledge, 1999.

Barnes M., T. Brannelly, L. Ward, and N. Ward. "Conclusion: Renewal and Transformation – The Importance of an Ethics of Care." *Ethics of Care: Critical Advances in International Perspective*, edited by M. Barnes, T. Brannelly, L. Ward, and N. Ward, Policy Press, 2015.

Barnett, David. "The Poverty of Verbatim Theatre." *Irish Theatre Magazine* 5, 2005, pp. 16–19.

Berg, Maggie and Barbara Seeber. *The Slow Professor: Challenging the Culture of Speed in the Academy*. University of Toronto Press, 2016.

Berry, Paschal. "No End Date: Timeframes and Expectations." *The Relationship is the Project: Working with Communities*, edited by J. Lillie, K. Larsen, C. Kirkwood, and J. Brown, Brow Books, 2020, pp. 151–158.

Botham, Paola. "From Deconstruction to Reconstruction: A Habermasian Framework For Contemporary Political Theatre." *Contemporary Theatre Review* 18.3, 2008, pp. 307–317.

Botham, Paola. "Witnesses in The Public Sphere: Bloody Sunday and the Redefinition of Political Theatre." *Political Performances, Theory and Practice*, edited by Susan Haedlicke, et al., Editions Rodopi, 2009, pp. 35–53.

Bottoms, Stephen. "Putting the Document into Documentary." *The Drama Review*, 50.3, 2006, pp. 56–68.
Bowditch, Caroline. "Access and Inclusion" *The Relationship is the Project: Working with Communities*, edited by J. Lillie, K. Larsen, C. Kirkwood, and J. Brown, Brow Books, 2020, pp. 51–58.
Burbules, Nicholas and Rupert Berk. "Critical thinking and Critical Pedagogy: Relations, Differences and Limits." *Critical Theories in Education*, edited by T. Popkewitz and L. Fendler, Routledge, 1999, pp. 45–66.
Callaghan, Dympna. "The Aesthetics of Marginality: The Theatre of Joan Littlewood and Buzz Goodbody." *Theatre and Feminist Aesthetics*, edited by Karen Laughlin and Catherine Schuler, Associated University Press, 1995, pp. 258–285.
Cañas, Tania. "Ethics and Self-Determination." *The Relationship is the Project: Working with Communities*, edited by J. Lillie, K. Larsen, C. Kirkwood, and J. Brown, Brow Books, 2020, pp. 41–50.
Cantrell, Tom. *Acting in Documentary Theatre*. Palgrave MacMillan, 2013.
Cantrell, Tom. "Playing for Real in Max Stafford-Clarke's Talking to Terrorists." *Studies in Theatre and Performance* 31.2, 2011, pp. 167–180.
Case, Sue-Ellen. *Feminism and Theatre*. London: Routledge, 1995.
Cohen-Cruz, Jan. *Engaging Performance, Theatre as Call and Response*. Routledge, 2010.
Decent, Campion. *Embers*. Playlab, Brisbane, 2008.
Duggan, Patrick. "Others, Spectatorship, and the Ethics of Verbatim Performance." *New Theatre Quarterly* 29.2, 2013, pp. 146–158.
Fisher, Judi and Beth Shelton. *Face to Face: Making Dance and Theatre in Community*. Spinifex Press, 2002.
Frieze, James. "Naked Truth: Theatrical Performance and the Diagnostic Turn." *Theatre Research International* 36.2, 2011, pp. 148–162.
Gallagher, Ann. *Slow Ethics and The Art of Care*. Emerald Publishing Ltd, 2020.
Goodman, Lizbeth. "Comic Subversions: Comedy as Strategy in Feminist Theatre." *The Polity Reader in Cultural Theory*, Polity Press, Blackwell Publishers, 1992, pp.242–247.
Goodman, Lizbeth. *Contemporary Feminist Theatres: To Each Her Own*. Routledge, 1993.
Hankivsky, O. *Social Policy and the Ethic of Care*. UBC Press, 2004.
Heddon, Deirdre. *Autobiography and Performance*. Palgrave MacMillan, 2008.
Heddon, Deirdre. "To Absent Friends." *Political Performances: Theory and Practice*, edited by Susan Haedicke, et al., Editions Rodopi, 2009, pp. 111–136.
hooks, bell. *Feminist Theory from Margin to Centre*. South End Press, 2000.
How, Alen. *Critical Theory*. Ed. Ian Craib. Palgrave MacMillan, 2003.
Kanpol, Barry. *Critical Pedagogy An Introduction*. Bergin & Garvey, 1994.
Kincheloe, Joe. *Critical Pedagogy*. Peter Lang Publishing Inc, 2008.
Laughlin, Karen and Catherine Schuler. "Introduction." *Theatre and Feminist Aesthetics*, edited by Karen Laughlin and Catherine Schuler, Associated University Presses, 1995, pp. 9–21.
Lillie J., K. Larsen, C. Kirkwood, and J. Brown. The Relationship is the Project: Working with *Communities*. Brow Books, 2020, ISBN: 9781925704198.
Luckhurst, Mary. "Verbatim Theatre, Media Relations and Ethics." *A Concise Companion to Contemporary British and Irish Drama*, edited by Nadine Holdsworth and Mary Luckhurst, Blackwell Publishing, 2008, pp. 200–222.

Megson, Chris. "Verbatim Practices in Contemporary Theatre: Symposium Report." *Backpages, Contemporary Theatre*, 2005, pp. 529–532.

Miller, Suzie. "Adrift: The Story of Writing Transparency." *Storyline* 33, 2013, pp. 78–83.

Paget, Derek. "Acts of Commitment: Activist Arts, the Rehearsed Reading and Documentary Theatre." *New Theatre Quarterly*, 2010, pp. 173–193.

Scott, Joan. "The Evidence of Experience." *Feminist Approaches to Theory and Methodology*, edited by Sharlene Hesse-Biber, Christina Gilmartin, and Robin Lydenberg, Oxford University Press, 1999, pp. 773–797.

Simola S., J. Barling, and N. Turner. "Transformational Leadership and Leader Moral Orientation: Contrasting an Ethic of Justice and an Ethic of Care." *The Leadership Quarterly* 21, 2010, pp. 179–188.

Stuart Fisher, Amanda. "'That's Who I'd Be, If I Could Sing': Reflections on a Verbatim Project with Mothers of Sexually Abused Children." *Studies in Theatre and Performance* 21.2, 2011, pp. 193–208.

Stuart Fisher, Amanda. "Trauma, Authenticity and the Limits of Verbatim." *Performance Research: A Journal of the Performing Arts* 16.1, 2011, pp. 112–122.

Summerskill, Clare. *Creating Verbatim Theatre from Oral Histories*. Routledge, 2021.

Taylor, Philip. "Doing Reflective Practitioner Research in Arts Education." *Researching Drama and Arts Education*, edited by Philip Taylor, and Falmer Press, 1996, pp. 25–58.

Taylor, Philip. *The Drama Classroom*. Routledge Falmer, 2000.

Thompson, James. "Politics and Ethics in Applied Theatre: Face-to-Face and Disturbing the Fabric of the Sensible." *Ethics and the* Arts, edited by P. Macneil, Springer Science and Business Media, 2014, pp. 125–135.

Valentine, Alana. *Bowerbird: The Art of Making Theatre Drawn from Life*. Currency Press, 2018

Waters, Steve. "Political Playwrighting: The Arts of Thinking in Public." *Springer Science and Business Media* 30, 2011, pp. 137–144.

Watt, David. "Local Knowledges, Memories, and Community: From Oral History to Performance." *Political Performances, Theory and Practice*, edited by Susan Haedicke, et al., Editions Rodopi, 2009, pp. 189–212.

Wink, Joan. *Critical Pedagogy: Notes from the Real World. 3rd*. Pearson Education Inc, 2005.

Young, Stuart. "Playing with Documentary Theatre: Aalst and Taking Care of Baby." *New Theatre Quarterly* 25, 2009, pp. 72–87.

Ziarek, Ewa. "At the Limits of Discourse – Heterogeneity, Alterity and the Maternal Body in Kristeva's Thought." *Language and Liberation: Feminism, Philosophy, Language*, edited by C. Hendricks and K. Oliver, State University of New York Press, 1999, pp. 324–345.

Afterword

We began this book by telling you this is our love letter to storytelling. Of course, one of the gifts of a community-engaged process is that storytelling is just the beginning. Narratives are how we form a connection with others, but then what we do with that connection can be immense. As playwrights and researchers, we value storytelling found through conversation in all its forms. Across a kitchen table, in a supermarket aisle, over a fence, or shared between audience and performer.

We have written this book during the height of the COVID pandemic, a topic which has already birthed countless verbatim projects. In this setting, the value of connection and community engagement has become more important than ever. It has been a devastating time for every industry, but performing artists have felt unique and acute grief. They are often outside the realms of government support because of their contract employment, and events have faced endless delays and cancellations. But of course, artists are nothing without the drive to innovate, and the new hunger for community connection has meant community-engaged artists are now facing fresh demand. Urgent and interesting questions have provoked the industry into fresh relevance. Can we do this work online? Can we create micro outcomes with small communities to help create a sense of cohesion and unity in this time of division and isolation? How can theatre model a type of conversation that brings communities closer together, not in homogeneity but in celebration of our glorious diversity? Of course, verbatim theatre methodologies in community-engaged contexts can greatly assist in providing solutions.

This book has been the culmination of several decades of shared work in the industry and research. As we publish the book, the industry, and the verbatim theatre form are once again being challenged to innovate. It's an exciting time, rich with possibility. Still, several key principles will remain critical. An ethical praxis will be mandatory. Conversations and interviews will remain the primary mode of stimulus for verbatim-based creative work. Overall, the practice will still call upon its working artists to remain nimble, open, and innovative.

Community-engaged practice calls upon artists to develop a very specific set of skills. One must be knowledgeable in the principles of sociology, conflict resolution, dramaturgy, ethical journalism, and theatrical aesthetics. This form typically breeds a special kind of leadership that traverses vulnerability, courage, and theatrical craft. If you have read this book from front to back and are a relative newcomer, it can be overwhelming. We hope that the examples and reflections from our own projects and case studies have helped to contextualise and make more accessible the creative practice we are discussing. Of course, every project is different and calls upon different skill sets that are highly contextually dependent. It's only in reflecting that the knowledge you have gained from such an experience truly becomes embodied. In the moment, community-engaged artists are usually instinctive, operating from a space that engages listening for aesthetics (even outside of interviews). At the start of any verbatim or community-engaged project, Sarah and David (still) feel a mix of nerves and excitement. Because every project is different, "mastery" of a key set of skills is almost impossible. Instead, we are constantly engaged in an evolving learning process.

With that, we are excited by the idea of contributing this book back to the community of practitioners, researchers, and emerging artists. If an artist is daring enough to step into this field, we promise you it's immensely fulfilling.

Sarah and David
2023

Index

AAAF *see* Australia Alopecia Areata Foundation (AAAF)
Abbs, Peter 89, 172
Ackerly, Brooke 173
Ackroyd, Judith 19, 24
acting company vs participating community 144–147, 149–152
active listening 30
Acts of Courage 26
aesthetics 65–85; interviewing, importance of 74–77; Listening for Aesthetics 68–74; of marginality 166; verbatim interview 66–68
Agger, Ben 170
Agitational Propaganda (Agitprop) 15–16, 21, 114; to understand political performance, using 34–35
Ainsworth, R. 144
Akram, S. 125
Alienation 145–146
Alrutz, Megan 5, 30
Amazing Race, The 27
Anderson, Michael 17, 170, 181
applied theatre 20
April's Fool 6, 78–79, 93, 179; community immersion 94; interview staging 118–119; play and real meet 153–154; rehearsal 146, 147; re-telling 123; script structures 135; transcribing interviews 90; voicing stories 96
Armchair Expert 85
Artsworx USQ 8
ASCA (Adults Surviving Child Abuse, now the Blue Knot Foundation) 47

Aston, Elaine 172
audience 157–158; as hero 139–140; impact of 159–161, 163–164
Australia Alopecia Areata Foundation (AAAF) 46, 55, 56
Australian Alopecia Areata Foundation 8
Australian Drama Curriculum 30
Australian Friends of the Camino 9
Australian National Anthem 131
Australian Plays Transform 7, 8
Australian Writer's Guild 154
authenticity, and ethics 176–181
autobiographical theatre 23

Bachelor, The 27
bald heads & blue stars 7–8, 35, 46, 89; audience impact 159–161; character-narrated realism 123; collective choruses 125–126; community immersion 54–56; conspectus of opinions 130–131; documentation 187; monologues 119–120; play and real meet 154; script structures 135; transcribing interviews 89, 90; voicing stories 95
Barnes M. 175
Barnett, David: "Poverty of Verbatim Theatre, The" 179
Barranger, Milly 16
Beck, Jaime 25
Behrndt, Synne K. 4
belonging, dramaturgy of 18, 20, 75–76
#BeMoreMartyn 25
Bennett, Susan 73
Berk, Rupert 170
Berry, Paschal 186

Black Diggers 132; script structures 135–136
Bleiker, Roland 114
Blister 8–9, 48, 92, 181; audience impact 159–161; devising through discussion 99–101; rehearsal 146–147; re-telling 121–123
Bloody Sunday 25
Blue Blouse Movement (1923–1933) 15
Blue Cow Theatre 53
Blue Mountains Gazette 46
Blythe, Alecky 26
Boal, Augusto 20, 44; "People's Theatre" 19; "Theatre of the Oppressed" 19
Boomtown 6
Booth, Lee-Gwen 53
Botham, Paola 16, 114, 179; *From Deconstruction to Reconstruction* 179
Bottoms, S. 27
Bottoms, Stephen 178, 179
Brecht, Bertolt 19, 34, 44, 116
Brockett, Oscar 16
Brown, Brene 76; *Unlocking Us* 85
Brown, Rich 89
Bryant, Dean: *Gaybies* 134–135
Bryant, Dylan 11
Burbules, Nicholas 170
Burton, David 19, 68, 131; *April's Fool* 6, 78–79; "Performance 'Training' in the Dirt: Facilitating Belonging in a Regional Community Musical Theatre Event" 7

Callaghan, Dympna 166
Called to Account 25
Campaign, The 17, 43, 52, 168; legacy of work 162; rehearsal 147–149
Cantrell, Tom 23, 25; *Acting in Documentary Theatre* 177
Carter, D. 19
Case, Sue-Ellen 172
Castagno, Paul 3
Cell 26 26
character-narrated realism 123
Chou, Mark 114
Christian, Claire 11, 21, 31, 44, 65, 102, 157, 167, 174, 176; *It's Been A Pleasure, Noni Blake* 50–51; *Talking to Brick Walls* 65–66, 121, 129–130, 162; *Virginity Mologues, The* 74, 97
Churchill, Caryl 142

Civil Conversations Project 76
Cohen-Cruz, Jan 29, 42, 166; *Boal Companion, A* 4
collaborative creative development 94–102; devising through discussion 97–103; formal creative developments 95–97; voicing stories 95–97
collective choruses 125–130
Comin Home Soon 49
community: map 140; of the production, expansion of 155–157; representation 167–168; understanding 35–37; well-being, fostering 22–23
community-engaged practice, verbatim methodologies for: community well-being, fostering 22–23; value to the artist 20–22
community-engaged theatre 18–20; artist 5, 26
community-engaged workshopping with young people 102–105
community immersion 2, 11, 13, 22, 23, 25, 34, 42–63, 74, 75, 87, 117, 142, 165, 170, 175, 181, 182; accessibility to the project, ensuring 51–54; case studies of 54–61; collected materials and artefacts 93–94; connection, maintaining 50–51; conversations 48–49; creative service, providing 49–50; definition of 42–43; documenting 92–94; engaging in activities 47–48; intentions of 45–46; journals 92–93; media outlets 46–47; participants, preparing 51–54; peak bodies, contacting 46; practical activities/reflective tasks 61–63; strategies and practices of 46–54; support services 46–47; values of 43–44
consensus vs conspectus 130
conspectus 130–132; consensus vs 130
critical pedagogy 29, 30, 44, 169–172, 174; dialogue of 170
critical theory 29, 169–172, 174
Croome, Rodney 43, 53; *From This Day Forward: Marriage Equality in Australia* 52
Cross Sections: audience impact 161
Currency Press 26

danger zones 77–78
Dead Man Brake: collective choruses 128
Decent, Campion 11, 17–18, 21, 52, 53, 91, 102, 114, 158, 167–168, 181; *Campaign, The* 17, 43, 52, 147–149, 162, 168; *Embers* 18, 77; *Picnic at Hanging Rock* 18; *Unprecedented* 43
Deep Cut 25
define adult: activities 105–110; community-engaged workshopping with young people 103, 105
devising through discussion 97–103
dialogic listening 98
diegetic realism 121
diegetic theatricality/diegesis 116, 139
direct address 115, 138
documentary theatre 25
Dolan 173, 174
double silencing 51
Downes, B. 20
Dragon 111
Drama Australia Journal 6, 87
dramaturg 4–5, 101, 105
dramaturgy: of belonging 18, 20, 75–76; dramaturgical boundaries 33; dramaturgical integrity 150; dramaturgical questions 114, 138–139; dramaturgical robustness 43; dramaturgical structure 134–136; heterarchical 136; of a play 4–5, 6, 20, 25, 32, 63, 75, 77, 78, 95–97, 102, 115, 117, 119, 125, 137, 159, 180, 195; of the work 145
DreamBIG Children's Festival, Adelaide 9
Driving into Walls 80; theatricality and imagination 133
Duggan, Patrick 114

Empire Theatre Projects 6
Engaged Verbatim Theatre Praxis 2, 3, 28, 168–176
Enoch, Wesley 11; *Black Diggers* 132, 135–136; *Seven Stages of Grieving, The* 18, 115
Enquirer 25
Epic Theatre 114
Eternity 8, 180; amalgamated characters 124; collective choruses 126; community immersion 58–60, 93–94
ethical conundrums 77–78
ethical practice 3, 28–29, 165–191; authenticity in performance 180–181; celebration 186–188; documentation 186–188; letter of consent, creation of 188–189; "real" material in performance 178–180; role-playing unethical behaviour 189–190; theory, development of 168–176
ethics: authenticity and 176–181; of care 45, 169, 174–176; definition of 165; reflective questions on 190–191; relational 165
ethnodrama 24
ethno theatre 24
Evans, Dan 11, 18, 21, 98, 167; *I've Been Meaning to Ask You* 105; *Let's Be Friends Furever* 48–49
Exodus Greater Manchester Refugee Arts Partnership, The 26
Exodus Onstage 26
ExpressWay Arts 9

facilitator 4, 5, 9, 60, 94, 105, 150, 174
Fast Cars and Tractor Engines 17, 26
Federal Theatre Project (FTP) 16, 19, 21
feminist theatre practice 21, 29, 43, 44, 169, 172–174
Fidler, Richard: *Conversations* 85
Fisher, Judi: *Face to Face: Making Dance and Theatre in Community* 186
Flanagan, Hallie 16
Forsyth, Alison 23
Foxon, Chris 3–4
Fredriksson, Lennart 71, 73
Fresh Air 85
Friere, Paulo 44
Frieze, James 179
FTP *see* Federal Theatre Project (FTP)
"Function of Verbatim Theatre Conventions in three Australian plays, The" 6

Gallagher, Ann: *Slow Ethics and the Art of Care* 175
Gallagher, Kathleen 15
Garde, Ulrike 15–17; "Short History of Verbatim Theatre, A" 17
Gaybies: script structures 134–135

Giroux, Henry 44
Gladiator Games 178
Goldbard, A. 19
Gonzalez, A. A. 26
Goodbody, Buzz 166
Goodman, Lizbeth 172, 173; *Contemporary Feminist Theatres* 173
Good Room, The 75, 132–133, 162
Gordon, Sue 10
Gough, Louise 102, 135
Grand Designs 32
Gray, Ross 22
Griefcast, The 85
Gross, Teri: *Fresh Air* 85
Grummet, Jace 10
Guantanomo: Honour Bound to Freedom 25
"Guidelines for Working Ethically in Verbatim Theatre Processes" 167
Gurreeboo, Yasmin 134

Hall, Jacquelyn 68
Hankivsky, Olena 45, 175
Harper, Todd 53
Haseman, Brad 69
Hazlehurst, Noni 52
headphone verbatim 26, 91
Heddon, Deirdre 68, 170, 171, 173
Hegel's theory of dialectics 170
Heim, C. 19
Hello, Goodbye and Happy Birthday 26
Hero's Journey: script structures 136–138
Hibberd, M. 115
Hilbers, J. 22
Hill, A. 27, 28
Hoare, Lynne 5, 30
Hogan, A. 125
Holden Street Theatres 9
Holderness, Graham 15
Holloway, Tom: *Beyond the Neck* 14
Home 25
Hopf, C. 69
Horchschild, Arlie Russell 76
Horin, Ros: *Through the Wire* 17
How, Alen 169, 171
How I Built This 85
Hunter, Kate 138

imagination 132–133
I'm Still Here! 24
I'm Your Man 17, 26

In Defence of the Discourse 174
informed consent 182–186
Ingram, Amy 75, 98; *I've Been Meaning to Ask You* 105
Innes, Christopher 15, 16
interview(s/ing): case study 78–80; in classroom environment, negotiating 83; frequently asked questions 80–83; importance of 74–77; practical activities 83–85; staging 117–119; transcribing 88–92; verbatim 66–68
Introduction, An 173
I Should've Drunk More Champagne 98; script structures 136; theatricality and imagination 132–133
Ivonoffski, Vrenia: *I'm Still Here!* 24
I Want To Know What Love Is 98; legacy of work 162
Izod, J. 115

Jarman, Robert 53
Jefferies, P. 76
Jeffers, Alison 114
Jonas-Simpson, Christine: *I'm Still Here!* 24
juxtaposition 130–132

Kanpol, Barry 170
Kaufman, Moises: *Gross Indecency* 178–179
Kaufman, Moisés 16, 89, 156–157
Keene, Daniel 52
Keeping Up With The Kardashians 27, 32
Kilbron, R. 115
Kincheloe, Joe 170
Korkmaz, Selma 68
Kristeva 171
Kushner, Tony 142

La Boite Theatre Company 10
Laramie Project, The 27, 80, 89, 173; community of the production, expansion of 156–157; diegesis 116
Laughlin, Karen 173
Leach, Robert 15, 16
Lead Artist 150
learning 171
Leffler, Elliot 77
legacy of work 161–162
Lerner, Harriet 76

letter of consent, creation of 188–189
Lilie, Jade: *Relationship is the Project, The* 182
Lillie, Jade 5, 18; *Relationship is the Project, The* 42
Listening for Aesthetics 76; applying strategies to assist in generating story 71–72; engaged audience member 73–74; mutual storyteller 72–73; paying attention to dramatic action of participant's story 68–69; responding in improvised manner to stories 69–71; traditional interviewer 72
literal theatrical, making 117–133; amalgamated characters 124–125; collective choruses 125–130; interview, staging 117–119; monologues 119–121; re-telling 121–124
Littlewood, Joan 166
Living Newspaper, The 16, 114; to understand political performance, using 34–35
Lloyd, Cariad: *Griefcast, The* 85
LockDown 9
Lockdown project 151
Logan Project, The 7, 131, 187
London Road 114
Lott, Martha 134
Luckhurst, Mary 25, 26, 178

MacMillan, Duncan: *Every Brilliant Thing* 44
Mailman, Deborah: *Seven Stages of Grieving* 18; *Seven Stages of Grieving, The* 115
Maron, Marc: *WTF* 85
Martin, Carol 23, 24
MasterChef 27
McCallum, J. 18
McCormack, Jess: *Choreography, and Verbatim Theatre* 114
McDonald, Janet 131; "Performance 'Training' in the Dirt: Facilitating Belonging in a Regional Community Musical Theatre Event" 7
Mee, Sean 128
Megson, Chris 23; "Verbatim Practices in Contemporary Theatre" 65
"Me Too" movement 76
Meyerhold 19

Micah Projects 47
Micich, Danielle 133
Millar, Damien: *Modern International Dead, The* 181
Miller, Suzie 11, 36–37; *Cross Sections* 37; *Driving into Walls* 80, 133; *Transparency* 67–68, 177
mimetic realism 121
mimetic theatricality/mimesis 116
Mitchell, Gail 25; *I'm Still Here!* 24
monologues 119–121
Monsour, Aleea 9
Mother 52
Mount Isa Blast, The 7, 131
multiple roles 116–117, 139
Mumford, Meg 15–17; "Short History of Verbatim Theatre, A" 17
Mundy, Cath 128
musical theatre 114
Mutnick, Deborah 4
My Octopus Teacher: diegesis 116

narrative-generating questions 69
New Theatre Quarterly 13
New Writing: The International Journal for the Practice and Theory of Creative Writing 8
Nicholson, Helen 30
Nightline Project, The 26, 91–92
Nomadland 28, 61
nonfiction theatre 23

Oades, Roslyn 11, 17, 26, 138; *Nightline Project, The* 26, 91–92
Olympic Opening and Closing Ceremonies 23
On Being 85
oral histories 26–27
Orr, S. 30, 31
O'Toole, John 24, 69
Otter Ai 111

Padman, Monica: *Armchair Expert* 85
Paget, Derek 13–17, 23, 26, 45, 67, 74, 114, 166, 181
Palani, Ari 9
participating community vs acting company 144–147, 149–152
Pascoe, Robin 133
Peace Train 130
Peacock Theatre 53
"People's Theatre" 19
Perel, Esther 34

Perth Theatre Company 145
Peters, Sarah 20, 28, 71, 75; *Time* 10–11, 79–80
Phillips, Carla 10
Philpott, Lachlan: *Alienation* 145–146
Piscator, Erwin 19, 44
Playlab Press 6, 8
playwriting 2–4, 8, 18, 20, 21, 29, 44, 49, 53, 61, 66, 92, 96, 113–140, 145, 146, 150, 161; activities 138–140; literal theatrical, making 117–133; script structures 133–138; "traditional" verbatim theatre conventions 114–117
Playwriting Australia: *Duologue* program 53
podcasts: using to discuss verbatim theatre 33–34
Pointed Heads: collective choruses 127
Pollock, Della 67, 68
Power Within, The 7; collective choruses 127–128
Prospect Theatre for Young People (PTFYP) 10
PTFYP *see* Prospect Theatre for Young People (PTFYP)
Public Pedagogy Journal 9

QMF *see* Queensland Music Festival (QMF)
Queensland Music Festival (QMF) 16, 127, 128, 131; *Mount Isa Blast, The* 47–48; *Queensland Music Festival Signature Community Works/Events* (2013–2019) 6–7, 48, 49, 93, 150, 180, 187
Queensland Regional Arts Development Fund 8
Queensland Theatre 8

Radiolab 34
Raz, Guy: *How I Built This* 85
Real Housewives 32
reality-based theatre 23
reality television 27–28; using to discuss verbatim theatre 32–33
Reese, Sam 68
rehearsal 2–3, 7, 9, 10, 26, 49, 56, 58, 60, 61, 127, 142–164, 176, 184, 192; acting company vs participating community 144–147; audience impact 159–161; in early days 143–152; frequently asked questions 163–164; legacy of work 161–162; post-show activities 163–164
Reinelt, Janelle: "Promise of Documentary, The" 25
relational ethics 165
relearning 171
research-based theatre 24–25
restored village performances 23
re-telling 121–124
reviewers 157–158
riffing 110
Riots, The 25
role-playing unethical behaviour 189–190
Rossiter, Kate 132
Round Heads: collective choruses 127
Ru Paul's Drag Race 27
Russell, Steve 128

Salamanca Arts Centre 53
Saldaña, Johnny 23, 24; *Dramatizing Data* 26
SBS Australia: SBS On Demand 7
Scholten, Matt 21, 52, 53; *Campaign, The* 17, 43, 52, 147–149, 162, 168
Schuler, Catherine 173
Schutzman, Mady: *Boal Companion, A* 4
Scott, Joan 173–174
script structures 133–138; story-led 134–136
Sea Stories 26, 152
Serial: diegesis 116
Seven Stages of Grieving, The 115
Shawl, Nisi: *Writing The Other: A Practical Approach* 62
Shelton, Beth: *Face to Face: Making Dance and Theatre in Community* 186
Shepherd, Dax: *Armchair Expert* 85
Shreeve, A. 30, 31
Sibley, Frank 68
Simola S. 175
Soans, Robin 77
Social Alternatives 159
Springgay, Stephanie: *Walking in/as Publics* 9
stage directions, exercises in 139
Stephenson, Jenn: *Insecurity: Perils and Products of Theatres of the Real* 24
Stevens, Cat: *Peace Train* 130
Stibbard, Lucas 8
St Mary's In Exile 8, 47, 180, 184–185;

community immersion 56–58; devising through discussion 101–102; play and real meet 154; re-telling 123–124; transcribing interviews 90; voicing stories 96
Stories of Love and Hate 17, 26
story-led script structures 134–136
Strayed, Cheryl 76
Stuart Fisher, Amanda 22, 31, 73, 114, 173, 180; *That's Who I'd be* 181
Stuck 10; activities 105–110; community-engaged workshopping with young people 104, 105; documentation 187
Summerskill, Clare 26; *Creating Verbatim Theatre From Oral Histories* 27, 167
Survivor 27

Tactical Questioning 25
Talking to Brick Walls 65–66; collective choruses 129–130; legacy of work 162; monologues 121
Tasmanian Gay Law Reform Group 52
Tasmanian Theatre Company 53
Taylor, L. 23
Tectonic Theatre Project 89
TED Radio Hour 34
That Boy: script structures 134
theatre artists 29–30
theatre-of-fact 23
theatre of the real 23–24; with screen-based forms, porosity of 27–28
theatre of witness 23
theatricality 132–133
Thompson, James 166
Threepenny Opera, The: collective choruses 127
Through the Wire 17
Time 10–11, 79–80, 182, 185–186; transcribing interviews 90; voicing stories 96
Time Is Now, The 9–10; amalgamated characters 125; community immersion 60–61
Tippett, Krista: *On Being* 85
Today We're Alive 17
Toonan, Nick 43, 53
Toowoomba Chronicle, The 55, 56
To Witness Mimesis 121
"traditional" verbatim theatre conventions 114–117; diegetic theatricality 116; direct address 115; multiple roles 116–117
transcribing interviews 88–92
transcription software, notes and recommendations on 110–111
Transparency 67–68, 177
tribunal theatre 25–26
Truman, Sarah E.: *Walking in/as Publics* 9
truth, manipulation of 176–178
Turner, Cathy 4, 94, 98
Turner, Jay 128
Turvey, George 3–4
twelve2twentyfive 7, 46–47; interview staging 117–118; transcribing interviews 90

Under This Sky 7, 131, 187
Ungar, M. 76
unlearning 171
Unlocking Us 85

Valentine, Alana 11, 17, 45–46, 177, 183; *Comin Home Soon* 49; *Dead Man Brake* 128
verbatim theatre: in Australia 17–18; definition of 13–15, 26; ethical practice of 28–29; historical mapping of 14–20; links to pedagogy 30–31; origin of 15; questions and exercises 29–37; using podcasts to discuss 33–34; using reality television to discuss 32–33
Verbatim Theatre and Healthy Ageing 183
Virginity Mologues, The 74, 97
voicing stories 95–97, 102

Wake, Caroline 13, 15–17, 51, 92; "Headphone Verbatim Theatre: Methods, Histories, Genres, Theories" 26; "Short History of Verbatim Theatre, A" 17
war and battle re-enactments 23
Ward, Cynthia: *Writing The Other: A Practical Approach* 62
Watermark 152; public reading of 155
Watt, David 15–17, 181
Watts, Richard 146
We Live Here 114
Well Made Play, The: script structures 136–138

Wenger, E. 144–145
Wenger, Etienne 31
Where Should We Begin? 34
Wilkinson, Linden 17, 170, 181; *Day in December, A* 46, 88; *Today We're Alive* 17
Wink, Joan 170, 171
Witham, Barry 16
Works Progress Administration (WPA) 16

WPA *see* Works Progress Administration (WPA)
Wright, Tom 11, 132; *Black Diggers* 18
WTF 85

Yugambeh Museum Language and Research Centre 128–129

Zhao, Chloe 28, 61
Ziarek, Ewa 171

For Product Safety Concerns and Information please contact our EU representative GPSR@taylorandfrancis.com
Taylor & Francis Verlag GmbH, Kaufingerstraße 24, 80331 München, Germany

www.ingramcontent.com/pod-product-compliance
Lightning Source LLC
Chambersburg PA
CBHW050535300426
44113CB00012B/2115